Helping Working Families:
The Earned Income Tax Credit

Helping Working Families: The Earned Income Tax Credit

Saul D. Hoffman
Laurence S. Seidman

2003

W. E. Upjohn Institute for Employment Research
Kalamazoo, Michigan

Library of Congress Cataloging-in-Publication Data

Hoffman, Saul D., 1949–
    Helping working families : the earned income tax credit / Saul D. Hoffman,
Laurence S. Seidman.
        p.   cm.
    Includes bibliographical references and index.
    ISBN 0-88099-253-0 (pbk. : alk. paper)—ISBN 0-88099-254-9
    (hardcover : alk. paper)
    1. Earned income tax credit—United States.   2. Working poor—United States.
I. Seidman, Laurence S.   II. Title.
HJ4653.C73 H624   2002
336.24'216—dc21

                                                                    2002013843

© 2003
W. E. Upjohn Institute for Employment Research
300 S. Westnedge Avenue
Kalamazoo, Michigan 49007-4686

The facts presented in this study and the observations and viewpoints expressed are
the sole responsibility of the authors. They do not necessarily represent positions of
the W. E. Upjohn Institute for Employment Research.

Cover design by Alcorn Publication Design
Index prepared by Nairn Chadwick
Printed in the United States of America.

Dedication

To our wives and children—

Susan, Jake, and Nathaniel

Ann, Jesse, and Suzanna

Contents

Figures

Tables

Acknowledgments

We would never have written this book were it not for the enormous expansion of the Earned Income Tax Credit program in 1993— the culmination of President Clinton's campaign pledge in 1992 to "make work pay." That increase, along with the subsequent reform of the welfare system in 1996, made the EITC arguably the most important income transfer program in the United States. It also made our original Upjohn Institute monograph, *The Earned Income Tax Credit: Anti-Poverty Effectiveness and Labor Market Effects*, a bit outdated. Our book, published in 1990, was, as far as we know, the first broad-based research by economists on the EITC. It covered almost everything that was then known about the economic impact of the EITC in a slim 91 pages.

But the expansion of the EITC also presented us with an opportunity to revise and expand our original monograph and incorporate the many policy changes and research efforts that occurred in the 1990s and early 2000s. We are grateful to Kevin Hollenbeck of the Upjohn Institute who first suggested to us the idea of updating our original monograph. We thank the Upjohn Institute for their financial support of our work, and Timothy Bartik and Kevin Hollenbeck of the Institute staff for their many, very useful comments on earlier drafts. We also benefitted from the comments of our colleagues at the University of Delaware and from conversations with many EITC experts, especially Janet Holtzblatt of the U.S. Department of the Treasury.

We could not, of course, have written this book without the many, many scholars who have studied the EITC program in the 1990s and the early 2000s. The work they produced is substantial and of a consistently high quality. We have done our very best to give it a fair and honest treatment. We thank all the contributors for their efforts and apologize, in advance, for those who may think that we did their work less than justice.

Our book was copyedited by Bob Wathen who did an admirable job of cleaning up our prose. Richard Wyrwa of the Upjohn Institute supervised the production of the book, and we are grateful to him for his attention to details and willingness to work with us on many issues. Erik Helm of the University of Delaware helped us put together many of the more complicated graphs, especially those in Chapter 1 and Chapter 8. We are grateful to him for his assistance.

Introduction

When we first wrote about the Earned Income Tax Credit (EITC) in 1990, it was still a little-known and lightly funded government program that played a relatively minor role in the government's broad set of antipoverty policies. The EITC, as it is usually known, had been around since 1975, when it was introduced as a small "work bonus" for very low income working families. It had barely been revised or expanded in the intervening years. Despite the cutbacks of the Reagan years, welfare thoroughly dominated the antipoverty policy approach. Expenditures on Aid to Families with Dependent Children (AFDC) and Food Stamps, the two most well-known transfer programs, were about $20 billion each and Medicaid, the medical assistance program for the poor, added another $70 billion. In contrast, total payments under the EITC were about $7.5 billion and the average recipient family received just $601. It was still several years before candidate Bill Clinton would promise "to end welfare as we know it" and 6 years before welfare reform, in a form that truly was the end of welfare as we had known it, would actually come to pass.

Yet, even then, the EITC was clearly something different. Unique among income-transfer programs for the poor, the EITC conditioned its benefits on earnings. Families without earnings received nothing, reflecting its linkage to work. Benefits actually increased with family earnings through a portion of the income distribution, before eventually phasing out at higher incomes. This was just the opposite of the traditional welfare programs like AFDC and Food Stamps, which provided maximum benefits to families without earnings and then reduced benefits at a very high rate as family earnings increased. Married couples as well as single parents were eligible for EITC under identical rules—another difference from AFDC, which provided far more generous treatment of single-parent families than married couples. In fact, the EITC wasn't technically a welfare program. It was a tax credit, administered by the Internal Revenue Service (IRS), not through the welfare system. And nearly unique among tax credits, it was refundable, which meant that poor working families could fully realize its benefits, even if they owed little or no taxes.

1

For these reasons, and many more, the EITC was even then emerging as a government antipoverty program that both liberals and conservatives could support. It could be broadly seen as endorsing work, since its benefit structure rewarded rather than penalized work, at least among the poorest of its recipients. Conservative politicians, weary of the low workforce activity of AFDC recipients, found that very appealing. Liberals viewed it not as a replacement for traditional welfare, but as a supplement and as a potential source of cash assistance for the working poor, a group often overlooked by most poverty programs. Others noted that it could function as a kind of substitute for a higher minimum wage and that it could do so without the concerns about higher minimum wages reducing employment opportunities and with better targeting of its benefits to low and moderate income households. The EITC operated without a large bureaucracy and without the welfare offices that neither clients nor administrators liked. It was fast becoming, as we wrote then, "a rallying point in redirecting poverty policy." We noted that its "time in the national agenda has clearly come," and we predicted that it would grow and change.

We were certainly correct about that! Indeed, it has grown and changed, well beyond even our own expectations. Who could have predicted then that, a decade later, the EITC, and not AFDC, would be the centerpiece of antipoverty programs? How did that happen?

Two major policy actions were decisive in this change in emphasis. The first was change in the EITC program itself, the result of an unusual alliance of conservatives and liberals, a linking of "conservative values" with "liberal funding." The decade began with an important EITC expansion. This increase, which came under the Bush Administration, was effective in 1991. Then came candidate Clinton who had promised not only to reform welfare but also "to make work pay," a phrase that signaled his interest in helping the working poor. He made good on this latter promise in 1993, when he proposed and Congress passed a major increase in the EITC.

By 1996, when the changes were fully phased in, the program was almost unrecognizable from its former modest self. As a result of the two sets of changes, the earnings subsidy rate had nearly tripled from 14 percent to 40 percent for a family with two children. The maximum credit had more than doubled and now exceeded $3,000 for a family with two children, nearly three and a half times higher than the maximum in 1990. Adults without children, who had been ineligible for

EITC benefits, were offered a modest credit. The total number of families receiving benefits jumped by nearly 70 percent to more than 20 million in 1998. Total EITC expenditures nearly quadrupled to $25 billion in 1995 and over $30 billion in 2000 (U.S. Committee on Ways and Means 2000).

The second important policy change was the "end of welfare as we knew it." Welfare reform was a high priority of the Clinton Administration, but it waited in the wings while the ill-fated health care reform initiative was advanced and ultimately defeated. When the administration did finally present a specific welfare reform program in the summer of 1994, it was a casualty of the November 1994 elections when the Republicans took control of the House of Representatives. The president's welfare reform proposal was never considered. The House Republicans included a very conservative version of welfare reform as a major element in their Contract with America, and they passed an ambitious and wide-sweeping reform. That particular version was vetoed by the president, but the president signed a somewhat modified and slightly milder version of welfare reform in the summer of 1996.

That law, the Personal Responsibility and Work Opportunity Reconciliation Act of 1996, effectively abolished rather than reformed welfare. Effective July 1, 1997, AFDC, the primary cash assistance program for the poor since the mid 1930s, was replaced with the Temporary Assistance for Needy Families (TANF) program. While TANF is essentially similar in its overall benefit structure to AFDC—it provides maximum benefits to families with no income—it is not a legal entitlement as AFDC was, and it imposes strict time limits on lifetime usage as well as other requirements that each state may choose to impose. Most states have revamped their programs, substituting employment activities for check-writing. Almost all states now require recipients to move quickly into available jobs. Nearly half of the states now require TANF applicants to participate in job search or other work-related activities as a condition of eligibility. Strict penalties for noncompliance have been imposed in most states. There is little doubt that the world of welfare has changed dramatically and probably permanently.

Following welfare reform and buoyed by the strong economy and low unemployment rates of the mid and late 1990s, welfare rolls have plummeted. The number of welfare recipients fell sharply from 13 million in 1996 to under 6 million in mid-year 2000; the number of families fell similarly, from 4.6 million to 2.2 million. The TANF caseload is now less than one-ninth of the number of households who receive EITC benefits.

As a result of these two important and related policy changes—the expansion of EITC and the reform of welfare—the EITC has emerged as the largest cash transfer program for the poor and the near-poor. There is little doubt that it will retain that status in the foreseeable future.

In this volume, we offer an overview of the EITC as it stands early in the twenty-first century after the tumultuous decade of the 1990s. We describe, analyze, evaluate, summarize, and critique the EITC in the year 2001, and we also make recommendations for changes on the basis of our analysis. The enormous expansion of the program has brought both a great increase in research about the EITC and its impact on the economy as well as controversy and criticism, both among economists and politicians. A more generous program naturally has more substantial impacts, and not all of them are necessarily positive. High implicit tax rates of the EITC, created by the need to phaseout the more generous benefits it now provides, are suspected of providing substantial work disincentives among some recipients. President Bush has spoken of the tax system as the "tollbooth on the road to the middle class"; ironically, some argue that the EITC phase-out rate is now part of the toll. Others contend that substantial marriage penalties are imbedded in the program, while still others allege that the EITC is subject for excessive fraud.

Our own view, reinforced by the many studies we have reviewed, is that the EITC is a government program that, on the whole, works and works well. That alone is no small achievement in the policy world of antipoverty programs, many of which have a well-documented history of failure and/or unanticipated negative effects. The EITC continues to offer substantial and meaningful earnings supplements to low and moderate income households. It successfully pushes many working families out of poverty. It is a viable and attractive alternative to an increase in the minimum wage. It does all of this, we will show, while creating relatively few substantial problems of its own. It is, however, not perfect, and we offer a set of very specific suggestions for revising the problems we do identify.

The accomplishments of the EITC are many and they are discussed throughout this volume. Chief among them are the following.

- The EITC provided cash assistance to a total of over 18 million households and provided them an average of about $1,625 in the year 2000. These households included about 6 million working-poor households who received an average of over $1,450 and another 3.75 million near-poor households who received an average of $1,650.

- The EITC reduced the poverty rate in 1999 by 1.5 percentage points. About 4 million persons were lifted out of poverty as a result of the cash assistance they received from the EITC.

- As an income-transfer policy for poor households, the EITC is clearly preferable to the minimum wage. For workers in the poorest households, the EITC operates exactly like an increase in the minimum wage, but without the potentially troubling increase in the wage price of labor that may reduce employment opportunities. For such a worker with two children, the effective minimum wage in 2000 was not its statutory rate of $5.15, but rather $7.21, courtesy of the 40 percent wage subsidy provided by the EITC. Additionally, the EITC targets its benefits to low and moderate income households with far more precision than the minimum wage does.

- The EITC has increased the labor force participation of many groups. For example, all estimates indicate that the EITC has increased labor force participation among single mothers, among married women whose husbands have low incomes, and among married men with children. While other factors such as welfare reform and the strong economy are undoubtedly important contributing factors, the EITC has had a major impact on the sharp increase in the labor force participation of single mothers and may well be the leading causal factor.

- Estimates of the impact of the EITC on the hours of work of current workers are relatively small in absolute value, whether positive or negative. There is no empirical evidence that the EITC has had serious adverse effects on hours of work among current workers, as some critics have claimed.

- Concerns about the negative impact of the EITC on marriage appear not to be warranted at this time.

There are, however, some emerging problem areas.

- The EITC penalizes work among workers with incomes at the high end of the EITC schedule, typically a family with earnings in the $25,000 range. Like any income support program, EITC benefits eventually decrease as a family's income increases. For families with two or more children, this "phase-out" rate is 21 percent. When combined with the federal income tax and the payroll tax, this adds up to a total marginal tax rate of about 50 percent. There is growing evidence that this high tax rate has discouraged work in married-couple families with moderate incomes.

- The EITC imposes substantial financial marriage penalties. If a childless full-time minimum wage worker marries a full-time minimum wage worker with two children, they suffer an EITC marriage penalty of more than $1,600 compared to what they could have if they remained single. In the unlikely event that they each had two children, their EITC financial sacrifice to marry would be $5,600! EITC marriage bonuses are possible but appear to be less common in practice.

- The EITC still leaves larger families with low wage workers in poverty. A married couple with two children and a single wage earner working full time at $6.50 an hour is still poor even after adding in its $4,000 EITC income.

- The eligibility criteria are needlessly complex. This is especially true regarding whether or not a household has "a qualifying child" and thus is eligible for the more generous benefits available to households with children. As a result, compliance issues have arisen. Some estimates suggest that as much as 25 percent of EITC payments are "in error," meaning that they do not comply with a strict interpretation of the complex EITC rules.

These problems are not, in fact, independent. This dependence is, in fact, a virtue when attempting to improve the program: a revision that addresses one problem also contributes to solving the others. In Chapter 8, we propose three very specific changes to alleviate these problems: 1) reducing the current EITC phase-out rate for a family with two or more children; 2) establishing a separate, more generous EITC schedule for married couples; and 3) providing a new rate schedule for families with three or more children. These three simple changes go a long way toward alleviating the above problems.

As is perhaps inevitable in writing about important public policies, the ground is constantly shifting. When we began our research in the summer of 2000, the Clinton Administration had proposed changes in the EITC, but no legislation was passed. As we completed our work in the summer of 2001, the major tax cut legislation of the Bush Administration had just been passed. The legislation included three changes that affected the EITC and/or its interaction with the broader tax code: 1) a new 10 percent tax bracket for the first $12,000 of income for a married couple, effective in 2001; 2) a refundable child tax credit, worth up to $1,200 for a family with two children, also effective in 2001; and 3) a change in the EITC benefit schedule for married couples, effective in 2002 and phased in slowly through 2007. The legislation also calls for these changes and all the other changes in the legislation to be eliminated in 2011, although few knowledgeable observers believe that will actually occur.

The tax cut of 2001 did not change the basic structure of the EITC, and our best guess is that the unique structure of the EITC will emerge from the first decade of the 2000s relatively unchanged as compared with the 1990s. Its basic benefit structure, conditioned on earnings and with benefits that first increase with earnings, is now well-established. There may, of course, be changes in benefit rates and other program details, although none appear to be on President Bush's current economic agenda. We hope that the analyses we present will serve not only those who want to know about the EITC as it stands now but also help understand the likely impact of any changes that may be implemented in future years. To that end, we have tried to emphasize general analytical principles. At the same time, we have tried to present a relatively complete account of how the EITC works and what is currently known about the impacts of the EITC. We hope that this volume will be a useful source book for anyone interested in learning about the EITC.

Throughout the book, whenever we use specific numbers to describe the EITC program, we have used the EITC as it stood in the year 2001. That year is the most current for which, at the time of this research, all EITC program parameters, including the various income thresholds that are an integral part of the benefit schedule, were known. We took full account of the tax code changes in 2001 that affected the EITC in 2001 but not of those that become effective only in future years.

Chapter 1 provides an overview of the history and operation of the EITC. It focuses especially on the unique EITC benefit formula and its implication for marginal tax rates. We include there a full discussion of the newest tax code changes and how they alter the EITC landscape. Chapter 2 looks at the EITC recipient population—who they are, how much they work, what they earn, and what they get from the EITC program. It also examines the impact of the EITC on the poverty rate. In Chapters 3 through 7, we evaluate the impact of the EITC program. In Chapters 3 and 4, we look at the impact of the EITC on individual behavior—labor supply and wage rates in Chapter 3 and marriage in Chapter 4. In Chapter 5, we compare the EITC to other antipoverty and transfer programs, including the minimum wage and TANF. Chapter 6 examines the impact of the EITC on the economy from the standpoint of its efficiency cost. Transfer and tax policies alter the relative prices that individuals face and in the process change the behavior of both recipients (who get the benefits) and taxpayers (who finance the benefits). These changes can end up costing the economy something in addition to the apparent dollar expenditures of the program itself; those additional costs are what economists call efficiency cost. Finally, Chapter 7 looks at the compliance problems of the EITC.

Based on the evaluations presented in Chapter 3 through 7, we offer ideas about how to strengthen the EITC program in Chapter 8. We firmly believe that the program works well in most respects but that modest changes would make a difference. We make a specific proposal to reform the EITC program in a very few selective ways. We then simulate the impact to assess the cost of the reform and see how it would be likely to change the program. Our approach is, of course, not the only way to accomplish reform. Other reforms have been proposed and we describe some of the well-known alternative proposals. We also discuss changes in the EITC program that will become effective after 2001.

Finally, in Chapter 9, we look both backwards at what the EITC has accomplished and forward toward what can be done to strengthen it.

1
An Overview of the Earned Income Tax Credit

The EITC provides a cash benefit through the tax system to low income working households. Unless the household actually earns labor income, it is ineligible for the credit. To receive an EITC benefit, a household must have positive labor earnings and total income less than a specified ceiling. Figure 1.1 shows the fundamental difference between the EITC and welfare. Panel A shows a simplified EITC schedule: when earnings are zero, the benefit is zero; as earnings increase, the benefit increases until a maximum benefit is reached; and then, as income continues to increase, the benefit is phased out. Panel B shows a simplified welfare schedule: when earnings are zero, the benefit is at its maximum, and as income increases, the benefit is phased out.

The size of the EITC depends on the number of children in the household. Throughout this chapter, we often focus on a family of four with two children and use the numerical values that apply to such a family.

Figure 1.2 shows a simplified EITC schedule that makes it easier for nonspecialists to remember the key magnitudes of the current EITC

Figure 1.1 The Relationship Between Earnings and Benefits Under EITC and Welfare

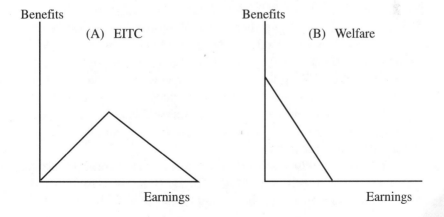

Figure 1.2 Simplified EITC Schedule, Family with Two or More Children

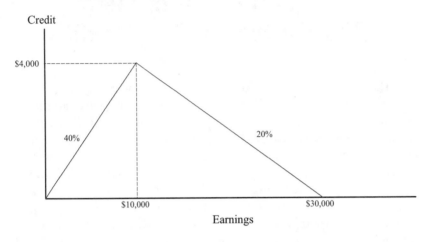

program. The simplified schedule presents round numbers and percentages that are roughly accurate for a family with two or more children in 2001 (note that the figure omits the small flat range that connects the phase-in range and the phase-out range under the actual EITC; this flat range is an optional component of an EITC). The family receives an EITC of $40 for each $100 of wage income it earns until its wage income reaches $10,000 and its EITC benefit reaches $4,000. Further family income (from either labor or capital) causes a phase-out of the credit; the credit is reduced $20 for every additional $100 of income the family obtains so that the credit falls to zero when the family's income reaches $30,000. Note that the phase-in of the EITC depends on labor earnings, whereas the phase-out depends on income (whether from labor or capital). Because the phase-in requires labor earnings, we label the horizontal axis of all EITC figures in this chapter "earnings," even though the phase-out depends on income. It should be noted, however, that if the family's investment income (for example, interest, dividends, and capital gains) exceeds $2,450, the family is *ineligible* for the EITC. Thus, the EITC excludes families with significant investment income.

The EITC is a *refundable* tax credit on the federal personal income tax. Like any tax credit, it enables an eligible household to reduce the tax it would otherwise pay. For example, if a household's tax would have been $800, but its EITC is $600, then the household must only pay $200 in tax. Refundable means that if the tax credit exceeds the tax the household would otherwise owe (the tax before credit), then the government pays the household the difference. For example, if a household's tax (before EITC) is $200 and its EITC is $600, then the government will pay the household $400.

A HISTORY OF THE EITC

The EITC began quietly and modestly in 1975—so quietly that it was virtually unnoticed by the general public for many years, in sharp contrast to welfare and the minimum wage. Under the original version, a household with at least one child received a supplement of 10 percent of its wage earnings until earnings reached $4,000 and the credit reached $400; then, for each $100 of income above $4,000, the credit was reduced $10 so that the credit completely phased out when household income reached $8,000. By comparison, for a household with two children today, the phase-in rate is 40 percent, not 10 percent, and the maximum credit is roughly $4,000, not $400 (today's maximum is much larger even when adjusted for inflation).

One rationale often given for the EITC is that it offsets the burden of the Social Security payroll tax for low income households. But why not simply exempt the first few thousand dollars of wage income from the payroll tax? One reason is that this exemption would complicate the employer's task of implementing the payroll tax for Social Security. Another is that an exemption might weaken the political claim of these workers to Social Security benefits upon retirement. Another is that such an exemption would be poorly targeted because many workers with low wage income are members of families that are high income due to the labor or investment income of other family members. Thus, the EITC can be viewed as a well-targeted vehicle for offsetting the burden of the payroll tax on low income workers.

Historically, however, the initiative for the enactment of the EITC in the 1970s came mainly from conservatives who viewed the EITC as an alternative to welfare (Howard 1997, Ventry 2000). The driving force behind the EITC was Senator Russell Long, the conservative chairman of the Senate Finance Committee. Long came to propose an EITC in the early 1970s in reaction to liberal welfare programs and to moderate welfare reform proposed by the Nixon Administration—the controversial Family Assistance Plan (FAP)—which proposed a low guaranteed income coupled with a work requirement. Long believed that the welfare system discouraged work, that any guaranteed income would exacerbate the problem, and that the FAP work requirement would not be enforceable. Howard wrote:

> When FAP was reconsidered in 1972, Long proposed an alternative. His "workfare" bill declared all employable persons ineligible for cash assistance. They would instead have to find work or accept a government job paying 60 percent of the minimum wage. By setting the wage scale so low, Long clearly intended to minimize the need for public jobs. As an added incentive, Long stipulated that workers earning low wages in the private sector would be eligible for a 10 percent work bonus. Heads of households with children would be eligible for a cash payment equivalent to 10 percent of their income as long as family income was less than $4,000. (p. 67)

This 10 percent work bonus (for earnings up to $4,000) appears to be the earliest actual EITC proposal. The first EITC, enacted 3 years later in 1975, was in fact a 10 percent credit on earnings up to $4,000.

The testimony before Long's committee in early 1972 of another conservative, then-Governor Ronald Reagan, may have contributed to Long's development of the 10 percent work bonus proposal. Although most of Reagan's testimony focused on his conservative approach to welfare in California, it contained a passage in which Reagan suggested that the federal government should exempt low income families from income taxes and give them a rebate for their Social Security taxes. Long endorsed Reagan's general testimony, and several months later proposed the 10 percent work bonus.

Although the House passed Nixon's FAP, the Senate Finance Committee rejected it in favor of Long's workfare proposal (including the work bonus), and the House and Senate could not agree on a welfare reform law. In 1973, Long introduced the work bonus proposal, not in the context of welfare reform, but as an offset to an increase in Social Security taxes. In this context, liberals voted for it and it passed 57 to 21. Its failure to become law, however, may have been due to the opposition of liberal House members who remembered its conservative workfare origin. The work bonus lay dormant until 1975.

The recession of 1975, resulting partly from the world oil price shock of 1974, gave Long an opportunity as Congress contemplated legislation to combat the recession. The main provision of the Tax Reduction Act of 1975 was a tax rebate to all households to stimulate consumption spending. Virtually unnoticed, however, Long attached to the bill a new refundable 10 percent tax credit for poor families—the "Earned Income Tax Credit." Thus, the EITC became law, not as part of a debate on social welfare legislation, but as part of an effort to respond to a recession. With most other Americans receiving a new income tax rebate, it seemed only fair to give some cash assistance to the working poor, all of whom were subject to the payroll tax, but many of whom did not pay any income tax. Hence, the new tax credit had to be "refundable" in order to reach them. Although Long played the key role, it should be noted that it was the moderate chairman of the House Ways and Means Committee, Al Ullman, who initially attached a version of the EITC to the administration's tax package. Howard (1997) wrote:

> Regardless of the precise explanation, the important points to note are that the EITC was a small part of a larger revenue bill; that no hearings were held or votes taken specifically concerning the EITC; that it generated little debate and reflected little input from interest groups; that moderate to conservative members of the revenue committees were instrumental to its passage; that it appealed simultaneously to proponents of welfare reform and tax relief for the working poor . . . (p. 72)

Howard concluded this way:

> Although all the traditional explanations for new social programs stress the rare and the extraordinary, what sets the EITC apart is how mundane and ordinary were its origins. Politicians who were moderate to conservative on social policy . . . were responsible for the timing and structure of the EITC. The key figure was Long, a strategically located member of the Senate Finance Committee and a conservative Democrat. Long transformed the family assistance supplement into the work bonus, kept the work bonus idea alive between 1972 and 1975, and successfully portrayed the EITC as an amalgam of welfare reform and tax relief for low-

income workers. He did not have to publicize the merits of his proposal or engineer any groundswell of popular support. He did not have to win the president's endorsement, knit together a coalition of support in Congress, or even engage in explicit log-rolling. Instead, Long had to find the right legislative vehicle to essentially hide the EITC and the right language to portray its objectives to anyone who noticed. He then used his power as Senate Finance chairman, which happened to reach a high water mark in 1975, to guarantee passage of this tax credit. (p. 74)

The EITC hardly grew over the next decade (U.S. Committee on Ways and Means 2000). At the end of the 1970s the phase-in range was raised from $4,000 to $5,000, thereby raising the maximum credit from $400 to $500. The late 1970s were a period of high inflation, however, so the adjustment mainly offset inflation. Total credits rose only from $1.3 billion in 1975 to $2.1 billion in 1985. The first real growth occurred in the second half of the 1980s. In the mid 1980s the phase-in rate was raised from 10 percent to 14 percent, the phase-in range was raised so that the maximum credit increased from $550 in 1985 to $953 in 1990, and the phase-out rate was reduced from over 12 percent to 10 percent. Total credits rose from $2.1 billion in 1985 to $7.5 billion in 1990.

The EITC's conservative origins delayed its acceptance by liberals, but eventually liberals came to appreciate the merits of the EITC. Liberals found that conservatives would oppose any expansion of welfare because it aided people who didn't work, but they would accept an expansion of the EITC because it aided only people who worked. Liberals might want to aid both groups, but they eventually decided that it made sense to join with conservatives to use the EITC to aid people who worked. Similarly, conservatives opposed liberal efforts to increase the legal minimum wage, partly because of its cost to small businesses but also because its impact was poorly targeted—beneficiaries were often teenagers from affluent homes. Liberals realized they could make political headway with the well-targeted EITC, in contrast to welfare and the minimum wage. By 1990, liberals had become supporters of the EITC despite its conservative origins. In 1990, the EITC enjoyed strong support across the entire political spectrum (Hoffman and Seidman 1990). The stage was set for a dramatic expansion.

Two major EITC expansions were enacted in 1990 and 1993. The 1990 expansion (enacted by a Democratic Congress and signed by a Republican president) raised the phase-in rate from 14 percent to 18.5 percent in 1993 for a family with one child and to 19.5 percent for a family with two or more children, thereby providing a small additional credit (1 percent) for the second child for the first time. The expansion raised the maximum credit from $953 in 1990 to $1,511 in 1993 for a family with two or more children. Total credits rose from $7.5 billion in 1990 to $15.5 billion in 1993. The 1993 expansion (enacted by a Democratic Congress and signed by a Democratic president) raised the phase-in rate from 18.5 percent to 34 percent for a family with one child in 1995 and from 19.5 percent to 40 percent for a family with two or more children in 1996, thereby raising the additional credit for the second child from 1 percent to 6 percent. The expansion more than doubled the maximum credit from $1,511 in 1993 to $3,556 in 1996 for a family with two or more children. For the first time, a small credit (7.65 percent up to a maximum of $323 in 1996) was given to a family with no children (provided the head was between ages 24 and 65). Total credits rose from $15.5 billion in 1993 to $28.8 billion in 1996. Thus, the two expansions nearly quadrupled total credits from 1990 to 1996 (from $7.5 billion to $28.8 billion).

This rapid expansion in the first half of the 1990s resulted in criticism from some conservatives (Ventry 2000) in the second half of the 1990s. In 1995 Senator Roth (R-DE), chairman of the Senate Finance Committee, expressed the view of some conservatives when he said (Ventry 2000 p. 1005): "The EITC was to create incentives for low-income parents to work. It was that simple. But as they say about too much of a good thing becoming dangerous, such is what happened to this once well-intended program."

One concern was an IRS study reporting a high "error rate" for the EITC: perhaps 25 percent of EITC payments were technically incorrect according to a strict interpretation of the complex EITC rules concerning the definition of a qualifying child, the required filing status, and the determination of which family member should file for the EITC. Ironically, some of this complexity resulted from well-intentioned efforts to improve the targeting of the EITC. In response to the apparently high error rate, hearings were held in both houses of Congress. Other concerns were that the EITC might be imposing a significant marriage penalty, discouraging recipients on its phase-out range from additional work, and costing taxpayers too much.

Despite these concerns, the EITC has retained enough support to avert any repeal of its two expansions. Its phase-in rates have been maintained (34 percent for a family with one child and 40 percent for a family with two or more children), and its maximum credit has risen automatically with inflation from $3,556 in 1996 for a family with two or more children to $4,008 in 2001. Total credits increased from $28.8 billion in 1996 to a projected $30.7 billion in 2001.

The tax act of 2001 maintained the EITC phase-in rates and maximum credits and reduced the marriage penalty (beginning in 2002) by making benefits larger for married couples.

MECHANICS OF THE EITC

In this section, we explain how the EITC works and its interaction with the income tax and the child tax credit (CTC). We use the numerical parameters of the EITC program and the tax system for the year 2001. We include all changes for the year 2001 that were the enacted in the tax act of 2001 (passed by Congress in May 2001 and signed into law by the president on June 7). The phase-in and phase-out thresholds are automatically adjusted each year for inflation so these numbers will increase automatically beyond 2001. The tax act of 2001 reduced the EITC marriage penalty beginning in 2002, but this change does not affect our analysis of the 2001 EITC program. In a section at the end of this chapter, we describe the changes in the EITC that were adopted in the tax act of 2001 but did not go into effect until after 2001. The EITC for a family varies with the number of children. Throughout this section, we will use the numerical values that apply to a family of four with two children.

There are three distinguishing features of an EITC. First, if a household has no labor earnings, it receives no credit. Second, the EITC begins with a phase-in range where the credit rises as the household's labor earnings rise. Third, the EITC ends with a phase-out range where the credit falls as income rises.

Note that the phase-in of the EITC depends on labor earnings, whereas the phase-out depends on income (from both labor and capital). Because the phase-in requires labor earnings, we label the horizontal axis of all EITC figures in this chapter "earnings," even though the phase-out depends on income. Note, however, that under the current EITC, if the family's investment income (for example, interest, dividends, and capital gains) exceeds $2,450 (in 2001), the family is ineligible for the EITC. *Thus, the EITC excludes families with significant investment income.* One feature of the current EITC is a flat range between the phase-in range and the phase-out range. When the EITC was enacted in 1975 there was no flat range, but the EITC has contained a flat range for many years.

Figure 1.3 shows the EITC schedule for 2001 for a household with two or more children. If the household's earnings are zero, its credit is zero. The phase-in rate is 40 percent, so when the household earns its first $100, it receives a credit of $40; it continues to receive $40 for each additional $100 of earnings until earnings reach $10,020 and the credit reaches $4,008 (40 percent of $10,020). There is a stationary range from $10,020 to $13,090 where the credit remains $4,008. The phase-out begins at $13,090. The phase-out rate is 21.06 percent; for each additional $100 of income, the credit is reduced by $21.06. Because the maximum credit is $4,008, it takes $19,031 of additional income to phase out the credit completely (because $4,008/0.2106 = $19,031). Thus, when earnings reach $32,121, the credit is zero (be-

Figure 1.3 EITC Schedule, Family with Two or More Children (2001)

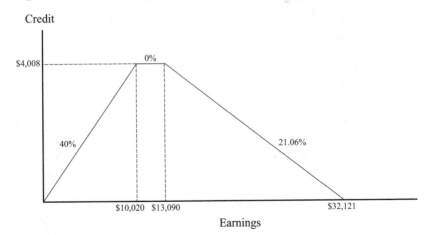

cause $13,090 + $19,031 = $32,121), so *the EITC phase-out income* is $32,121.

Under the 2001 EITC schedule, the credit C for a household with two or more children with labor earnings E and total income Y is given by[1]:

$C = 0.40E$	if $E \leq \$10,020$.
$C = \$4,008$	if $\$10,020 \leq E$ and $Y \leq \$13,090$.
$C = \$4,008 - 0.2106 \, (Y - \$13,090)$	if $\$10,020 \leq E$ and $\$13,090 \leq Y \leq \$32,121$.
$C = 0$	if $Y \geq \$32,121$.

With this 2001 EITC schedule, there is a nice round number example for a household with two or more children: if the household's income is $25,000, its EITC is $1,500 (because C = 4,008 − 0.2106 (25,000 − 13,090) = 1,500). Thus, we can summarize the current EITC schedule this way: the maximum credit is $4,008 when earnings are between $10,020 and $13,090; the credit phases down to $1,500 when income reaches $25,000; and the credit phases out to $0 when income reaches $32,121. See Appendix A for the algebra of a general EITC schedule.

The "Marginal Tax Rate" Generated by the EITC

Whenever any government benefit phases down as a person earns additional income, the phase-down reduces the person's net gain from earning additional income. For example, suppose that, when a person earns an additional $100, the government benefit is reduced $20. Then, the person's net gain from earning the additional $100 is $80. It is *as though* the person were being taxed 20 percent on the additional earnings. Economists therefore describe this situation by saying the person faces a *marginal tax rate* of 20 percent.

But, of course, the person is not actually being taxed. The person is not making a payment to the government. The government is making a payment to the person, and the person is better off because of the program. Economists may not realize that, when they say the EITC imposes a marginal tax rate of 21.06 percent, some listeners may be misled into thinking that the EITC makes the person pay the government 21.06 percent of any additional earnings and that the EITC therefore reduces the person's income and makes the person worse off. In fact, the EITC always raises a person's income and makes the person better off than he would be without the EITC.

The marginal tax rate, however, does tell how much a person gains by earning another $100. If the marginal tax rate is 21.06 percent, then the person gains $78.94 by earning another $100. Thus, a high marginal tax rate may discourage individuals from making the effort to earn more. Even if they do earn more, they may be discouraged because their net gain is less than their additional earnings. It is therefore important to analyze the pattern of marginal tax rates generated by the EITC.

Figure 1.4 shows the pattern of marginal tax rates. Look first at the phase-out range from $13,090 to $32,121. In the phase-out range, for every additional $100 of income, the EITC is reduced $21.06, so the household's net gain (after earning an additional $100) is only $78.94. This net gain of $78.94 is the same that an ordinary taxpayer would obtain if she were in a 21.06 percent tax bracket. Thus, the EITC recipient in the phase-out range faces a marginal tax rate of 21.06 percent. As we emphasized above, this marginal tax rate of 21.06 percent does not mean that families in this income range (between $13,090 and $32,121) are hurt by the EITC; on the contrary, they are helped by it—they receive an EITC payment from the government that raises their income.

**Figure 1.4 EITC Marginal Tax Rates, Family with Two or More
          Children (2001)**

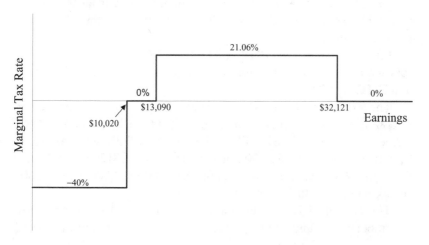

In the phase-in range from $0 to $10,020, the EITC recipient faces a negative marginal tax rate equal to −40 percent (a marginal subsidy rate of +40 percent) because, for every $100 of earnings, the household gains $140. Thus, the current EITC for a household with two or more children is characterized by three marginal tax rates: −40 percent in the phase-in range, 0 percent in the stationary range, and +21.06 percent in the phase-out range.[2]

THE EITC, THE CHILD TAX CREDIT, AND THE INCOME TAX

In this section, we ignore any other tax credits or taxes in order to focus on the EITC, the child tax credit (CTC), and the income tax. A working family of four with two children receives an EITC if its income is less than $32,121. If its earnings are above $10,000, it also receives a CTC. At the same time, if its earnings are above $19,200, it faces an income tax rate of 10 percent until its income reaches $31,200, at which point the tax rate jumps to 15 percent; this schedule determines its *tax-before-credits* (TBC), that is, its tax before deducting the two credits. The household's net payment to the government therefore equals TBC − CTC − EITC. If this amount is negative, it means the household receives a net payment from the government equal to EITC + CTC − TBC. Thus, the family's net receipt from or payment to the government, and the combined marginal tax rate it faces, depends on the interaction of the EITC, CTC, and TBC. In this section we analyze this interaction.

Figure 1.5 shows the EITC, CTC, and TBC schedules for a household with a husband, wife, and two children in 2001. It also shows the sum EITC + CTC.

The TBC is zero until $19,200 because of the standard deduction, $7,600, and four personal exemptions ($2,900 each) totaling $11,600 ($7,600 + $11,600 = $19,200). The tax act of 2001 set a tax rate of 10 percent on the first $12,000 of taxable income ($12,000 of income above $19,200); when income reaches $31,200 ($12,000 + $19,200), the tax rate jumps to 15 percent.

The tax act of 2001 made the CTC refundable, so there are now two important refundable tax credits implemented through the federal

Figure 1.5 EITC, CTC, and TBC Family of Four with Two Children (2001)

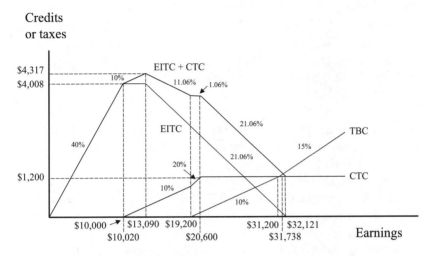

personal income tax: the EITC and the CTC (Seidman and Hoffman 2001). The CTC equals 10 percent of the excess of earnings over $10,000, *plus* the amount needed to cancel the TBC (CTC = 0.1 [earnings − $10,000] + TBC), *up to a limit* of $1,200 (2 × $600 per child). As shown in Figure 1.5, the CTC begins at earnings of $10,000 and phases in at a 10 percent rate until earnings reach $19,200 (where the TBC schedule begins with the new first-bracket rate of 10 percent) and the CTC reaches $920. The phase-in rate then jumps to 20 percent (the additional 10 percent is due to the 10 percent needed to cancel the new first-bracket tax rate under the TBC) until income reaches $20,600 and the CTC reaches $1,200 (because the CTC = 0.1[earnings − $10,000] + TBC = 0.1[$20,600 − $10,000] + 0.1 ($20,600 − $19,200) = $1,060 + $140 = $1,200). Thereafter, the CTC remains constant at $1,200 until the family's income is very high, after which it phases out (not shown in the figure).

The EITC + CTC schedule is also shown in Figure 1.5. From $0 to $10,000 (where the CTC begins), it coincides with the EITC schedule with a phase-in rate of 40 percent. Over the tiny range from $10,000 to $10,020, not visible on the figure, it has a phase-in rate of 50 percent (40 + 10). From $10,020 to $13,090 (where the EITC phase-out begins) its phase-in rate is 10 percent, due entirely to the

CTC (because the EITC is constant over this range). At $13,090, EITC + CTC is at its maximum value of $4,317 (an EITC of $4,008 and a CTC of $309). From $13,090 to $19,200, the EITC + CTC phase-down rate is 11.06 percent (21.06 − 10); from $19,200 to $20,600, 1.06 percent (21.06 − 20); from $20,600 to $31,121 (where the EITC phases out to zero), 21.06 percent (21.06 − 0); at $32,121, EITC + CTC reaches $1,200 and then remains constant (until a high income), after which it phases out (not shown).

If EITC + CTC is greater than TBC, the household receives a net payment from the government. This is the case until income reaches $31,738.[3] Thus, a family of four must earn more than $31,738 before its TBC exceeds EITC + CTC.

Figure 1.6 shows the marginal tax rate facing the family as a consequence of the interaction of the EITC, CTC, and TBC. From $0 to $10,000, the marginal tax rate equals −40 percent (due to the EITC alone); over the tiny range from $10,000 to $10,020, −50 percent (due to the EITC and CTC phase-in rates of 40 percent and 10 percent); from $10,020 to $13,090, −10 percent (due to the CTC alone); from $13,090 to $19,200, 11.06 percent (because the EITC phases out at 21.06 percent rate but the CTC phases in at a 10 percent rate); from $19,200 to $20,600, 11.06 percent (the income tax rate is 10 percent

Figure 1.6 Marginal Tax Rate, Family of Four with Two Children (2001)

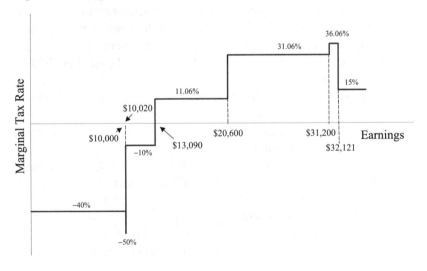

and the EITC phase-out rate is 21.06 percent, but the CTC phase-in rate is 20 percent, so 10 + 21.06 − 20 = 11.06); from $20,600 to $31,200, 31.06 percent (the income tax rate is 10 percent, the EITC phase-out rate is 21.06, and the CTC is constant); over the small range from $31,200 to $32,121, 36.06 percent (the EITC phase-out rate of 21.06 percent plus the income tax rate of 15 percent); and above $32,121, 15 percent (due to the income tax alone).

PROVISIONS OF THE 2001 EITC[4]

This section gives a brief description of the main provisions of the 2001 EITC program. We discuss these provisions in greater detail in Chapter 7 on compliance issues. The tax act of 2001 adopted several changes that will begin *after* 2001—these changes will be noted in the next section.

Table 1.1 shows the earned income credit parameters for 1975–2001. The table shows how the size of the EITC varies with the number of children. Prior to 1993, eligibility required at least one child, but a small credit was established in 1993 for workers without children (the worker must be over the age of 24 and under 65). There was a single schedule until 1990 regardless of the number of children, but the credit for a household with more than one child was made larger than the credit for a household with one child beginning in 1991. All income thresholds have been indexed annually for inflation since 1987. Note particularly the numerical values for 2001, which vary with the number of children.

A "qualifying" child must satisfy a relationship test, a residency test, and an age test. The child may be a stepchild, descendent of a child, or a foster or adopted child of the taxpayer. The child must have the same place of abode as the taxpayer for more than half the taxable year, and the household must be located in the United States. Finally, the child must be under 19 (24 for a full-time student) or be permanently and totally disabled.

Several provisions are aimed at excluding persons with significant investment income so that the EIC targets low-income workers. Thus, a household is ineligible for the EITC if its investment income ("disqualified" income) exceeds $2,450 in 2001 (this threshold is indexed

Table 1.1 Earned Income Credit Parameters, 1975–2002
(Dollar amounts unadjusted for inflation)

Calendar year	Credit rate %	Minimum income for maximum credit ($)	Maximum credit ($)	Phase-out rate %	Phase-out range ($) Beginning income	Ending income
1975–78	10.00	4,000	400	10.00	4,000	8,000
1979–84	10.00	5,000	500	12.50	6,000	10,000
1985–86	14.00	5,000	550	12.22	6,500	11,000
1987	14.00	6,080	851	10.00	6,920	15,432
1988	14.00	6,240	874	10.00	9,840	18,576
1989	14.00	6,500	910	10.00	10,240	19,340
1990	14.00	6,810	953	10.00	10,730	20,264
1991						
One child	16.70	7,140	1,192	11.93	11,250	21,250
Two children	17.30	7,140	1,235	12.36	11,250	21,250
1992						
One child	17.60	7,520	1,324	12.57	11,840	22,370
Two children	18.40	7,520	1,384	13.14	11,840	22,370
1993						
One child	18.50	7,750	1,434	13.21	12,200	23,050
Two children	19.50	7,750	1,511	13.93	12,200	23,050
1994						
No children	7.65	4,000	306	7.65	5,000	9,000
One child	26.30	7,750	2,038	15.98	11,000	23,755
Two children	30.00	8,425	2,528	17.68	11,000	25,296
1995						
No children	7.65	4,100	314	7.65	5,130	9,230
One child	34.00	6,160	2,094	15.98	11,290	24,396
Two children	36.00	8,640	3,110	20.22	11,290	26,673
1996						
No children	7.65	4,220	323	7.65	5,280	9,500
One child	34.00	6,330	2,152	15.98	11,610	25,078
Two children	40.00	8,890	3,556	21.06	11,610	28,495
1997						
No children	7.65	4,340	332	7.65	5,430	9,770
One child	34.00	6,500	2,210	15.98	11,930	25,750
Two children	40.00	9,140	3,656	21.06	11,930	29,290

Table 1.1 (continued)

Calendar year	Credit rate %	Minimum income for maximum credit ($)	Maximum credit ($)	Phase-out rate %	Phase-out range ($) Beginning income	Phase-out range ($) Ending income
1998						
No children	7.65	4,460	341	7.65	5,570	10,030
One child	34.00	6,680	2,271	15.98	12,260	26,473
Two children	40.00	9,390	3,756	21.06	12,260	30,095
1999						
No children	7.65	4,460	347	7.65	5,670	10,200
One child	34.00	6,800	2,312	15.98	12,460	26,928
Two children	40.00	9,540	3,816	21.06	12,460	30,580
2000						
No children	7.65	4,600	353	7.65	5,800	10,380
One child	34.00	6,900	2,353	15.98	12,700	27,413
Two children	40.00	9,750	3,888	21.06	12,700	31,152
2001						
No children	7.65	4,760	364	7.65	5,950	10,710
One child	34.00	7,140	2,428	15.98	13,090	28,281
Two children	40.00	10,020	4,008	21.06	13,090	32,121

SOURCES: Values from 1975–1999; U.S. Committee on Ways and Means 2000 (p. 809, table 13–12). Values from 2000 and 2001; *1040 Instruction Booklet,* Internal Revenue Service.

for inflation). Disqualified income is the sum of interest (taxable and tax exempt), dividends, net rent and royalty income, capital gains net income, and net passive income that is not self-employment income. The EITC phases out according to "modified" adjusted gross income (AGI). Modified AGI includes tax-exempt interest and nontaxable distributions from pensions, annuities, and individual retirement accounts, and it disregards a variety of losses (such as net capital losses and net losses from trusts and estates, nonbusiness rents and royalties).

Taxpayers file for an EITC or refund, like other tax credits, on their annual federal income tax returns. Note that although the return is due by April 15, a taxpayer can file her return as early as January 1 and therefore receive a refund before April 15. Many EITC recipients (not surprisingly) do file early and receive early refunds from the U.S. Treasury. Since 1979, an advanced payment option has been offered that would permit taxpayers to receive the credit in their paychecks, rather than waiting until their annual returns are filed and processed. The advanced payment option would therefore be a kind of negative withholding. This option requires administrative tasks of the employer. In practice, very few taxpayers have elected to request the advanced payment option. The once-a-year payment of the EITC may encourage saving, the purchase of durables, and social mobility (Smeeding, Phillips, and O'Connor 2000; Romich and Weisner 2000; Barrow and Mc-Granahan 2000).

Table 1.2 indicates who is projected to receive the EITC in 2000. In 2000, 18.4 million taxpayers will receive an EITC or refund, totaling $30 billion. Roughly 72 percent of the EITC expenditure goes to taxpayers who file as singles or heads of households and 28 percent to married taxpayers. The EITC is well targeted: most of the EITC expenditure goes to working households with less than $30,000 of income.

Table 1.3 shows the growth in the EITC since its inception in 1975. The most rapid growth has occurred since 1990. From 1990 to 2000 (projected), the number of recipient families has risen about 50 percent (from 12.5 million to 18.4 million; see Figure 1.7). One source of the increase in recipients was the creation of the childless EITC in 1993. Over that decade, the total amount of credit has quadrupled (from $7.5

Table 1.2   Distribution of Earned Income Credit, 2000, by Income Class

Income class	Joint returns		Head of household and single returns		All returns	
	Number	Amount ($)	Number	Amount ($)	Number	Amount ($)
$0–$10,000	592	1,041	4,490	4,575	5,082	5,616
$10,000–$20,000	1,187	2,993	4,724	10,056	5,910	13,049
$20,000–$30,000	1,747	3,196	3,312	5,989	5,059	9,185
$30,000–$40,000	1,026	996	1,143	970	2,169	1,966
$40,000–$50,000	172	130	17	12	189	141
$50,000–$75,000	29	43	0	0	29	43
$75,000 and over	0	0	0	0	0	0
Total	4,754	8,398	13,685	21,602	18,459	30,000
Percent distribution by type of return	25.8	28.0	74.2	72.0	100.0	100.0

SOURCE: U.S. Committee on Ways and Means 2000 (p. 812, table 13–13).

Table 1.3 Number of EITC Recipients and Amount of Credit, 1975–2002

Year	Number of recipient families (thousands)	Total amount of credit (million $)	Refunded portions of credit (million $)	Average credit per family ($)
1975	6,215	1,250	900	201
1976	6,473	1,295	890	200
1977	5,627	1,127	880	200
1978	5,192	1,048	801	202
1979	7,135	2,052	1,395	288
1980	6,954	1,986	1,370	286
1981	6,717	1,912	1,278	285
1982	6,395	1,775	1,222	278
1983	7,368	1,795	1,289	224
1984	6,376	1,638	1,162	257
1985	7,432	2,088	1,499	281
1986	7,156	2,009	1,479	281
1987	8,738	3,391	2,930	450
1988	11,148	5,896	4,257	529
1989	11,696	6,595	4,636	564
1990	12,542	7,542	5,266	601
1991	13,665	11,105	8,183	813
1992	14,097	13,028	9,959	924
1993	15,117	15,537	12,028	1,028
1994	19,017	21,105	16,598	1,110
1995	19,334	25,956	20,829	1,342
1996	19,464	28,825	23,157	1,481
1997	19,391	30,389	24,396	1,567
1998[a]	20,273	32,340	27,175	1,595
1999[a]	19,440	29,965	25,800	1,541
2000[a]	18,439	30,002	26,148	1,625
2001[a]	18,502	30,662	26,763	1,657
2002[a]	18,233	31,010	26,916	1,701

[a] Estimated

SOURCE: U.S. Committee on Ways and Means 2000 (p. 813, table 13–14).

Figure 1.7 Number of EITC Recipient Households, 1975–2000

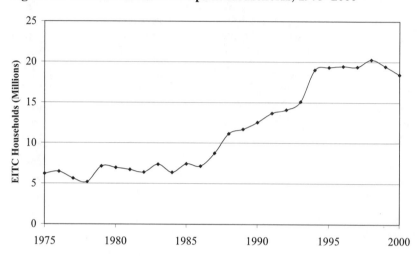

billion to $30.0 billion) and, as shown in Figure 1.8, the real (inflation-adjusted) average EITC per family has doubled. From 1990 to 2000, the nominal credit per family increased from $601 to $1,625, a multiple of 2.7 (by comparison, the consumer price index (CPI) increased by a multiple of only 1.3 so, if the credit had simply kept up with the CPI, it would have risen from $601 to $781). Figure 1.8 shows both the rise in nominal credit and the inflation-adjusted rise in "real" credit. The refunded portion of the credit was about 87 percent of the total credit in 2000 ($26.1 billion out of $30.0 billion), indicating the great impor- tance of "refundability." The refunded 87 percent is categorized as a "budget outlay," and the remaining 13 percent as a "tax expenditure." Thus, the EITC budget outlay greatly exceeds the EITC tax expendi- ture.

Since 1991, Congress has specified that the EITC is not to be counted as income or as a resource for determining the eligibility or amount of benefit of AFDC, Medicaid, Supplemental Security Income, food stamps, or low income housing programs.

The Census Department excludes the EITC in its official count of poverty, in contrast to cash transfers, which are counted in assessing whether a household lies above or below the official poverty line.

Several provisions have been adopted to improve compliance and enforcement in the EITC program. The welfare reform act of 1996

Figure 1.8 Average EITC Benefits per Recipient Household, 1975–2000

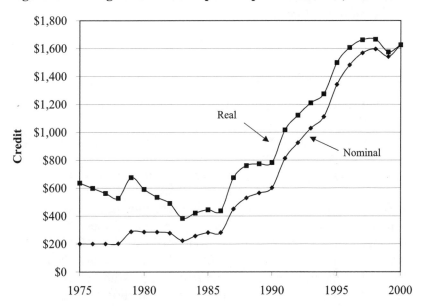

(the Personal Responsibility and Work Opportunity Reconciliation Act) contained new rules concerning taxpayer identification numbers (while preserving some rules that were already in effect). Individuals are ineligible for the credit if they do not include their taxpayer identification number and their qualifying child's number (and, if married, their spouse's taxpayer identification number) on their tax return. For the EITC, a taxpayer identification number is defined as a Social Security number issued to an individual by the Social Security Administration. If an individual fails to provide a correct taxpayer number, the error is treated as a mathematical or clerical error by the IRS. The Taxpayer Relief Act of 1997 included provisions that: 1) deny the EITC for 10 years to taxpayers who fraudulently claimed the EITC and for 2 years for EITC claims that are the result of reckless or intentional disregard of rules or regulations; 2) require EITC recertification for a taxpayer who is denied the EITC; 3) impose due diligence requirements on paid preparers of returns involving the EITC; 4) require information sharing between the Treasury Department and state and local governments regarding child support orders; and 5) allow expanded use of the Social Security Administration records to enforce tax laws, including the

EITC. The Balanced Budget Act of 1997 increased the IRS authoriza-
tion to improve enforcement.

THE TAX ACT OF 2001[5]

The tax act of 2001 made several changes in the EITC beginning
after 2001.

As we will further explain in Chapter 4, the EITC imposes a marriage penalty on many low income couples: the EITC certain couples
receive if they are married is less than the sum of the two EITCs they
would receive if they were single. To address this problem, the tax act
of 2001 provides a more generous credit schedule for married couples
beginning in 2002. Both the beginning and end of the EITC phase-
out range is increased by $1,000 from 2002–2004, by $2,000 from
2005–2007, and by $3,000 from 2008 on. Figure 1.9 shows the impact
of the fully phased-in reform for married couples with two children as
if it had been in effect in 2001. If a 3 percent inflation rate is assumed,

**Figure 1.9 Comparison of 2001 and Modified EITC, Married Couple,
Two Children**

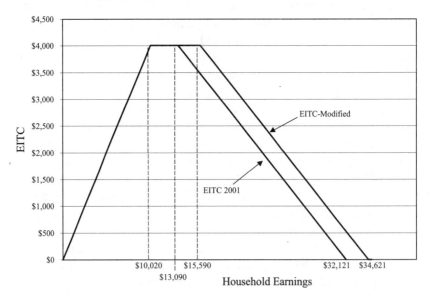

$3,000 in 2008 would be equivalent to about $2,500 in 2001, so the reform would have shifted the beginning and end of the phase-out range $2,500 to the right in the figure (the beginning of the phase-out range would shift from $13,090 to $15,590). The impact of this change is only on households with earnings greater than $13,090, the income at which the phase-out range began in 2001. Benefits are increased by $526.50 (equal to the 21.06 percent phase-out rate × $2,500) at all incomes between $15,590 and $32,121 (the income at which all EITC benefits were lost under the old schedule). The change in the schedule also provides a benefit of between $0 and $526.50 to households with income between $13,090 and $15,590, and between $32,121 and $34,621.

As we will see in Chapter 7, the EITC has a compliance problem partly due to confusion with several complex provisions concerning eligibility. The tax act of 2001 adopts several measures to reduce confusion. We simply note these measures here and will explain them in Chapter 7. The act simplifies the definition of "qualifying child" and modifies the present-law tie-breaking rules. Beginning in 2004, the IRS is authorized to use "math error authority" to deny the EITC if the Federal Case Registry of Child Support Orders indicates that the taxpayer is the noncustodial parent of the child.

Finally, the tax act simplifies the calculation of the EITC by replacing modified AGI with AGI. It simplifies the definition of earned income by excluding nontaxable employee compensation from the definition for the purpose of the EITC. It also repeals the present-law provision that reduces the EITC by the amount of an individual's alternative minimum tax.

STATE EITC PLANS

Nearly a third of the states have enacted their own state EITCs as a supplement to the federal EITC (National Center for Children in Poverty 2001; Johnson 2001). The welfare reform act of 1996 assigned states a greater role in providing opportunities for low income people; as a consequence, 11 states plus the District of Columbia have either enacted new EITCs or expanded existing ones since 1997. State EITCs are financed from general revenue or from the federal TANF block grant enacted under the 1996 welfare reform act.

All but two states simply "piggyback" on the Federal EITC by providing a state EITC equal to X percent of the federal EITC credit. This approach avoids subjecting potential recipients to another round of filling out complex EITC schedules. Once a household has gone through this process for the federal income tax return, the household is automatically entitled to X percent of this amount on its state income tax return. Table 1.4 lists the states with EITC provisions as of 2001 and provides information about program details. As seen there, the state credit ranges from a low of 4–5 percent in several states to a high

Table 1.4 State EITC Programs, 2001

State	Percentage of federal EITC
Colorado	10
District of Columbia	10
Illinois[a]	5
Indiana	3.4 of gap between earnings and $12,000
Iowa[a]	6.5
Kansas	10
Maine[a]	5
Maryland	15 (refundable) 50 (non-refundable)
Massachusetts	15
Minnesota[b]	20–42
New Jersey[a, c]	10
New York	20
Oregon[a]	5
Rhode Island	25
Vermont	32
Wisconsin	4 (one child) 14 (two children) 43 (three children)

[a] State credit not refundable.
[b] Minnesota credit is not explicitly set as a percentage of federal EITC. Percentages shown are range of credit across income levels. Average credit is approximately 25% of federal credit.
[c] New Jersey credit limited to families with income < $20,000.

of 43 percent in Wisconsin for families with three or more children. Ten percent is the most common subsidy rate, currently chosen in five states. Like the federal EITC, most (but not all) states make their EITC refundable. Recent research (National Center for Children in Poverty 2001) found that these state EITCs have increased the income-to-needs ratio of poor families by an average of about 4–5 percent.

SUMMARY

The EITC has moved from relative obscurity when it began in the mid 1970s to center stage today. After a decade and a half in the shadow of welfare and the minimum wage, the EITC emerged in 1990 as an antipoverty policy that commanded strong support across the political spectrum, and this support generated two major expansions in 1990 and 1993. Its conservative support derives from the fact that the EITC provides assistance only to families that actually work, and its liberal support derives from the fact that the EITC effectively targets assistance on low income families with children. Although some conservatives have become critical of certain aspects of the EITC following these expansions, the EITC has continued to maintain sufficiently broad political support to avert any repeal of the expansions, and the tax act of 2001 included an increase in EITC benefits for married couples beginning in 2002.

Notes

1. Although we have used a formula to describe the 2001 EITC schedule, the actual schedule consists of discrete brackets in a table on the personal income tax return. The formula closely approximates the numbers the taxpayer would actually obtain from the tax return table.
2. For a household with one child, the three marginal tax rates are -34 percent in the phase-in range, 0 percent in the stationary range, and $+15.98$ percent in the phase-out range. For a household with no children, the three marginal tax rates are -7.65 percent in the phase-in range, 0 percent in the stationary range, and $+7.65$ percent in the phase-out range.
3. Let E^* be the income at which the household's net payment under the income tax is zero. We find E^* as follows. At $Y = 31,200$, TBC $= 0.1(31,200 - 19,200) = 1,200$; also, CTC $= 1,200$. But EITC > 0 because it phases out to zero at 32,121. Thus, E^* must be greater than 31,200, so at E^*, TBC $= 1,200 + 0.15$

$(E - 31{,}200)$. EITC $= 4{,}008 - 0.2106$ $(E - 13{,}090)$. TBC equals CTC + EITC where $1{,}200 + 0.15$ $(E - 31{,}200) = 1{,}200 + 4{,}008 - 0.2106$ $(E - 13{,}090)$. Solving for E yields $E^* = 31{,}738$.

4. The material in this section is based on the 2000 *Green Book,* pages 808–813 (U.S. Committee on Ways and Means).

5. The material in this section is based on the "Summary of Provisions Contained in the Conference Agreement for H.R. 1836, the Economic Growth and Tax Relief Reconciliation Act of 2001," Joint Committee on Taxation, May 26, 2001.

2
Who Benefits from the EITC?

In this chapter, we examine the demographic and economic characteristics of the EITC population. We present information about who receives the EITC and the amount of credit various groups receive, as well as about the labor supply and earnings of EITC recipients. This information goes well beyond what is available from IRS tables, which are largely limited to the distribution of the credit across income classes and provide relatively little information about the characteristics of the recipient families themselves. We also discuss what the EITC accomplishes in terms of reducing poverty and income inequality.

DATA AND METHODS

To examine the EITC recipient population, we use data from the Panel Study of Income Dynamics (PSID). The PSID is a nationally representative survey that has been interviewing families of all ages about a wide range of economic, demographic, and sociological matters annually since 1967. The original sample included an over-sample of low income families, so it is well-suited in terms of sample size for analyses of low and moderate income populations. In 1997, the last year for which data was available at the time of these analyses, over 6,000 families were interviewed by the PSID.

We use the PSID in our analyses of the EITC because it provides a nationally representative sample of the entire age range of the population, has extensive information about personal characteristics and labor market activity, and has accurate and thorough information about household income.[1] Although the PSID collects information on many detailed sources of income, it does not ask directly about whether a family received income from the EITC program and, if so, how much the credit amounted to. This is common practice with surveys of household income, including the Current Population Survey (CPS). Indeed, because of the way the EITC is received via the tax system, often as a reduction in taxes paid rather than as a refundable cash transfer, it is not clear that families would be able to report this information accurately.

The PSID does, however, include all the information necessary for us to compute eligibility and the amount of the credit received. The key parameters of the EITC formula are age of the householder, number of children, earned income, taxable income, and "modified" AGI (AGI plus a portion of business and farm losses).[2] All of this information is available in the PSID.

Our analysis of EITC participation is based on data for 1996, which was collected in 1997. This is the last year available in the PSID as of late 2000.[3] Fortunately, the EITC in 1996 was virtually identical to the EITC in 2001. All phase-in and phase-out rates were exactly the same and the incomes that define the three credit regions have been adjusted for inflation since 1996 and nothing else. So, in this respect, the EITC population in 1996 ought to closely mirror the EITC population in 2001. There are, however, some complicating factors. First, the unemployment rate was lower in 2001 than in 1996—5.4 percent in 1996 versus approximately 4.5 percent in 2001. And second, the low income labor market has been affected by the replacement of AFDC with TANF and the accompanying state-level reforms that have imposed time limits and work requirements. The likely net result is that some portion of families that we find ineligible for EITC because they had no earnings may, in fact, have been eligible in 2001.

There are also some inherent difficulties in comparing EITC estimates from the PSID or any household survey with the official IRS figures. First, a single household may contain multiple tax-filing units, for example households with subfamilies, other adult relatives, and/or teenagers.[4] In 1996, there were approximately 100 million households in the United States but 120 million tax returns. Households in the PSID may include other family members whose income and or/earnings are typically combined with those of the primary family to produce an estimate of total family income. In computing EITC eligibility, however, we have assumed that other family members file separate tax returns, and we have included only the earnings and income of the primary adult(s) as part of that household's income for tax purposes.[5] This is probably a good approximation to actual tax-filing behavior. Second, since there is no direct information about EITC receipt, we necessarily assume that all eligible taxpayers receive the credit and that no ineligible families do so. Our EITC participation rate is, therefore, best regarded as an estimate not of the population that may actually receive the EITC but of the one for which the EITC is *intended*.

This population differs from the actual EITC population for two reasons. First, some eligible recipients may not claim the credit because they fail to file a tax return, typically because they owe no net income taxes. In 1996, for example, a married couple with two children owed no tax if its income was less than $16,900.[6] In the early 1990s, the IRS computed the EITC on a return even if the return failed to claim it; now the IRS sends a notice of potential eligibility to a taxpayer who has failed to claim a credit for which he appears to be eligible.[7] Relatively little is known about current nonparticipation in the EITC. Estimates of eligible nonrecipients for 1990, when the potentially eligible population was much smaller, range from 13.6 percent to 19.5 percent (Scholz 1994).[8] Since that time, there has been an extensive outreach program to encourage eligible low income households to file and claim the EITC, including, for example, milk-carton advertising and aggressive outreach programs by interest groups. Additionally, the participation rate may have increased on its own because participation is now more valuable and because the somewhat higher income households who are now eligible are more likely to file in any event. It is, therefore, likely that the fraction not claiming the award has fallen, but there are no firm data about this.

Second, a substantial amount of EITC payments are paid in error, most often, it appears, to taxpayers who do not have a "qualifying" child[9] and who are, therefore, either ineligible or eligible for the much smaller payments available to households without children. Studies indicate that approximately 25 percent of EITC dollars were paid in error in 1994 and 1997 (McCubbin 2000) and perhaps as much as one-third of EITC dollars were paid in error in 1999 (IRS 1999). It is difficult to assess what proportion of EITC recipients were ineligible. In 1994, only about 10 percent of the overpayments were due to income errors among eligible recipients, while about 60 percent were due to qualifying child errors (McCubbin 2000). This suggests that much of the excess payments in that year were made to taxpayers who were probably ineligible for EITC payments.

THE EITC RECIPIENT POPULATION IN 1996

For 1996, IRS tabulations show that the EITC was received by 19.5 million taxpayers or about 16.3 percent of the 120 million returns received. Based on earnings, income, age, and the number of dependent children as reported by households in the PSID, we estimate that 13.1 percent of all households were eligible to receive the EITC in 1996.[10]   When, however, we adjust the IRS figure to allow for the inclusion of ineligible recipients and the omission of nonrecipient eligibles, the two estimates are very similar. If 25 percent of recipients are ineligible and 10 percent fail to claim the credit, then the corresponding estimate is 13.4 percent, just 0.3 percentage points different than the PSID estimate.[11]   If 20 percent are ineligible and 7.5 percent fail to claim the credit, then the corresponding figure is 14.0 percent. Thus, the PSID appears to provide an accurate estimate of the intended EITC population. It will, however, necessarily differ from the actual EITC recipient population in some ways.

Table 2.1 shows our estimates of the EITC eligibility of all households in 1996 by the range of the EITC in which they fell and, for ineligible households, the reason they were ineligible. Just over 3 percent of households had incomes and family characteristics that placed

Table 2.1 EITC Receipt Status of the Population, 1996

Receipt status	Share of population (%)
Eligible, total	13.1
Phase-in range	3.3
Stationary range	1.3
Phase-out range	8.4
Ineligible, total	86.9
Demographically ineligible	
< Age 25, no children	5.3
> Age 64, no children	18.6
Income or earnings ineligible[a]	
Zero earnings	6.3
Income > Maximum	56.7

[a] All income or earnings ineligible households are demographically eligible.
SOURCE: Panel Study of Income Dynamics.

them on the phase-in range of the credit, 1.3 percent were on the stationary range, and 8.4 percent of the population—nearly two-thirds of those eligible—were on the phase-out range. The ineligibles fall into three groups. Our classification scheme looks first at demographic eligibility and then at earnings or income eligibility, so that households who are ineligible for both reasons are included in the demographic category. We find that about one-quarter of all households were demographically ineligible because they had no children age 18 or younger and failed to meet the minimum and maximum age cutoffs. The vast majority of these demographic ineligibles were elderly, a group the EITC (with its emphasis on earned income) is largely not expected to cover. About 80 percent of the demographically ineligible households also failed the earnings tests. This leaves a relatively small group—about 3 percent of all families—who would be eligible for the EITC except for the age restrictions. About two-thirds of these families were elderly (1.7 percent of all families) and one-third (1.3 percent) were under the age of 25. Another 6 percent of all households satisfied the demographic criteria of the EITC but had no earned income. Finally, 57 percent of households were demographically eligible but had incomes that exceeded the EITC maximum for their family situation.

The EITC population is similar to the low and moderate income population, but it differs from it in several important ways. Obviously, households with low incomes but no earnings are ineligible. So, too, are families with low earnings but substantial nonlabor income and households without children in which the primary adult is either under age 25 or over age 64. Many households without children and with modest earnings will nevertheless be ineligible because their income exceeds the 1996 maximum of $9,500.

Table 2.2 provides further information about the characteristics of EITC households in 1996. Overall, we estimate that one household in seven is eligible for the EITC. About one in 12 white households are eligible, one in four black households, and one of every two Hispanic households. (Note that the PSID construction of race/ethnicity in 1997 differs from the Census Bureau; white and black here are non-Hispanic, and the groups are mutually exclusive.) Not unexpectedly, single-parent families with children have high rates of receipt—just under 50 percent for men and over 60 percent for women. Among married-couple families with children, nearly one in five receives the EITC.

Table 2.2 EITC Receipt and Average Credit by Selected Family Characteristics, 1996

	Proportion receiving EITC (%)	Share of EITC population (%)	Average credit ($)
All	13.1	100	1,327
Race			
White (non-Hispanic)	8.5	50.8	1,188
Black (non-Hispanic)	24.4	22.2	1,322
Hispanic	49.5	20.7	1,711
Other	17.7	6.3	1,206
Family/marital status			
Married with children	18.7	35.3	1,597
Married, no children	2.5	5.4	167
Single female with children	60.7	35.9	1,615
Single male with children	47.5	10.0	1,544
Single, no children	4.7	13.5	157
Age of household head			
<25	17.5	7.3	1,507
25–34	20.3	30.5	1,353
35–44	19.8	35.7	1,525
45–54	12.5	18.7	1,146
>55	3.2	7.7	588
Number of children			
None	3.8	18.8	160
One	27.7	30.0	1,198
Two	28.4	28.9	1,782
Three or more	37.6	22.3	1,900
Poverty status			
Poor	35.7	41.3	1,456
Non-poor	9.0	58.7	1,237
Poverty ratio			
<1	35.7	41.3	1,456
1–1.5	35.3	25.8	1,650
1.5–2	26.9	21.0	973
>2	7.6	11.8	805

NOTE: Methods for determining poverty ratio are discussed in the text.
SOURCE: Panel Study of Income Dynamics.

Given the low income thresholds for households without children, very few of them qualify for benefits—2.5 percent for married couples and less than 5 percent for single individuals.

Because of the earned income requirement and because the credit could be received at an income as high as $28,495 in 1996 for families with two children, the EITC is not particularly sharply targeted at families that are in poverty. It is certainly best understood as a program for low and moderate income families, rather than poor families. The poverty ratio brackets shown in Table 2.2 are the ratio of family income to the official poverty needs standard for a family of given size.[12] We sometimes refer to this measure as the "income-to-needs" ratio. In computing household income, we follow the official Census Bureau practice of including all cash income and income from other family members, but we exclude EITC benefits themselves because they are technically a tax. This method is consistent with the way taxes are treated in computing a family's income, although conceptually the excluded EITC is much like the cash transfers that are included.[13] We estimate that only about 35 percent of poor families are eligible for the credit and a similar percentage of families between 100 percent and 150 percent of the poverty threshold. More than one in four families at 150 percent to 200 percent of the poverty threshold are eligible. Overall, nine percent of nonpoor families are eligible for the EITC.

Why are so many poor families ineligible for the credit? Several reasons are illustrated in Figure 2.1. About one-third of all poor households are demographically ineligible, that is, they do not have a qualifying child and fail the age test. Most of these are elderly households. About 30 percent are demographically eligible but have no earnings. Finally, a small group—about 2.5 percent of poor households—are demographically eligible and do have earnings, but they are ineligible because their earnings or taxable income is too high. Almost all of these are families with no children, and their ineligibility is not a function of some odd and unanticipated interaction: the maximum income for eligibility for them ($9,500) is less than the poverty threshold for a two-person family. Moreover, not all of them are two-person families; in the PSID, about 10 percent of families with no children had a family size of three or more.

As shown in Table 2.2, column 2, half of all EITC recipient households are white and about one-fifth are black and one-fifth Hispanic.

Figure 2.1 EITC Status of the Poverty Population, 1996

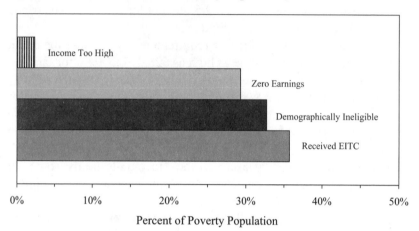

Nearly 60 percent of recipients are single-parent households; less than one-fifth are childless. Two-thirds are ages 25–44. Only about 40 percent of the EITC population is poor, but another quarter have income less than 150 percent of the poverty line. Twelve percent have an income more than twice the poverty line.

The average credit received (column 3) computed from the PSID is $1,333, which is about 11 percent below the IRS average credit of $1,480 in 1996. Again, since the populations naturally differ, the average credit is not necessarily likely to be identical. Strategic misrepresentation of earnings, income, and family status is consistent with the higher average credit derived from tax filings than from the PSID.[14] The average credit received is about 50 to 55 percent of the maximum for families in each category for number of children; the higher credit for families with three or more children must reflect their lower income since the EITC is currently adjusted only through two children. We find that Hispanic households receive the largest credit, with non-Hispanic black families about $400 lower and non-Hispanic white families $525 lower. Again, these differences reflect income and/or family size differences. We do find that poor families get a substantially larger credit than non-poor families, although the credit for near-poor families (100–150 percent of poverty level) is greater than it is for poor families. This pattern of benefits that increase with income is a natural consequence of the EITC formula, which provides its maximum benefit to households that, depending on their family size, are at or just above the poverty threshold.

By combining the proportions of the EITC population in column 2 with the average credit in column 3, we can compute the proportion of total credits going to various groups. Figure 2.2 shows this proportion by race/ethnicity, family status, and the ratio of family income to the poverty threshold. We find that 45 percent of EITC dollars are received by non-Hispanic white households, 22 percent by non-Hispanic black households, and about 27 percent by Hispanic households. Households without children receive less than 2.5 percent of EITC dollars, even though they account for 19 percent of the recipient population. Well over half of all credits go to single-parent families, especially female-headed families. Finally, we find that EITC dollars are far better targeted than EITC receipt. Forty-five percent of dollars go to poor households, and more than three-quarters of all dollars go to households with incomes at or below 150 percent of the poverty line.

Table 2.3 presents information about the earnings, income, and labor supply of EITC recipients in 1996, for all recipients and separately by EITC range. The average income of EITC recipients was about $20,000, and earned income was just under $13,000. Transfer income accounts for about three-fourths of the difference between total income and earned income; the remainder comes from the income of other family members.[15] The average recipient household's income placed it at about 25 percent above the poverty level. Labor supply

Figure 2.2 Percent of EITC Dollars Received by Selected Family Characteristics, 1996

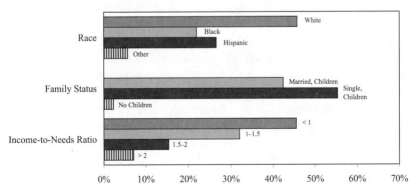

Table 2.3 Income, Earnings, and Employment Status of EITC Recipient Households, 1996

	All	Phase-in	Stationary	Phase-out
Total family income[a]	$20,361	$8,700	$16,447	$24,478
Earned income	$12,906	$3,025	$8,804	$17,460
EITC income	$1,328	$1,002	$2,380	$1,296
Poverty ratio	1.24	0.69	1.01	1.49
Poor	41.3%	85.6%	65.6%	20.0%
Employment status of householder				
Employed	94.5%	91.2%	94.0%	95.9%
Weeks worked	38.8	27.6	38.0	43.3
Hours per week	37.9	31.8	36.4	40.5
Employment status of spouse				
No spouse	59.3%	76.3%	66.1%	51.6%
Employed	22.5%	11.5%	21.1%	27.1%
Weeks worked[b]	20.2	13.7	21.3	21.3
Hours per week[b]	17.6	11.7	21.5	18.4
Family labor supply				
Single earner	81.5%	93.7%	84.2%	76.3%
Two earners	18.5%	6.3%	15.8%	23.7%
Annual hours worked	1,906	1,096	1,816	2,242
Percent of EITC households	100%	25.6%	9.9%	64.5%

[a] Poverty status includes income from all household members, but does not include EITC income.
[b] Average computed for all wives.
SOURCE: Panel Study of Income Dynamics.

was substantial. The householder, defined here as the husband in a married-couple household and a single adult otherwise, worked an average of 38 hours per week and 39 weeks per year. Only five percent of householders did not work at all during the year; in those cases, another primary adult in the household must have worked in order to qualify for the EITC. About 55 percent of the wives in EITC recipient families worked but, because only 40 percent of EITC households are married-couple families in the first place, less than a quarter of the families have a working spouse and less than a fifth have more than a single earner. On average, wives worked part time (less than 20 hours) and part year (about 20 weeks). This implies that working wives worked essentially full time and full year.

What most distinguishes these households is not their labor supply but their wage rate and the number of earners. The implied household wage rate is about $6.77 per hour. Total household labor supply is 1,900 hours, which is about the average for a full-time, year-round worker in 1996 and is about 900 hours less than for non-elderly, non-EITC households. The difference in average annual work hours between householders in EITC households and in non-elderly, non-EITC households is about 280 hours; the rest of the difference between the two groups is due to differences among working wives in number of hours worked and differences in the proportion of wives working.

For households on the phase-in range, total income and earned income are necessarily low, with average wage rates at $4.25. These are typically single-parent households, where the worker is often combining work with welfare or with transfer income from other sources. Note, for example, that this group's earned income of about $3,000 is much less than half its annual family income of about $8,700. Virtually all of these households are poor. Annual labor supply of householders is less than 900 hours and, because so few of these households have more than a single worker, total household labor supply is less than 1,100 hours. The EITC makes a substantial addition to income for these households, boosting it by more than 12 percent.

Across the other two EITC ranges, all employment measures increase. Weeks of work and hours of work increase very sharply for both householders and spouses, and there is also a large jump in the proportion of married-couple families and families with two earners. Average wage rates for householders increase as well, to $6.36 for workers on the stationary range and to $9.08 for workers on the phase-out range. Household labor supply doubles between the phase-in and phase-out range.

Even so, there are some labor supply differences between households in the phase-out range and non-elderly, non-EITC households. The labor supply of householders in the two groups are quite similar—the EITC phase-out range households report working more hours per week, but fewer weeks, so that total annual hours are virtually identical. The non-EITC households are more likely to be married (59 percent vs. 51.6 percent), and they are much more likely to have an employed spouse (46 percent vs. 27 percent). They are therefore twice as likely to have two earners. Total household labor supply differs by about 550 hours, almost all due to the hours contributed by spouses.

A possible concern about the EITC is that it subsidizes somewhat higher wage workers who choose for some reason to work fewer hours. The average household wage of EITC recipients, computed from the earnings and labor hours in Table 2.3, is $6.77, which is clearly quite modest. Table 2.4 provides further information on the wage and hours distribution for household heads and wives. Among household heads, the modal wage category is less than $6.00 and the median is less than $7.50. Only 5 percent earn more than $15.00 per hour, an hourly wage that clearly implies much less than full-time, full-year work. Among working wives, almost two-thirds earn less than $6.00 and just about 5 percent earn more than $15.00 per hour. The distribution of annual work hours, shown at the bottom of the table, confirms this pattern. Among household heads, about one-quarter worked less than 1,000 hours, including in that category the 5.5 percent who did not work at all. About equal proportions worked 1,000 to 2,000 hours and more than 2,000 hours, 37 and 38 percent, respectively. Among wives, hours worked are much more modest. Forty-five percent did not work, and the working wives are relatively evenly distributed across the work

Table 2.4 Wage and Hours Distribution, EITC Recipient Households, 1996

	Household heads (%)	Wives (%)
Wage rate		
Did not work	5.5	44.6
<$6.00	38.4	35.4
$6.00–$7.50	14.1	6.4
$7.50–$10.00	19.4	7.3
$10.00–$15.00	17.2	3.6
>$15.00	5.4	2.7
Annual work hours		
Did not work	5.5	44.6
1–500 Hours	8.8	11.4
500–1000 Hours	10.6	12.1
1000–1500 Hours	11.8	9.5
1500–2000 Hours	26.3	14.6
>2000 Hours	37.0	7.8

SOURCE: Panel Study of Income Dynamics.

hour categories. Eleven percent worked fewer than 500 hours and another 12 percent worked 500 to 1,000 hours. Only a bit under one-quarter of all wives in EITC households worked at least 1,500 hours per year.

CHANGES IN THE EITC RECIPIENT POPULATION

As was discussed in Chapter 1, the EITC program was substantially expanded as part of the Budget Reconciliation Act of 1993. Phase-in rates for families with children were increased in annual increments between 1994 and 1996, when they reached the rates that continue to apply. Phase-out rates were also increased, so that, after adjusting for inflation, the maximum income for eligibility was unchanged for families with one child and increased by about 12 percent for families with two or more children. Additionally, households with no children in which the householder was between the ages of 25 and 64 were made eligible for the first time, although benefits remain quite low. The total number of families receiving the EITC increased by about 4 million (about 26 percent) between 1993 and 1996. Using our 1996 estimates of the characteristics of the recipient population, we estimate that about three-quarters of that increase was due to the extension of benefits to childless households.

To see how the expansion of the EITC altered the nature of the recipient population, we use the PSID again to draw a sample of EITC-eligible households in 1991, several years before the reforms. The EITC in 1991 was essentially the same as in 1993. We use exactly the same procedures we used for 1996 to identify EITC eligibility and the amount of the credit for which a household would be eligible. Again, we identify the EITC-eligible population, rather than the actual EITC recipient population, which may differ because of both nonparticipation by eligible household and receipt by ineligible households. With the PSID, we estimate that 9 percent of households were eligible to receive the EITC in 1991. Figures from the IRS (U.S. Committee on Ways and Means 2000) show 14.1 million recipients out of 113 million returns, or 12.4 percent. When this figure is adjusted for ineligible recipients and for eligible nonfilers, the IRS and PSID proportions are again quite close. If one-third of recipients are ineligible and 15 percent of those eligible failed to file, the IRS figure is equivalent to an eligible proportion of 9.6 percent of households.

Table 2.5 summarizes some of the major differences, both in the composition of the EITC population and the distribution of EITC benefits in 1991 and 1996.[16] As seen in the first two columns, the EITC population has shifted toward households on the phase-out range, increasing from half to nearly two-thirds. This shift is almost entirely due to two factors: the higher income eligibility level of families with two or more children and the very low income level ($5,950) at which the phase-out range begins for households without children. This is corroborated in the distributions of households by number of children and the poverty ratio. Households without children now account for 18.8 percent of all recipient households, with almost all of the decline among other families coming from the reduced representation of families with one child. The distribution by poverty ratio categories shows a five-percentage-point drop in the proportion of households with an income 100 to 150 percent of the poverty line but an offsetting increase in the proportion between 150 and 200 percent of the poverty line.

In terms of expenditures, the EITC has actually become better focused on lower income households. Forty-five percent of all dollars went to poor households in 1996, compared with 40 percent in 1991; this is undoubtedly due to the big increase in the phase-in rates. At the higher end of the EITC income distribution, the proportion of benefits going to households with an income more than twice the poverty line has fallen in half, from about 14 percent to 7 percent. Households on the phase-in and stationary ranges now get a smaller proportion of total benefits—down from 56 percent to 37 percent. Finally, families with two or more children now get more than 70 percent of all benefits, compared with about 60 percent in 1991.

THE IMPACT OF THE EITC ON THE POVERTY RATE

The official poverty rate in the United States is based on a comparison of a household's income to a level of income that has been established as necessary to achieve a minimal acceptable (i.e., poverty-level) standard of living.[17] That standard of living, which is called the poverty threshold or poverty standard, was constructed in 1964 as part of

Table 2.5 Characteristics of the EITC Population, 1991 and 1996

	Share of EITC population (%)		Share of EITC benefits (%)	
	1991	1996	1991	1996
EITC range				
Phase-in	32.3	25.6	25.7	19.3
Stationary	17.5	9.9	30.3	17.7
Phase-out	50.2	64.5	43.9	62.9
Race				
White (non-Hispanic)	64.5	50.8	64.6	45.5
Black (non-Hispanic)	29.7	22.2	29.7	22.1
Hispanic	—	20.7	—	26.7
Other	5.8	6.3	5.7	3.3
Family/marital status				
Married, children	37.7	35.3	35.7	42.4
Married, no children	0.0	5.4	0.0	0.7
Single parent, children	62.3	45.9	64.3	55.3
Single, no children	0.0	13.5	0.0	1.6
Age of household head				
<Age 25	12.9	7.3	11.6	8.3
25–34	42.4	30.5	43.0	31.1
35–44	29.5	35.7	29.5	41.0
45–54	10.1	18.7	10.1	16.2
>55	5.1	7.7	5.9	3.4
Number of children				
None	0.0	18.8	0.0	2.3
One	43.1	30.0	42.9	27.1
Two	34.8	28.9	34.6	38.7
Three or more	22.1	22.3	22.6	31.9
Poverty status				
Poor	39.2	41.3	40.1	45.3
Non-poor	60.8	58.7	59.9	54.7
Poverty ratio				
<1	39.2	41.3	40.1	45.3
1–1.5	30.6	25.8	31.9	32.1
1.5–2	16.2	21.0	13.3	15.4
>2	14.0	11.8	14.7	7.2

SOURCE: Panel Study of Income Dynamics.

the initial effort to measure the extent of poverty in the United States and progress in eliminating it. The official U.S. poverty threshold was based on the minimum cost of a nutritionally adequate diet, as estimated by the U.S. Department of Agriculture. This income was then adjusted for other basic needs by multiplying by three on the basis of budget studies that showed that low income families spent approximately one-third of their income on food. Further adjustments are made for family size, age (elderly/non-elderly), and farm residence. Annual adjustments are made for inflation. Any household with total income below the resulting income level is officially considered poor. In 2001, this income level was about $17,600 for a family of four and about $8,800 for a single-person household.

The income used in the poverty calculation includes all conventional sources of earnings and income, including cash transfers, but it excludes all in-kind transfers and all taxes as well as other sources of income such as unrealized capital gains and the value of health insurance supplements to wage and salary income. It is therefore best understood as a pre-tax, post-cash transfer measure of household income. Thus, for example, welfare and Social Security benefits are included in household income because they are received as a cash transfer, but food stamps and Medicaid benefits are excluded, because they are in-kind benefits.[18] While the EITC functions as a cash transfer and therefore might quite arguably be included in household income, it is technically a tax credit. Thus, it is excluded from the standard measure of income used for computing the poverty rate, just like all other taxes. As a result, the EITC cannot, by construction, have any direct effect on reducing the official U.S. poverty rate.[19]

The Census Bureau does, however, publish a set of alternative poverty measures based on different treatment of various excluded items. Currently, there are 16 such alternative poverty measures; the EITC figures prominently in several of them, thus these measures can be used to estimate its impact on the poverty rate.[20] It is, however, not possible to compare the official poverty rate with the poverty rate adjusting only for the EITC; rather, the Census Bureau tabulations show the EITC impact relative to an alternative baseline poverty rate. Figure 2.3 shows one of these estimates of the impact of the EITC on the poverty rate for the time period from 1991 to 1999. In this comparison, the baseline is the poverty rate when household income is adjusted to in-

Figure 2.3 Reduction in Poverty Rate Due to EITC, 1991–1999

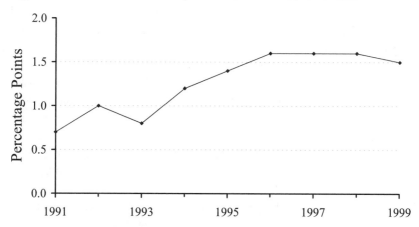

clude estimated capital gains and losses (which has virtually no impact on the poverty rate) and is net of all taxes except the EITC. This adjustment increases the poverty rate by about 1.0 to 1.2 percentage points relative to the official poverty rate, depending on the year because the adjustment for taxes paid reduces household income by more than the inclusion of capital gains. The alternative comparison is the same income concept, but now including all income received from the EITC. The numbers shown in the figure are the difference between these two poverty rates; this provides an estimate of the net reduction in the poverty rate due to the EITC cash transfer. This is a static exercise in the sense that it does not account for any behavioral changes on work and/or marriage that might be partially offsetting.[21]

On the basis of these two adjusted income measures, the EITC reduced the poverty rate in 1999 by 1.5 percentage points, which means that about 4 million persons were lifted out of poverty as a result of the cash assistance they received from the EITC. This is not trivial, but neither is it an enormous overall impact. There are two reasons for this modest impact on the poverty rate. First, recall that only about 35 percent of all poor households receive any cash assistance at all via the EITC. The EITC is not fundamentally a transfer program for the poor since its eligibility criteria exclude many poor households. Second, the EITC benefit structure offers modest benefits to the poorest households and provides its maximum benefits to families just on either side of the poverty threshold. As shown in Table 2.2, what we call near-poor households (those with an income-to-needs ratio between 1.0 and 1.5) actually receive almost $200 more in EITC benefits than poor households.

We do estimate that the EITC has a substantial impact among the poor households who do receive benefits. We estimate that just under one-quarter of poor EITC recipient households are boosted out of poverty by the EITC. This is, unfortunately, a very rough estimate, in part because EITC receipt is based on household status, while the poverty estimates are based on an individual count. We estimate that about 6 million poor households receive EITC benefits and, from the Census Bureau analyses, we estimate that 4 million persons were lifted out of poverty by the EITC. It is not clear, however, how many households are represented by those 4 million persons. Our estimate of 25 percent of recipient households lifted out of poverty assumes that the 4 million persons resided in 1.5 million households.

The poverty impact of the EITC has been essentially constant since 1995, the year after EITC benefits were substantially increased (Figure 2.3). Between 1991 and 1993, when EITC benefits were considerably smaller, the impact on the poverty rate was between 0.7 and 1.0 percentage points.

The EITC also figures in an alternative set of poverty rate calculations. In this comparison, the baseline poverty rate is the rate when household income is reduced by excluding all cash transfers and subtracting estimated federal taxes and is increased by including capital gains and the value of health insurance supplements to wage and salary income. The exclusion of cash transfers increases the poverty rate about 7 percentage points, while the other changes have relatively small impacts (half a percentage point or less). The alternative rate is based on this income plus estimated EITC benefits. This comparison yields a similar estimate for the impact of the EITC on reducing the poverty rate during the 1990s—roughly 1.5 percentage points in recent years and 1.0 percentage point in the early 1990s. This measure is also available back to 1979, during a time period when the EITC was a very small program. Throughout the 1980s, the EITC impact on the poverty rate ranges from 0.2 to 0.4 percentage points.

SUMMARY

We have used data from the PSID for 1996 to describe the demographic and economic characteristics of EITC recipient households. Our estimates describe the population of EITC-eligible households, rather than of recipient households. Our estimate of the proportion eligible for EITC benefits in 1996 (13.1 percent) is therefore substantially lower than the proportion reported by the IRS. When we adjust for reasonable estimates of ineligible recipients and eligible nonclaimers, however, our estimate is remarkably close to the IRS figure.

We find that about one-quarter of recipient households are on the phase-in range of the EITC, one-tenth are on the stationary range, and the remainder—nearly two-thirds of all recipients—are on the phase-out range. About 25 percent of households, mostly elderly, are demographically ineligible for the EITC because they have no children and do not meet the age requirement for childless households. About 6 percent of households do meet the demographic eligibility requirements but have no earnings. The extension of eligibility to childless households, age 25–64, has altered the overall composition of EITC households. Childless households now account for nearly one-fifth of all households, although they get less than 2.5 percent of all expenditures because their benefits are so modest. The overall population of EITC households is about 50 percent non-Hispanic white, with roughly equal proportions of non-Hispanic blacks and Hispanics.

As a poverty program, the EITC is clearly limited by its focus on households with earnings. We find that only about 35 percent of poor households received benefits from the EITC in 1996. About one-third of all poor households are demographically ineligible; most of these are elderly households, a group that the EITC is certainly not designed to serve. About 30 percent of poor families were demographically eligible but had no earnings in 1996. In many ways, the near-poor fare better from the EITC. Households with an income between 100 percent and 150 percent of the poverty line are just as likely to receive EITC benefits as poor families, and their greater earnings often enable them to receive a substantial grant. These near-poor families received an average credit of $1,650, almost $200 more than poor families.

The labor market activity of EITC recipient households is not terribly different from that of nonrecipient households. The householder in an EITC household worked an average of 39 weeks and 38 hours per week, and the average total annual hours worked for head and spouse was over 1,900 hours. What most distinguishes household labor supply of these families is the lack of a second earner. Nearly 60 percent of these families are either single-parent families or single-person households; in all, less than one-fifth had more than a single earner.

Finally, the EITC has made a modest contribution to the reduction of poverty in the United States, reducing it by about 1.5 percentage points or 4 million people. The impact is muted, because more than 60 percent of poor households are ineligible for the EITC.

A program as large as the EITC has now become may begin to have an impact on the economic behavior of the households it serves. This kind of impact has been the norm for safety-net programs, such as AFDC. In the next chapters, we turn to these issues, examining the impact of the EITC program on labor supply behavior and marriage.

Notes

1. For a discussion of the continuing representativeness of the PSID, see Fitzgerald, Gottschalk, and Moffitt (1998). The authors concluded that the PSID remains representative for most purposes. For a general discussion of the PSID, see Hill (1992).
2. In 1996, this portion was 50 percent; in 2001, it is 75 percent.
3. We use the early release 1997 family file.
4. A 1998 study by the IRS (Weber 1998) found that, of the nearly 115 million returns in 1993, over 9 million were filed by someone who was a dependent of another taxpayer.
5. We do not need to take explicit account of the other family members because the PSID sample, when weighted, is nationally representative of all households. This means that individuals like them are already appropriately accounted for in the PSID sample and thus in our estimates. For example, they may be the primary householders in a PSID household.
6. This is the sum of the standard deduction ($6,700) and the per person exemption of $2,250. In 2001, the corresponding figure is $7,500 + (4 × $2,900) = $19,100.
7. In order to receive the credit, a taxpayer would then have to file an amended return, which might well be a daunting task.
8. Scholz's analysis pre-dates the expansion of the EITC to childless households. Nothing at all is known about EITC participation among this group.

9. A "qualifying" child is a child under age 19 (or under age 24, if a full-time student) who lived with the claimant for at least half the year. Only one tax filer can claim a particular child as a qualifying child even if more than one meets all requirements. See Chapter 7 for a full discussion of compliance issues.

10. In computing eligibility, we do take account of modified AGI, by adding back into household income 50 percent of business and farm losses. Like most other researchers, we do not take account of ineligibility due to interest, dividend, and capital gains income greater than $2,000, because we lack decent information on this. This rule typically affects very few cases.

11. To get this figure, multiply 16.3 percent × 0.75 to find the proportion of the recipient population who were eligible. Multiplying that figure by 1.15 to adjust for eligible nonrecipients yields 13.4 percent.

12. The official poverty standard adjusts for family size in a nonlinear way to capture economies of scale. In 1996, the poverty standard was $10,233 for a two-person family, $16,036 for a four-person family, and $27,091 for an eight-person family. The poverty standards in the PSID differ slightly from the official numbers because they account for changes in family size during a calendar year.

13. The Census Bureau treats EITC income in exactly the same way we do in its calculation of poverty. It also publishes alternative poverty computations in which EITC income is included. We discuss those measures at the end of this chapter.

14. For example, claiming additional children can increase the credit. Overstating income through the end of the stationary range also increases the credit.

15. There is a fundamental inconsistency between the tax-filing unit that is the basis for the EITC and the household unit that is the basis for poverty calculations. All of our EITC calculations include only the income of the head and spouse, while calculations of total family and of poverty status include the income of all household members and, in the case of poverty status, their needs as well.

16. It is important to appreciate that the changes in the distributions between 1991 and 1996 reflect not only the changes in the EITC schedule but also changes in the underlying distribution of the population across characteristics on which EITC benefits are based.

17. See the Census Bureau web site at www.census.gov for information on current year poverty standards and a further discussion. Alternative thresholds, based on the cost of housing, have been proposed recently.

18. The argument for excluding the bonus value of food stamps is particularly weak, since food stamps are used as if they were cash by most recipients. This argument is far less compelling for the value of Medicaid.

19. This is true holding labor supply and earnings constant. It is, however, possible (see Chapter 3) that the EITC might affect household labor supply and earnings and thereby affect the poverty rate, either positively or negatively.

20. The Census Bureau uses essentially the same procedures that we use to estimate the EITC benefits received by households for its poverty computations. Like the

PSID, the CPS does not provide any direct information about EITC benefits. EITC benefits are estimated on the basis of income, earnings, age, and number of children, assuming (just as we do) that all eligible households receive the EITC and that no ineligible households do.

21. These potential impacts are discussed in Chapters 3 and 4.

3
The EITC and the Labor Market

It is well understood by both economists and policymakers that tax and transfer programs often have effects on individual behavior and that these effects may be large, often unintended, and sometimes counter to the aims and intents of the programs themselves. The potential impact of the welfare system on work, marriage, and fertility is the most famous of these, with hundreds of studies of its impact on labor supply, fertility, and marital status; see Moffitt (1992) for a summary. The impact of the tax system, especially its high marginal tax rates and the marriage penalty, has been a second major focus. See Alm, Dickert-Conlin, and Whittington (1999) for a recent summary of demographic effects; see Poterba (1998) and Slemrod (2000) for a recent summary of labor supply effects.[1]

When the EITC was a relatively small program in the 1980s and early 1990s, its behavioral impacts were consequently quite small, perhaps even ignorably small. With the very substantial increase in the EITC in 1994 and the large impact it now has on individual budgets, however, it is certainly possible that the EITC might now have more important behavioral effects. As with the welfare and tax system, there are two broad areas of likely impacts—labor supply and marriage. The labor supply impacts occur because the EITC substantially changes an individual's after-tax wage rate and net income. The marriage impacts exist because, depending on their particular circumstances, households stand to gain or lose considerable EITC benefits by marriage.

In this chapter, we describe the way the EITC may affect work, show the likely impacts, and then examine the growing empirical literature. We also examine the possible impact of the EITC on wage rates, via its impact on labor supply. In Chapter 4, we do exactly the same thing for marriage. In Chapter 8, we use these reviews as a basis for proposing a reform of the EITC program.

LABOR SUPPLY AND THE EITC

Labor supply refers to the number of hours an individual works in the labor market. *Labor force participation* is a related concept that measures whether or not an individual works in the labor market. Hours of work are often called the *intensive* labor supply margin, while labor force participation is the *extensive* labor supply margin.

The standard economic approach to labor supply behavior focuses on the effects of an individual's wage rate and of nonlabor income[2] on these two labor supply dimensions—whether or not to work and how many hours to work. We first discuss the standard economic approach to labor supply behavior and then show how labor supply choices might be affected by the EITC. Readers who are familiar with the basics of labor supply analysis, including indifference curves and budget constraints, may want to skip ahead to the next section or see Appendix B.

The basic idea in labor supply analysis is that individuals make choices about how much leisure they want to have and how much consumption of market goods and services they want.[3] It is assumed that individuals have sufficient latitude to choose their hours of work by choice of job, working an additional job, working part time, and so on. This assumption may be less true in the short run, but it is more so in the long run. There is an inevitable trade-off between having goods and services on the one hand and having leisure on the other since, to have more consumption, an individual must first earn the income to purchase the goods by giving up leisure time. A wide range of leisure time/consumption possibilities exist; the exact set of feasible combinations depend on an individual's wage rate and nonlabor income.[4]

In analyzing this problem, it is very useful to think of the wage rate as the price of an hour of leisure time. It is not, of course, a price that anyone pays in the traditional way. But, it is a price nonetheless, since taking one more hour of leisure means working one less hour and thus not earning an amount of income exactly equal to the wage rate.[5]

An individual's goal is to choose the best combination of goods and services and of leisure that is available, where "best" means that no other feasible combination would be preferred. It is possible to solve this problem in terms of marginal conditions that must hold at the best choice; there is a well-known economics formula that captures that idea (see Appendix B). This choice will depend on an individual's underlying preferences for goods and leisure, on the wage rate (price of leisure), and on the amount of nonlabor income he or she has.

For our purposes here, the exact details of this rule are relatively unimportant. What is more important is how the choice would change if there were a change in the wage rate or a change in nonlabor income. In order to analyze the EITC's possible impacts on labor supply, we need to extract the general rules and principles of how individual labor supply choices will respond to changes in wages and/or nonlabor income. Both are substantially affected by the EITC.

The Two Principles of Labor Supply Analysis

There are two basic analytical principles in labor supply analysis: one concerns the effect of a pure increase in nonlabor income and the other a pure increase in the price of leisure. Once these principles are understood, it is possible to readily apply them to a vast array of situations, including the impact of the EITC.

If Only Richer or Poorer

Suppose an individual is somehow made richer at his or her current hours of work but still has exactly the same wage as before. This could occur through an increase in nonlabor income or through a change in the structure of taxes or transfers that decreases an individual's net taxes or increases transfers, without changing the marginal tax rate.[6] Since the change makes an individual richer but doesn't change the price of leisure relative to consumption goods, he or she is likely to want to consume both more leisure and more consumption goods. In effect, the additional income is "spent" on both additional consumption goods and on additional hours of leisure. If hours of leisure increase, then hours of work must fall.

This is the first principle of labor supply analysis: Any change that makes an individual richer at his or her current labor supply without changing the wage rate will decrease labor supply. Any change that makes an individual poorer at his or her current labor supply without changing the wage rate will increase labor supply. This kind of change is called an income effect. The bigger the change in income, the bigger the total impact on labor supply.

The income effect applies both to hours of work and labor force participation. An increase in nonlabor income will reduce hours worked by current participants and could, if the income change is large enough, actually cause some workers to become nonparticipants (imagine winning the lottery and its impact on labor supply). Similarly, a decrease in nonlabor income will increase hours worked by current participants and could, if the income change is large enough, cause some nonworkers to enter the labor market.

If Only a Change in the Wage Rate

Now consider the opposite kind of change. Suppose that an individual's wage has increased, but that at the very same moment, nonlabor income is somehow reduced so that the worker is no richer at current hours of work. For example, if an individual is currently working 30 hours per week and the wage increases by $1.00, imagine that somehow $30 a week is simultaneously lost, leaving that individual with exactly the same income as before. This is exactly like having a higher price for leisure but being no richer. What effect will that have? The higher price means that leisure is now more expensive relative to consumption goods than it was before. This provides an incentive for individuals to cut back on leisure and consume more consumption goods. Since they are no richer, there is no offsetting impact. If hours of leisure fall, hours of work will increase.

This response is the second principle of labor supply analysis: An increase in an individual's wage rate that does not make him or her richer at current hours of work will increase labor supply. A decrease in an individual's wage rate that does not make him or her poorer at the current hours of work will decrease labor supply. This kind of change is called a substitution effect or a compensated wage effect.[7] The bigger the change in the wage, the bigger the total impact on labor supply. Substitution effects rarely occur in the real world by themselves, but they are an important component of many policies that affect wage rates.

Like the income effect, the substitution effect also applies to both hours of work and labor force participation. Thus, the substitution effect of a wage increase will increase hours of work among current workers and may also increase labor force participation, if the change in the wage rate is large enough. And if the wage rate falls, the substitution effect will decrease hours of work among current workers and may decrease labor force participation, if the change in the wage rate is large enough.

A Change in the Wage Rate

When an individual's wage rate changes, there is both a substitution effect and an income effect. A higher wage makes leisure more expensive, but it also makes an individual richer since, at the current hours of work, total income increases. The substitution effect of the wage increase causes hours of work to increase, while the income effect makes an individual richer and causes hours of work to fall. What happens when the two effects are put together? The total change in work hours when the wage increases is the sum of the changes arising from the income and substitution effects. The net result cannot be predicted: the income and substitution effects of a wage increase conflict.

The same logic applies in reverse when there is a decrease in the wage rate. Now the price of leisure is lower, but the individual is poorer. In this case, the substitution effect causes hours of work to fall, but the income effect of being poorer causes both leisure and consumption to fall, thus increasing hours of work. Again, the two effects conflict. If the substitution effect is stronger than the income effect, hours of work will fall when the wage falls. If the income effect is stronger, hours of work will rise.

A change in the wage rate also may affect the participation decision. Consider the situation of someone who is currently not working. That person has a wage rate—what he or she could earn if he or she took a job consistent with his or her skills and the status of the labor market. Now suppose this wage rate goes up. In this case, the substitution effect of a wage increase is an incentive to increase hours of work. The incentive may not be big enough to actually push a worker into the labor market, but the direction of the impact is clear. Usually there is an offsetting income effect when the wage increases but not in this case. Here, precisely because the individual isn't working to begin with, he or she isn't made any richer by the wage increase. Thus, in the case of a nonworking individual, there is only a substitution effect. A wage increase will increase the probability of labor market participation and a wage decrease will decrease that probability.

One final point: in all labor supply analyses, the relevant wage rate is not the market wage rate itself, but rather the *net marginal wage*.

The marginal wage is the wage that would be earned, net of all taxes or subsidies, if an individual worked one more hour. If w is the market wage and t is the marginal tax rate, then the net marginal wage is $w_m = w \times (1 - t)$; if there is a wage subsidy at rate s, then $w_m = w \times (1 + s)$. The distinction between the wage itself and the net marginal wage is important because many of the effects of the EITC operate via changes in the marginal wage rate.

How the EITC May Affect Labor Supply

The effects of the EITC on labor supply and labor force participation are complex and varied. That the EITC will affect these decisions is certainly plausible, since the EITC substantially alters the two factors that we know are the key determinants of those choices—the net after-tax wage rate and nonlabor income. The impact is complicated, however, by several factors. First, each of the three ranges of the EITC generates distinct and different potential labor supply effects. Second, the impacts are different for hours of work by workers already in the labor market and by potential workers who are not currently working. Finally, the impact is itself potentially problematic since the EITC is filtered through the tax system, thereby blurring its structure.

Hours of Work

For workers on the phase-in portion of the EITC schedule, the EITC subsidy acts exactly like an increase in a worker's wage rate. Here, the net marginal wage becomes $w \times (1 + c)$ where c, the EITC credit rate, equals 0.0765 for childless workers, 0.34 for workers with one child, and 0.40 for workers with two or more children. For current workers, there will be conflicting substitution and income effects, exactly like an increase in the wage rate. The higher wage provides an incentive to work more hours. But, the higher income (the dollar amount of the credit received at an individual's current hours of work) provides an incentive to work less. The net effect on hours of work is thus an empirical matter—it depends on which effect is stronger.

For workers on the stationary portion of the EITC schedule, the EITC acts exactly like a pure increase in nonlabor income with no accompanying change in the wage rate. Thus, there is an income effect that ought to have a negative effect on labor supply, but there is no potentially offsetting substitution effect. Since the maximum EITC benefit is quite substantial for workers with children, the effect on work hours for workers in this income range might well be large.

Finally, for workers on the phase-out range of the EITC schedule, the EITC operates as both a tax on the marginal wage rate and an increase in income. A worker's net wage becomes $w \times (1 - p)$ where p, the phase-out rate, equals 0.0765 for childless workers, 0.16 for workers with one child, and 0.21 for workers with two or more children. For example, if a worker with two children earns an additional $1,000, he or she will lose $210 of the credit, thus ending up only $790 richer. Despite this lower marginal wage, however, workers in the phase-out range are richer than they otherwise would be as long as they still receive a credit from the EITC program. Thus, in this range, there is a substitution effect of a lower wage and an income effect of being richer, both of which will reduce labor supply.

This particular configuration of incentives is the standard case of most income-tested transfer programs, such as AFDC, TANF, and food stamps. Those programs typically provide maximum benefits to individuals with little or no income and then reduce those benefits as family income rises. The benefits make the individuals better off and create an income effect that reduces labor supply, while the reduction in benefits with own earnings lowers the net marginal wage rate, creating a substitution effect that also reduces labor supply. There are, however, two important differences between EITC and the other income-tested programs in this respect. First, the phase-out rates in EITC are substantially lower than in these other programs and, second, the phase-out rates are applied not at very low earnings, as in most transfer programs, but at the somewhat higher levels that mark the beginning of the EITC phase-out range.

The theory of labor supply does identify some situations where the impacts of the EITC might be particularly strong. For workers on the phase-in range, the amount of the credit increases with income, so the income effect should increase as well. In contrast, the increase in the marginal wage rate is the same at all points along the phase-in range, so the substitution effect should be similar at all points. This suggests that the net effect on work might be more positive at very low incomes and somewhat less positive or negative at higher incomes within the phase-in range.

The most negative impact of the EITC would be on workers at or near the beginning of the phase-out range. They receive the maximum credit (or close to it) and also face a substantial reduction in their marginal net wage rate. For them, both income and substitution effects ought to be relatively strong. For workers at the high end of the phase-out range, the income effect will be much weaker because their credit is smaller, but the substitution effect will be the same.

Since all of the relevant EITC parameters increase with the number of children (through two), effects should increase with the number of children. Similarly, since the EITC phase-in and phase-out rates have increased over time, we would expect that the impacts have increased as well.

Labor Force Participation

For nonparticipants, the impact of the EITC also depends on where, prior to their own labor participation decision, their family income places them on the EITC range.

For a current nonworker in a household with no other earned income, the EITC increases the net marginal wage but without making the worker any richer at his or her current hours of work (which are zero). Thus, there is only a substitution effect. The EITC very definitely provides an incentive for nonworkers, such as these, to enter the labor market; the effect could well be large, especially for households with children where the wage subsidy is either 34 percent or 40 percent. This case would certainly apply to single mothers attempting to make a transition from welfare to work.

For a current nonworker in a household with other earnings that already place it on the phase-in range, the phase-in rate acts as a wage increase and creates a substitution effect that is an incentive to work. Possibly offsetting this, however, is the credit itself, for which the family is already eligible on the basis of the earnings of other household members. This operates like an increase in family income and creates a negative income effect. For these workers, the EITC effect on participation is unknown *a priori* and is, thus, an empirical question.

For a current nonworker in a household whose income places them on the EITC stationary range, there is an income effect that comes from the credit itself. That effect makes the household richer and will therefore reduce the incentive to work. In addition, there may also be a negative substitution effect, if their own labor supply would push them into the phase-out range. So, the impact is clearly negative for these workers.

Finally, for a current nonworker in a household already on the EITC phase-out range, the work incentives are clearly negative. The household is richer because of the credit, while the marginal net wage rate is lower because of the phase-out rate. Thus, there is both a substitution effect and an income effect, both of which provide negative work incentives. These effects could also operate to reduce labor force participation among current workers.

The largest positive effects on labor force participation ought to be for workers who are currently at the beginning of the phase-in range, where there is only a strong positive substitution effect. The largest negative effects on labor force participation ought to be for workers who are currently at the beginning of the phase-out range, where there are strong negative income and substitution effects.

All of these impacts on the hours of work of current workers and the labor force participation of current nonparticipants are summarized in Table 3.1. Also shown in the table are likely groups affected by the EITC in each range.

There is one final complication in analyzing the impact of the EITC on labor supply. All of these effects on the net marginal wage and on nonlabor income operate through the tax code. While the formulas that underlie the EITC clearly do result in changes in net marginal wages and family income, exactly as described above, it is not clear whether individuals are likely to perceive these marginal effects. Liebman (1998), for example, argued that taxpayers often regard the EITC as a lump-sum payment and do not clearly recognize that it could be higher or lower, depending on variations in their labor supply and/or income and earnings.[8] Nearly all EITC recipients receive the credit in a single payment as part of their annual tax refund check in the year following the year in which they earned the income entitling them to the credit. In contrast, the federal income tax and the payroll tax are withheld from each paycheck, and welfare benefits are received monthly. Because of the indirect way the EITC operates, the effects of

Table 3.1 Predicted Effects of the EITC on Hours of Work and Labor Force Participation

	Expected labor supply effect on	
EITC range of current household income	Hours of work of current workers	Labor force participation of current nonworkers

Phase-in	Substitution effect: +
	 Income effect: −
	 Net effect:?
		Substitution effect: +
		 Income effect:
		   0 (no other workers in
		     family)
		   − (other workers with
		     income)
		 Net effect:
		   + (no other workers in
		     family)
		   ? (other workers with
		     income)

	Impacted group: workers in low income families	Impacted group: single women on welfare; secondary workers in very low income families
Stationary	Substitution effect: 0 Income effect: − Net effect: − Impacted group: workers in low income families	Substitution effect: 0 or − Income effect: − Net effect: − Impacted group: secondary workers in low income families
Phase-out	Substitution effect: − Income effect: − Net effect: − Impacted group: workers in moderate income families	Substition effect: − Income effect: − Net effect: − Impacted group: secondary workers in low and moderate income families

the EITC could well be somewhat different than those that follow from a standard rational choice approach.

Evidence—The Effects of the EITC on Labor Supply

Methods

There is a very lengthy empirical literature in economics in the analysis of individual labor supply and how it is affected by wages, nonlabor income, taxes, and transfers.[9] There are several stylized facts from that literature that are helpful in identifying the likely impact of the EITC. First, the labor force participation decision is much more responsive to changes in wages and income than are decisions about hours of work. Heckman (1993), for example, in his review of the literature on labor supply has emphasized the importance of changes in the extensive margin (labor force participation) relative to the intensive margin (hours of work). Second, and consistent with that, women's labor supply decisions are more responsive to economic incentives than men's decisions are. This is especially true for married women. In many analyses, men's labor supply is largely unresponsive to changes in income and/or wages.

The first evidence on the likely labor supply impact of the EITC came from simulations that relied on labor supply parameters estimated in other related contexts. For example, in Hoffman and Seidman (1990), we used estimates of income and substitution effects for low income workers from the Seattle and Denver income-maintenance experiments that occurred in the mid-to-late 1970s. We then assumed that the low and moderate income families eligible for the EITC in 1988 would respond similarly to the wage and income changes created by the credit. We did not attempt to estimate the labor supply impact of the EITC directly or independently. A similar approach has also been followed by Dickert, Houser, and Scholz (1995).

Since then, there have been two broad approaches to determining the labor supply effects of the EITC. One approach involves the modeling of individual labor supply decisions in a framework that incorporates the income and wage changes created by the EITC. Statistical methods are then used to estimate behavioral responses. Combining the observed behavioral response with the actual changes in wages and nonlabor income created by the EITC provides an estimate of the impact of the EITC on labor supply. Some of these estimates attempt to characterize individual budget constraints fully, and they are called "structural" estimates. Other estimates are "reduced form," in that they do not attempt to fully characterize the budget constraints. The major benefit of this approach is that the resulting statistical estimates are not limited to the particular EITC formula or data on which they are based and can be used to predict the impact of future changes. The difficulties are primarily in implementation: it is enormously difficult to fully characterize the often complex budget constraints that face individuals and the multiple ways they changed during, for example, the 1990s. Additionally, these studies necessarily assume that individuals clearly perceive all of the wage and income changes of the EITC. Structural labor supply models of the EITC have been estimated by Meyer and Rosenbaum (2000) and by Dickert, Houser, and Scholz (1995). Reduced form labor supply models of the impact of the EITC have been estimated by Eissa and Liebman (1996) and Eissa and Hoynes (1998).

A second popular approach utilizes a *natural experiment* methodology. A natural experiment shares much in common with a traditional controlled experiment, like a medical drug trial, in which individuals are randomly assigned to treatment and control groups. In a experiment with random assignment, the effect of the treatment can be estimated simply as the difference between the two groups in the outcome of interest. There is no need for complex statistical analysis because random assignment eliminates all other, potentially confounding, differences between the two groups.

A natural experiment is essentially identical to a traditional experiment except that a natural experiment is not designed and controlled by an experimenter, but rather it is the result of some policy or some other action that affects one identifiable group but not some other otherwise similar group.[10] Here the treatment might refer to implementation of a particular law or policy that affects a particular group but not some other otherwise similar group. For example, minimum wage laws affect the wages and possibly the employment of less-skilled workers, but they arguably have little or no effect at all on the wages and employment of more-skilled workers. Thus, one way to determine the impact of the minimum wage on the employment of unskilled workers is to compare their employment rate to the employment rate of more-skilled workers.

In a natural experiment, the experimental and control group may have substantial pre-existing differences in the outcome of interest, something which is typically not true in a controlled experiment. For example, in the minimum wage example, the employment rate very likely differs between more-skilled and less-skilled workers even prior to any change in the level of the minimum wage. In that case, a simple comparison of the outcomes after the treatment reflects not just the treatment but also any pre-existing differences. Therefore, instead of comparing differences, researchers typically compare the *difference in the differences*, that is, the difference after the treatment with the difference before the treatment.[11] This difference-in-differences approach is now the standard method of evaluating a natural experiment in economics.

In the context of the EITC, researchers have identified a number of natural experiments that are useful for analyzing the labor supply impacts of the EITC. They all share a common structure—a comparison over time of some labor supply measure for two groups, one of which is eligible for the EITC, while the other is either not eligible for the EITC or is eligible for a markedly smaller EITC. Eissa and Liebman (1996) compared the labor force participation and hours of work of single mothers with that of single women without children. Eissa and Hoynes (1998) made the same kind of comparison for married women and married men. Ellwood (2000) compared labor force participation of single mothers with relatively low predicted wages (likely to be eligible for the EITC) with the labor supply of otherwise similar women with relatively high wages (ineligible for the EITC). He also compared the labor supply of different groups of married women, classified by whether their husband's income alone leaves the family on the phase-in, stationary, or phase-out region of the EITC schedule. In all of these cases, the impact of the EITC was estimated using the difference-in-differences approach.

It is important to appreciate both the strengths and weaknesses of the natural experiment approach in this context. There is no need to assume anything at all about how individuals perceive the EITC and its impact on net wages and their income. Researchers can be agnostic about what individuals know or do not know about the EITC. This is also true in traditional experiments; an experimenter need not have any particular theory about why a drug intervention may work in order to estimate whether it does, in fact, work. This is probably a strength of this approach, but it also ultimately limits its application to policy analysis. The results of natural experiments are narrowly tied to the particular treatment being investigated. Because they do not model or estimate the basis of the behavioral response (e.g., the income and substitution effects themselves) but only its aggregate impact, the experiments are not informative about what the effects would be if the

EITC were changed in some different way. They cannot be used for quantitative predictions of the impact of policies different from the natural experiment itself, although they may be useful for qualitative predictions.

Findings

Tables 3.2 and 3.3 summarize what we know from the economics literature about the labor supply effects of the EITC. Table 3.2 examines the effects on labor force participation, and Table 3.3 looks at the effects on hours of work. Appendix Tables B.1 and B.2 describe the studies in the tables further, including information about data and methodology plus interpretative notes. Our discussion focuses on the two text tables, but we urge interested readers to examine the two background tables.

A few words of introduction are in order. First, most of the studies are based on the EITC as of the mid 1980s or focus on the major expansion of the EITC in 1993. Especially in the natural experiment studies, the impacts are always marginal, that is, they identify the impact of a particular EITC change relative to the immediate status quo. Second, the tables are organized by population group—single mothers, married mothers, etc. It is reasonable to expect labor supply impacts to vary across these groups because they tend to face different EITC labor supply incentives and all of the natural experiments are structured around those differences. Still, the groups are not homogeneous and some dilution of effects is to be expected. Finally, the studies are consistently well done and virtually all are reliable. Some further editorial comments are included in the Appendix B tables.

Using the summary of data presented in Tables 3.2 and 3.3, we can draw the following conclusions about the impact of the EITC on labor supply.

- The empirical evidence is unusually consistent, with very few anomalous findings. Virtually all estimates are consistent with the underlying hypotheses generated from the economic model of labor supply behavior. This is an extremely important finding for thinking about reform of the EITC. Economic incentives do seem to matter.

- The findings are also quite consistent with the standard finding that decisions about hours of work are less responsive to

Table 3.2 Summary of Estimated Effects of EITC on Labor Force Participation and Employment Rate

Population group and study	Expected effects	Methods	Findings
Single mothers Dickert, Houser, and Scholz (1995) Eissa and Liebman (1996) Ellwood (2000) Meyer and Rosenbaum (1999, 2000)	Positive, because most nonworking single mothers face incentives of phase-in range of EITC.	Natural experiment by number of children and by quartile of predicted wage rate (Ellwood, Eissa and Liebman, Meyer and Rosenbaum). Structural models with taxes and transfers, including EITC and AFDC (Dickert, Houser, and Scholz; Meyer and Rosenbaum).	Consistently positive. • 1986 EITC expansion increased LFPR 2 to 4 percentage points (Eissa and Liebman). • 1993 EITC expansion and AFDC reform increased LFPR of low wage single mothers 18–23 percentage points compared to higher wage single mothers and to single women without children (Ellwood). • 6 to 7 percentage point increase in employment rate of single mothers between 1990 and 1996 compared to single women without children (Meyer and Rosenbaum 2000). • 1993 EITC expansion increased LFPR 3.3 percentage points (Dickert, Houser, and Scholz) • Change in income taxes if work (primarily EITC) increased LFPR of all single mothers by 1.5 to 2 percentage points, 1992–96, approximately 35% of total change in LFPR (Meyer and Rosenbaum 1999).

(continued)

Table 3.2 (continued)

Population group and study	Expected effects	Methods	Findings
Married Mothers Eissa and Hoynes (1998) Ellwood (2000)	Negative, because many married mothers face incentives of flat and phase-out ranges of EITC.	Natural experiment by number of children and husband's income (Ellwood; Eissa and Hoynes) Reduced form model with simulation of EITC effect (Eissa and Hoynes).	Negative overall, but depends on particular incentives. • 1993 EITC expansion and AFDC reform decreased LFPR of low wage married mothers by 3–7 percentage points compared to higher wage married mothers (Ellwood); decreased LFPR of less educated married mothers by 2–4 percentage points (Eissa and Hoynes). Reduced form estimate is smaller but still negative (Eissa and Hoynes). • LFPR for married women on phase-in range increased by 1.1 percentage points (Eissa and Hoynes); increased 13 percentage points for low wage married women with family income low enough to have positive work incentives (Ellwood).
Married Men Eissa and Hoynes (1998)	Weakly positive, because nonworking married men face incentives of phase-in range of EITC.	Natural experiment by number of children (Eissa and Hoynes). Reduced form model with simulation of EITC effect (Eissa and Hoynes).	Zero to positive, but very small. • 1993 EITC expansion increased LFPR of married men with children and with wife <12 years of education by 0.7–1.6 percentage points relative to married men without children. • Reduced form estimates are essentially zero.

NOTE: LFPR is labor force participation.

Table 3.3 Summary of Estimated Effects of EITC on Hours of Work

Population group and study	Expected effects	Methods	Findings
All EITC recipients Hoffman and Seidman (1990) Dickert, Houser, and Scholz (1995)	Mixed, depends on current earnings, which determine EITC range and resulting labor supply incentives.	Simulations (Hoffman and Seidman; Dickert, Houser and Scholz)	Negative, but relatively small. • 1988 EITC reduced annual hours of work 2% relative to EITC (Hoffman and Seidman). • 1996 EITC decreased annual hours of work 0% to 4.0%. Most estimates between 0% and −1.6% (Dickert, Houser, and Scholz). • Hours of work increase on phase-in range and decrease in flat and phase-out ranges (Hoffman and Seidman; Dickert, Houser, and Scholz).
Single mothers Dickert, Houser, and Scholz (1995) Eissa and Leibman (1996)	Mixed, but probably negative overall, depends on current earnings, which determine EITC range and resulting labor supply incentives.	Reduced form model (Eissa and Leibman) and simulations (Dickert, Houser, and Scholz).	Negative or zero. • 1986 EITC expansion had little or no effect on hours of work (Eissa and Liebman). • 1993 EITC expansion decreased hours of work 0.5% to 4.0%. Most estimates between −0.5% and −1.0% (Dickert, Houser, and Scholz).

(continued)

Table 3.3 (continued)

Population group and study	Expected effects	Methods	Findings
Married women Hoffman and Seidman (1990) Dickert, Houser, and Scholz (1995) Eissa and Hoynes (1998)	Mixed, but probably negative overall, since married women may face negative labor supply incentives of phase-out range.	Simulations (Hoffman and Seidman; Dickert, Houser, and Scholz) and reduced form labor supply model (Eissa and Hoynes).	Mostly negative, but depends on particular incentives. • 1988 EITC decreased annual hours of work of wives in EITC recipient families 3.6% (Hoffman and Seidman). • 1993 EITC expansion decreased annual hours of work of married women with children 1.5% to 11.4%. Most estimates between −1.5% and −4.0%. (Dickert, Houser, and Scholz). • 1993 EITC expansion decreased average hours of work 1% to 5%. Large positive effect (8–50%) for workers on phase-in range small negative effect for workers on flat range, possibly large negative (2–20%) for workers on phase-out range (Eissa and Hoynes).
Married men Hoffman and Seidman (1990) Dickert, Houser, and Scholz (1995) Eissa and Hoynes (1998)	Mixed, depends on current earnings, which determine EITC range and resulting labor supply incentives.	Simulations (Hoffman and Seidman; Dickert, Houser, and Scholz) and reduced form labor supply model (Eissa and Hoynes).	Negative overall, but quantitatively small; positive effects on phase-in range. • 1988 EITC decreased average hours of work 1.6% (Hoffman and Seidman). • 1993 EITC expansion decreased annual hours of work 0% to 3.2%. Most estimates between −1% and −2% (Dickert, Houser, and Scholz). • 1993 EITC expansion decreased average hours of work about 2%. Increase of 2 to 4% for workers on phase-in, no effect for workers on flat range and a decrease of 3% to 4% for workers on phase-out (Eissa and Hoynes).

changes in wages and income than are decisions about labor force participation. Virtually all estimated labor force participation effects are larger than hours of work effects.

- The EITC has increased the labor force participation of population groups that face positive work incentives. For example, all estimates indicate that the EITC has increased labor force participation among single mothers. This was true for the relatively modest EITC expansion of the mid 1980s and especially of the much more substantial expansion of the mid 1990s. The participation effects are consistent along a number of dimensions (e.g., less educated vs. more educated, low wage vs. high wage). Other groups who have faced positive incentives and whose labor force participation has increased include married men with children, for whom there is a small but positive effect, and married women whose husbands have very low incomes, for whom the estimates are much larger. While other factors such as welfare reform and the strong economy are undoubtedly important contributing factors, the EITC has had a major impact on the sharp increase in the labor force participation of single mothers and may well be the leading causal factor.

- The EITC has decreased the labor force participation of groups that face negative work incentives. Married women, many of whom are operating along the phase-out range, are the most conspicuous example of this. Estimated effects are not trivial, probably on the order of 3 to 5 percentage points.

- Estimates of hours of work effects among workers are relatively small in absolute value, whether positive or negative. This appears to be the case for single mothers of the mid 1980s and also for less-educated married men and married women in the mid 1990s. Estimated effects are larger for married men and women, presumably because more of them are located along the phase-out range. A reasonable estimate for the mid 1990s is a decrease in hours worked of about 2 to 4 percent among married men and women. There are no comparable estimates for the impact on single mothers in the 1990s.

- While hours of work fall among EITC recipients as a whole, they increase for workers along the phase-in range. Decreases in work hours are concentrated among workers along the phase-out range. The range of estimates of this negative effect is reasonably large and imprecise.

- Estimates from natural experiments tend to be consistently slightly greater than (in absolute value) estimates from regression models, whether those models are reduced form or structural.

- There is only a single estimate of the total impact of the EITC on total labor supply, including both changes in hours of work among current workers and changes in labor force participation. Dickert, Houser, and Scholz (1995) estimated that the 1996 EITC increased total labor supply, relative to the EITC in 1993, by about 20 million hours due to an increase of 75 million hours by previous nonparticipants, which offset a decrease of 55 million hours by current workers. This is a small net effect relative to total labor input in the economy.

THE IMPACT OF THE EITC ON WAGE RATES

Since, as we have seen, the EITC may affect labor supply decisions, it may also affect market wage rates, which depend on the interaction of labor supply and labor demand. Given what we know about the magnitude of the labor supply impacts, the effects are likely to be modest at most. Nevertheless, it is worth reviewing the issue briefly and seeing what the impacts could be and what they are likely to be.

Consider, for example, the labor market for the least skilled, lowest wage workers. It is certainly possible that many of these workers will be on the phase-in range of the EITC, in which they are receiving a credit that ranges from 7.65 percent if they are childless to 40 percent if they have two or more children. For these workers, as we discussed above, there are conflicting income and substitution effects, although the empirical evidence suggests that the net effect is likely to be small but positive. In addition, both theory and the empirical evidence suggests that labor force participation will rise among previously non-employed workers and that this effect will be reasonably large.

What impact will this have on the labor market equilibrium? What will happen to market wage rates for these less skilled workers? Figure 3.1 shows a representative very low wage labor market before and after the introduction of the EITC (or, equivalently, before and after a substantial increase in the EITC, as in the 1990s). The original equilibrium is at wage W_0^*, where demand curve D and supply curve S_0 intersect. The wage on the vertical axis is the market wage, which is the relevant wage for labor demand. We know that for workers on the EITC phase-in range, however, the credit rate of the EITC is exactly equivalent to a wage increase, and it is the net (after-tax and after-transfer) wage that is relevant for labor supply decisions. Because any market wage now corresponds to a higher net wage and because the relationship between wages and hours worked is positive, the impact of the EITC is to increase the supply of labor over market wage rates that correspond to the phase-in range. At these low wage rates, more labor is supplied at each market wage, so the supply curve shifts out to S_1.

Note that supply curve S_1 has an unusual shape—it is not parallel to S_0, but steeper. This reflects the expected pattern of income and substitution effects. The impact of the substitution effect derives from the credit rate, which is constant within the phase-in range, but the

Figure 3.1 The Potential Impact of the EITC on Wages in the Very Low Wage Labor Market

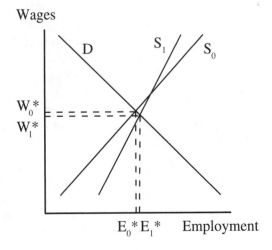

impact of the income effect, which derives from the actual amount of EITC income, increases as earned income increases. Thus, at relatively low wages, the positive substitution effect will probably dominate but, at higher wages, the negative income effect becomes larger so that the increase in supply is much smaller. When the substitution and income effects are equal in magnitude, the two curves intersect. Eventually, at wages high enough to place a worker on the EITC stationary range, there is only an income effect, which reduces labor supply. At that point, the new labor supply curve is above (or to the left of) the old supply curve.

In the figure, there is a small increase in labor supply in the wage vicinity of the old equilibrium wage, and that is probably the likeliest result. Thus, when the EITC is introduced or increased, the equilibrium market wage falls to wage W_1^*, where demand curve D and supply curve S_1 intersect. It is, therefore, certainly possible that the EITC could, by increasing labor supply among low wage workers, reduce their market wage rate. Even so, it is clear that the net wage is substantially increased.

Proceeding in exactly the same way, we expect, based both on economic theory and the empirical evidence, the EITC to decrease labor supply among workers on the stationary range and on the phaseout range. Thus, over these regions, the EITC would likely increase equilibrium wages.

In fact, all of these impacts are likely to be quite modest for several reasons. First, the changes in labor supply induced by the EITC are relatively small; the labor force participation impacts on nonworkers facing the phase-in range and on secondary workers on the phase-out range, which are certainly not trivial, are notable exceptions. Second, there is a relatively loose correspondence between the EITC range of a worker and the particular labor market in which he or she participates. For example, very low wage workers can be not only primary workers in households on the EITC phase-in range, but they can also be secondary workers in EITC households on the EITC stationary or phase-out range. In that case, the positive and negative labor supply impacts of the different ranges might well cancel each other out. This mixed impact also occurs because the EITC benefit schedules vary by the number of children; as a result, a given earned income corresponds to a different EITC region and thus different labor supply effects for different workers. Finally, EITC workers are themselves not necessarily the majority of any particular labor market. Many low and moderate wage workers are not eligible for the EITC. For instance, teenagers or secondary workers in middle-income families are ineligible, as are single adults with incomes greater than $10,700. The most likely result, then, is that the EITC has, at most, a very small negative impact on wages for low wage workers and a similarly small positive impact on wages for workers with slightly higher wage rates.

Table 3.4 provides some empirical evidence on this, using the 1996 PSID data that was the basis for the description of the EITC population in Chapter 2. In the table, workers are divided into wage brackets that correspond roughly to "very low" (< $6.00), "low to moderate" ($6.00–$7.50), and "moderate" ($7.50–$10.00). The sample here includes all heads of households and their spouses; it does not include other earners such as teenagers. For each wage bracket, the table shows the proportion of workers in that wage bracket who are on the various regions of the EITC or who are EITC-ineligible. The EITC range is computed here based on the husband's earnings alone for married couples and on family income for single households and for wives. This method has the impact of increasing the number of low wage workers who are placed on the phase-in and stationary range.

The table reveals that EITC-eligible workers are a minority in each of these three labor markets. Recipients of the EITC comprise just 52 percent of the participants in the lowest wage market, about 33 percent of the second bracket, and 30 percent of those earning $7.50 to $10.00

Table 3.4 The Percentage Distribution of Workers by EITC Range and Market Wage Rate, 1996

	Wage rate		
EITC status	<$6.00	$6.00–$7.50	$7.50–$10.00
Phase-in	24.5	5.2	2.2
Stationary	6.5	5.8	1.8
Phase-out	17.0	23.0	25.4
EITC-ineligible	52.0	66.0	70.6
Total	100.0	100.0	100.0

SOURCE: Panel Study of Income Dynamics.

per hour. Among EITC recipients, almost all phase-in households are necessarily in the lowest wage bracket, but these lowest wage workers are themselves distributed almost equally between the phase-in range (about 51 percent) and the latter two ranges (49 percent). For the other two EITC brackets, the correlation between wage bracket and EITC range is much tighter, with 70 percent of workers in the second wage bracket and 85 percent in the third bracket located along the phase-out range.

It may be surprising to see that so many low wage workers are EITC-ineligible. In the lowest wage group, almost all of the ineligibles are demographically eligible but have incomes that exceed the EITC maximum, despite their low wages. Almost all the head of households who are ineligible have no children, so they were income-ineligible in 1996 if their annual earnings exceeded $9,500. In the case of low wage wives, more than half had children, but most were income-ineligible on the basis of their husband's earnings. The average husband's earnings for these income-ineligibles was over $36,000.

SUMMARY

In this chapter, we examined the impact of the EITC on the labor market, including labor force participation, hours of work, and wage rates. By the mid 1990s, the EITC had been transformed from a very modest program into one that has a very substantial impact on individual incomes for many low and moderate income families. In the process, it altered the economic benefits of work for many individuals, some positively and others negatively.

The research of the last decade has helped clarify the nature of these effects. We now have particularly good information about the impacts of the EITC on work. It is clear that the EITC has increased labor force participation among workers who earn relatively low market wages and face the positive work incentives of the EITC phase-in range. This group includes single mothers, including women making a transition from welfare to work, and married women whose husbands have very low incomes. There are negative labor force participation impacts on married women as a whole, many of whom are operating along the EITC phase-out range and thus face markedly more negative work incentives than in the past. Hours of work among current workers are also affected, increasing for low wage workers and falling for workers with higher incomes. Hours of work effects, however, appear to be small relative to participation effects. It is quite possible that the overall EITC effect on labor supply has been positive, as a consequence of its substantial positive participation effect on the lowest wage workers.

It is certainly not impossible that the EITC could also affect market wages. Any program that operates on a substantial scale, as the EITC does, and that affects labor supply can have such an effect. In the case of the EITC, though, it is likely that the impact on wage rates is quite modest. In only a few cases are the estimated labor supply effects among EITC recipients large enough to make an impact. Even in those cases, most participants in low wage labor markets are EITC-ineligible, so the labor supply impact of the EITC on the market wage is further diluted.

The overall picture that emerges, then, is of a program that appears to operate fundamentally well and that transfers substantial sums of money to many low and moderate income families and does so with far more positive impacts than negative. This is certainly true, as we will show in Chapter 5, when compared with alternative transfer policies targeted at low wage workers and/or low income households.

Notes

1. For further discussion of the behavioral impact of the EITC, see Hotz and Scholz (2000) and the papers collected in Meyer and Holtz-Eakin (2001).
2. Nonlabor income is income that an individual has at zero hours of work and includes such things as transfer income and income from assets. In a family with a clear primary earner and secondary earner, the income of the primary earner is often treated as nonlabor income from the standpoint of the secondary earner. This treatment is appropriate if decision making about work is sequential, but not if it is simultaneous.
3. The traditional labor supply model is based on a two-way choice about time use between market work and leisure. It is often useful in the analysis to reinterpret leisure as housework or other productive household activities.
4. If w is the wage rate, p the price of consumption goods, V is nonlabor income, and T is the total amount of time available, then feasible combinations of consumption goods (C) and leisure time (L) must satisfy $pC + wL = wT + V$. The right-hand side of this equation is called full income—the maximum income an individual could have if he/she worked all T hours. The left-hand side shows

spending on consumption goods (pC) and leisure (wL). The equation indicates that total spending must equal full income.

5. As an example of this kind of logic, think about the cost of home-schooling a child. Actual monetary costs may be modest relative to, say, private school tuition, but foregone earnings of the "teacher" are very substantial.

6. The marginal tax rate is the tax rate that applies to the last dollar of earned income.

7. The substitution effects described here is a Slutsky substitution effect in which an individual's income is held constant when prices change. An alternative and more common substitution effect (Hicks substitution effect) holds an individual's income constant. The Slutsky substitution effect is much easier to describe without graphs. The analysis in Appendix B uses the Hicks substitution effect.

8. Liebman (1998) concluded, based on interviews he conducted as an IRS VITA (Volunteer Income Tax Assistance) volunteer in 1994, that there was relatively low awareness of the credit. He further noted, "While it is possible that recent publicity and outreach efforts (as well as the increased size of the credit) have increased awareness, interviews I conducted in 1996 with housing-project residents and recipients of Section 8 housing assistance show that while almost all housing-subsidy recipients understand exactly the relationship between their income and their rent, the few who are working and say they receive the EITC have no idea whether their tax refund would go up or down if their income increased." This, of course, is not intended to be definitive information about the knowledge of the EITC by potential recipients.

9. For a recent survey, see Blundell and MaCurdy (1999). An earlier useful discussion is Heckman (1993).

10. For a further discussion of natural experiments, see Rosenzweig and Wolpin (2000) and Angrist and Krueger (1999).

11. If x_1 and x_2 are the outcomes for the treatment group and y_1 and y_2 are the corresponding outcomes for the control group at times 1 and 2, then the difference-in-difference estimator is $DID = (x_2 - x_1) - (y_2 - y_1)$ which is the difference in the changes. Equivalently, $DID = (x_2 - y_2) - (x_1 - y_1)$, which is the change in the differences. The DID estimator depends critically on the further assumption that any other effects that occur over the length of the experiment affect both groups identically. This can be a problem if macroeconomic changes or other policies affect the control and treatment groups differently.

4
The EITC and the Family

The "marriage tax" has been much in the news in the 1990s and the early 2000s. A marriage tax exists whenever married couples end up paying more in taxes than they would if they were single. It is a natural feature of a tax system that is both progressive and treats a married couple as a tax-paying unit. A marriage tax occurs primarily in families where there are two earners that earn relatively similar amounts; single-earner families often receive marriage benefits from the tax system in the sense that they pay less tax than if they were single. In a two-earner family, the earnings of one spouse are taxed at rates that depend on the earnings of the other, so the progressive tax rates push the couple into a higher tax bracket than either would face as a single person. Adjustments in the tax code provide a separate, more favorable tax schedule for married couples, but that does not eliminate the marriage tax under all situations. Indeed, it is impossible to design a tax code that is progressive, treats a married couple as the tax-paying unit, and is marriage neutral.

Like the rest of the tax code, the EITC also imposes a marriage tax on some married couples who find themselves receiving smaller EITC benefits than if they were single. In addition, the EITC provides marriage bonuses to other married couples who receive higher EITC benefits than if they were single. As the program has become more generous, these impacts have become quite substantial. Unlike the positive income tax rate structure, the EITC in 2001 does not make any distinction at all between married couples and single individuals in terms of EITC rates and benefits. Because EITC benefits depend on the number of children (in a nonlinear way and capped at two children) and because benefits are phased out as income rises, single individuals can either gain or lose quite substantial credit amounts by marriage, depending on their particular family and earnings circumstances. Similarly, married couples may stand to gain or lose substantial amounts if they were to separate or divorce. These effects, which can be quite large under just the right circumstances, may potentially affect marriage decisions, but they may be deemed inappropriate and unfair even if they don't.

During the 2000 presidential campaign, both Al Gore and George W. Bush promised to eliminate the marriage tax. The Economic Growth and Tax Relief Act of 2001, passed in June 2001, included a set of provisions to reduce the marriage tax. The legislation addressed the marriage penalty in both the tax code as a whole and in the EITC. Effective in 2005 and fully phased in by 2008, the standard deduction for married couples will be increased to twice that of a single-person household and the upper income limit of the 15 percent tax bracket will also be increased to twice that of a single-person household. The EITC benefit schedule was also adjusted, with the creation of a separate married-couple schedule, which begins in 2002 and becomes fully effective in 2007. This adjustment will also reduce the marriage tax.

In this chapter, we examine the EITC from the perspective of the family. We first examine how the EITC marriage bonuses and penalties arise, using the EITC program as it existed in 2001 to construct a set of illustrative examples. Since the EITC marriage penalty reform of the 2001 tax cut legislation was not implemented until 2002, we do not include it in our analyses. We do, however, simulate the impact of the change by considering what impact it would have had, if it had been in place in 2001. We then consider how large these marriage bonuses and penalties are in practice, drawing on a set of studies that use representative data rather than illustrative cases. Finally, we review the evidence about whether marriage decisions themselves have been sensitive to the penalties and bonuses created by the EITC.

MARRIAGE BONUSES AND PENALTIES

Marriage bonuses occur whenever the EITC benefits of a married couple exceed the combined EITC benefits if each person were single. The most obvious case is one in which a low income single individual with earnings but without a qualifying child marries a low income (or even better, no income) individual with a qualifying child (or, even better, two qualifying children). In this case, the two original families are eligible for, at most, a very small credit, while the new family is eligible for a substantial EITC payment. Marriage penalties occur when an EITC-eligible single individual marries another low income individual who may also be EITC eligible. While their individual incomes enable them to receive two possibly substantial EITC payments, their joint incomes will place them well into or even beyond the phase-out range, while their new larger family size provides fewer or even no advantages. Thus, they collectively will receive substantially reduced EITC benefits. The extreme case occurs when both are eligible for the maximum EITC benefits as single households.

Table 4.1 provides a set of examples that identify the sources and magnitudes of EITC marriage bonuses and penalties, as of 2001.[1] The first row shows a case of EITC neutrality. If a single, low wage worker with children marries a nonworker without children, there are no EITC changes, precisely because the benefit formula is independent of marital status. The second row shows the EITC marriage bonus for the case of a single, childless, full-time, year-round minimum wage earner

Table 4.1 Illustrative EITC Marriage Bonus or Penalty, 2001

Situation	EITC marriage bonus ($+$) or penalty ($-$) ($)
(1) EITC eligible worker with children marries childless non worker	0
(2) Childless minimum wage worker marries non worker with two children[a]	$+3,977$
(3) Worker with $5,000 earnings and one child marries worker with $5,000 earnings and one child	$+600$
(4) Childless minimum wage worker marries minimum wage worker with two children[a]	$-1,613$
(5) Minimum wage worker with two children marries minimum wage worker with two children[a]	$-5,590$
(6) Worker with two children earning maximum income on EITC plateau marries worker with two children earning maximum income on EITC plateau[b]	$-6,765$
(7) Worker with two children earning $20,000 marries worker earning $50,000	$-2,553$

[a] Minimum wage worker @ $5.15/hour $\times$ 2,000 hours.
[b] EITC earnings maximum in 2001 = $13,090.

($5.15 per hour × 2000 hours) who marries a nonworker with two children. Given the EITC benefit structure, the two single individuals are eligible for $31 and $0, respectively, while as a married couple with two children, their income places them in the plateau region where they collect the maximum benefit of $4,008. Thus, they receive an EITC marriage bonus of $3,977. The third row illustrates the case of two low income workers, each with one child. They receive a much smaller bonus than the previous example, and it arises from the difference between the credit rate and the maximum incomes on which the credit can be earned for families with one and two children. Individually, each receives a credit of $1,700 (0.34 × $5,000), while together they are eligible for a credit of $4,000 (0.40 × $10,000). The break-even income in this kind of situation under 2001 EITC parameters is $5,894.[2] Beyond that, a marriage of equal earners each with one child generates EITC penalties.

Rows 4 through 6 illustrate EITC marriage penalties. In example 4, the same childless minimum wage worker now marries a minimum wage worker with two children. As two single tax-paying units, they are eligible for payments of $31 and $4,008, respectively. Jointly, by virtue of their higher income, they are eligible for only $2,426 ($2,426 = $4,008 − 0.2106 × [$20,600 − $13,090]), which yields a penalty of $1,613. In case 5, if both individuals had two children, they would each receive payments of $4,008 if they were single, but only $2,426 if married, for a total penalty of $5,590—more than 25 percent of their earned income. For two single individuals, each with two children and each earning an income exactly equal to the maximum income on the plateau region of the EITC, the marriage penalty would reach its maximum of $6,765 (illustrated in row 6).[3]

Finally, EITC penalties can also exist among some moderately high income families, as long as one of the partners has an EITC-eligible income. Row 7 shows a case like this in which a worker with two children and earnings of $20,000 marries a worker with an income of $50,000. Individually, they receive an EITC of $2,553 and $0, respectively. Together, their combined income of $70,000 greatly exceeds the EITC earnings cut-off level, and their combined benefit is thus $0.

In general, bonuses exist among low income, single-earner families and penalties among most low to mid income, two-earner couples

with children. Eissa and Hoynes (2000) showed that the EITC marriage penalty increases with the share of income contributed by the
second earner.

The examples in Table 4.1 are simply illustrative and do not, by
themselves, provide information about how important and widespread
either bonuses or penalties are. It is not clear, *a priori,* whether bonuses or penalties are more common; certainly, the cases illustrated in
the last two rows must be quite rare. The actual distribution of bonuses
and penalties depends on the distribution of households across wage
and demographic categories. To evaluate that, we need to turn to population data.

Determining the actual, as compared to illustrative, importance of
these EITC marriage bonuses and penalties is inherently complicated
because it requires observing or imputing an alternative marital status
for each household in order to compute and then compare its EITC
benefits in the two marital statuses. It is more complex yet if the bonuses and penalties affect marriage decisions. Suppose, for example,
that large bonuses encourage marriage and large penalties discourage
it. In that event, a sample of currently married couples will overrepre-
sent households with large potential bonuses and underrepresent
households with potential penalties, precisely because the bonus and
penalties affect which households are married.

There are three major questions about the EITC marriage bonus
and penalty that are of particular interest. First, how many households
receive EITC bonuses and how many suffer EITC penalties? Second,
which households receive the benefits or bear the penalties? The distribution by income bracket is of special interest here. Third, what is
the aggregate dollar amount of bonuses and penalties? There is good
information on the second and third questions, but basic information
on the first question is unfortunately not very useful.

There are two major empirical approaches to measuring EITC marriage bonuses and penalties. One method is similar to what is done in
most studies of marriage tax effects. It begins with a sample of currently married couples, "divorces" them in order to create a counter-
factual marital status, makes assumptions about custody of children
and other details in the divorced status, and then computes and compares taxes in the two marital statuses.[4] The analysis is static in the
sense that it assumes no labor supply response to the change in marital

status; for example, individual income is assumed to be unchanged when marital status changes, just as in the illustrative examples in Table 4.1. The other approach uses longitudinal data on individuals in order to compare EITC benefits before and after a change in marital status. In this case, bonuses and penalties are computed net of behavioral changes that accompany a change in marital status.

Ellwood (2000) used the latter approach, with data from the PSID for marriages that occurred between 1983 and 1991. The EITC benefits in the first full year after marriage were computed, inclusive of any changes in labor supply and fertility, and compared with EITC benefits in the last full year prior to marriage. Therefore, the bonuses and penalties he computed are potentially quite different from the static examples illustrated in Table 4.1 and in the "divorce" approach mentioned above. For example, if a married couple has a child, their EITC will increase under many circumstances, thus yielding both more situations of bonuses and also larger bonuses. Ellwood used the 1996 EITC formula to compute before and after benefits.[5] Because the marriages occurred well prior to the sharp increase in EITC benefits, the sample of marriages does not reflect and, thus, does not suffer from the potentially stronger marriage incentives created by the current EITC.

The standard "divorce" approach was adopted by the Congressional Budget Office (CBO 1997), Holtzblatt and Rebelein (1999, 2000), and Eissa and Hoynes (2000). The CBO study and the papers by Holtzblatt and Rebelein share some common features. They used data from the IRS Statistics of Income (SOI), a data source that is derived directly from tax returns and is particularly detailed and accurate. The procedures they followed are well-suited for measuring the total dollar bonuses and penalties of the EITC as well as their distribution but not for identifying the proportion of EITC recipient households with bonuses and penalties.[6] The studies first computed the impact of *all* taxes that change with marital status except the EITC and then computed the *marginal* impact of the EITC on whether a household has a net marriage bonus or penalty and on the amount of the bonus or penalty. This is perfectly appropriate for measuring the total dollar impact of the EITC on bonuses and penalties. But, with this procedure, a married couple receiving an EITC bonus or penalty is identified only if the EITC changes its net marriage bonus or penalty status, given the impact of all other taxes that change with marital status.

For example, suppose a married couple has a net marriage penalty of $1,000 without including the EITC and additionally loses $1,000 of EITC benefits. The married couple's net penalty/bonus status does not change by incorporating the EITC, so it would not be identified as a married couple suffering an EITC penalty. Neither would it be identified as a married couple experiencing an EITC bonus unless its EITC bonus was greater than $1,000. As a result, the methods used in these two studies will tend to underestimate the number of married couples with either EITC bonuses or EITC penalties.

The methods do not, however, affect estimates of the total dollar impact of EITC bonuses or penalties and, because the data are particularly good, these studies are very useful for that purpose. Eissa and Hoynes also provided estimates of total bonuses and penalties but no information about the proportion of married couples receiving bonuses or suffering penalties.

The estimates from these three studies necessarily depend on assumptions about residence, custody of children, and many smaller issues, all of which may affect the EITC and other taxes that the married couple would face if they were divorced. Eissa and Hoynes assumed that the wife retains custody of the children and computed the EITC on that basis. The CBO study assumed that divorcing parents with two or more children will divide the children between their households, thereby enabling both to have the qualifying children needed for more substantial EITC benefits. This assumption will likely increase the EITC receipt of divorcing households and thus ought to increase the number of married couples for whom EITC marriage penalties are computed and also the total dollar amount of penalties. The underlying assumption that children are divided across households is questionable.

Holtzblatt and Rebelein is by far the most thorough study to date. They emphasized four scenarios in all, but here we emphasize three of them: one in which children are allocated to the higher income spouse, one in which they are allocated to the lower income spouse, and a third in which they are allocated so as to minimize taxes.[7] The first case will likely lead to fewer divorced households receiving EITC because fewer divorced persons will have both sufficiently low earnings and children. Because fewer divorced persons will be eligible for EITC benefits, fewer married couples will be found to have EITC marriage penalties. In the second case, there will be more divorced households receiving the EITC because now more families have both low earnings and children. Thus, in this case, more married couples will be found to have EITC marriage penalties. In the final case, because divorced individuals receive the maximum EITC for which they could potentially be eligible, more married couples will be found to have EITC marriage penalties.

Because all of the studies are based on a sample of currently married couples (or marrying couples in Ellwood's study), the analyses necessarily incorporate any impact of bonuses and/or penalties on marriage and divorce decisions as well as on labor supply decisions. If there is any behavioral response to the potential bonuses and penalties, these samples will tend to provide an overestimate of bonuses and an underestimate of penalties.

The findings about EITC marriage penalties and bonuses from these studies are presented in Table 4.2. None of the studies provide a useful estimate of the proportion of married couples with a penalty or bonus. Ellwood's findings have an obvious upward bias toward finding bonuses that arise from post-marriage changes in fertility and labor supply. The CBO and Holtzblatt and Rebelein studies are biased against finding any impact because their approach is marginal. We emphasize these biases in the table by noting that the true estimates are "at most" or "at least" as the figures reported. Dollar estimates in these two studies are not, however, affected by that bias and are, therefore, quite useful.

We can draw the following conclusions about EITC marriage penalties and bonuses.

- In practice, the EITC penalizes marriage much more often than it rewards it. Ellwood found that at most 16 percent of married couples received a penalty and at most 11 percent received a bonus, with more than half of the bonuses due to post-marriage changes that increased EITC benefits. Holtzblatt and Rebelein's marginal impacts imply that at least 4 percent to 12 percent of married couples receive a penalty while at least 0.5 percent to 1.3 percent receive a bonus depending on the underlying assumptions.[8] The CBO estimates suggest that at least 6 percent of married couples receive penalties and at least 4 percent receive bonuses. Adjusting Ellwood's figures by eliminating

Table 4.2 Estimated EITC Bonuses and Penalties

Study	Data and method	Findings	Comment
Ellwood (2000)	Marriages from PSID that occurred between 1983 and 1991. Bonus and penalty calculated using 1996 EITC. Longitudinal before-after comparison, inclusive of impact of any behavioral changes.	16% of marriages have EITC marriage penalty. Average penalty = $1,505. Total penalty approximately $12 billion. No more than 11% of marriages receive marriage bonus. Average bonus = $1,367. Total bonus approximately $7.5 billion.	Method overstates bonuses relative to static approach. In more than half of marriages with bonus, bonus is due to birth of a child. Sample reflects new marriages, may not be representative sample of marriages.
Holtzblatt and Rebelein (1999, 2000)	IRS Statistics of Income sample of tax returns of married couples in 1995. Bonus and penalty calculated using 2000 EITC. Compare EITC benefits before and after "divorce" of married couples under varying assumptions about custody of children.	Method 1: EITC benefit to higher income spouse. • At least 3.7% of married couples have EITC penalty. Total penalty = $3.7 billion. • At least 0.5% of married couples have EITC bonus. Total bonus = $150 million. • $50 million net bonus for married couples with AGI <$15,000. More than half of penalty dollars for married couples with AGI >$30,000. Method 2: EITC benefit to lower income spouse. • At least 12% of married couples have EITC penalty. Total penalty of $20.7 billion. • At least 1.3% of married couples have EITC bonus. Total bonus = $5.1 billion.	Sample of currently married couples is problematic if EITC bonuses and/or penalties affect marriage decisions. Methodology identifies bonus or penalty only if they change taxpayer's net bonus/penalty status. This likely underestimates number of taxpayers with bonus/penalty. Very accurate income data and tax calculations.

(continued)

Table 4.2 (continued)

Study	Data and method	Findings	Comment
		• $3.4 billion net bonus for married couples with AGI <$15,000. $12.2 billion penalty for married couples with AGI >$50,000. Method 3: Dependents allocated to minimize taxes.	
		• At least 7.2% of married couples have EITC penalty. Total penalty = $14.3 billion	
		• At least 0.4% of married couples have EITC bonus. Total bonus = $60 million.	
Congressional Budget Office (1997)	IRS Statistics of Income sample of tax returns of married couples in 1993. Bonus and penalty calculated using 1996 EITC and tax laws. Compare EITC benefits before and after "divorce" of married couples.	At least 6% of married couples have EITC penalty. Total penalty = $12 billion. Total bonus = $0. Impossible to derive proportion with bonus from published tabulations.	Sample of currently married couples is problematic if EITC bonuses and/or penalties affect marriage decisions. Methodology identifies bonuses or penalties only if they change taxpayer's net bonus/penalty status. This likely underestimates number of taxpayers with bonus/penalty. Child allocation procedure divides children between divorced parents, allowing both spouses to qualify for EITC. This greatly increases estimated EITC marriage penalties and reduces EITC marriage bonuses. Least credible study.

(continued)

| Eissa and Hoynes (2000) | CPS sample of married couples with children for tax years 1984–1997. Compare EITC benefits before and after "divorce" of married couples. | Average EITC penalty post-1994 is approximately $500; average EITC penalty 1984–93 is less than $200. 1997 EITC provides bonuses for married couples with family income <$25,000, penalties for married couples with family income $25,000 to $50,000. No information of proportion of couples with penalty or bonus. | Sample of currently married couples is problematic if EITC bonuses and/or penalties affect marriage decisions. |

bonuses created by post-marriage behavioral changes (i.e., fertility) suggests that married couples with penalties outnumber married couples with bonuses by at least a two-to-one margin and probably more than that.

- Marriage penalties and bonuses can be large. Average penalties among married couples who are penalized certainly exceed $1,000 and may be as high as $1,500. Average bonuses for married couples with bonuses are also large, though probably somewhat smaller than average penalties.

- Marriage penalties increased as a result of the 1994 expansion of the EITC program.

- Estimates of aggregate EITC marriage bonuses range from essentially zero in CBO and Holtzblatt and Rebelein (method 1) to $5.5 billion to $7.5 billion in Holtzblatt and Rebelein (method 2) and Ellwood, respectively.[9] The higher estimates are based on stronger methods; the $5.5 billion in Holtzblatt and Rebelein is probably the most credible.

- Estimates of aggregate EITC marriage penalties range from less than $4 billion (Holtzblatt and Rebelein, method 1) to nearly $21 billion (Holtzblatt and Rebelein, method 2).[10] A $12 billion penalty, estimated by both Ellwood and CBO, is the mode, mean, and median. Since the two Holtzblatt and Rebelein procedures are based on strong, polar assumptions, $12 billion may be a reasonable estimate.

- EITC marriage bonuses are concentrated among lower income families (< $20,000). A very high proportion of penalties—certainly 50 percent or more—come from married couples with AGI of $30,000 or more. Some estimates suggest that much of the penalties come from families with AGI of $50,000 or more.

- Given the complexity of the tax code and the necessity to make assumptions about counter-factual situations that affect taxes, perfect answers are impossible when studying the impact of the EITC on marriage bonuses and penalties. The research, especially that based on IRS income data, does a very credible job of measuring the aggregate dollar impact of the EITC, but it does not provide a reasonable estimate of the proportion of married couples with an EITC bonus or penalty. That information would be particularly useful.

MARRIAGE PENALTY REFORM IN THE 2001 TAX ACT

The Economic Growth and Tax Relief Act of 2001 modified the EITC benefit formula for married couples, creating a separate benefit schedule for them for the first time. It did this by extending the beginning point of the phase-out range by $1,000 in 2002–2004, $2,000 in 2005–2007, and $3,000 in 2007 and thereafter.[11] Figure 1.9 (p. 30) shows what the impact of the fully phased-in benefits would be in terms of the EITC in 2001 for a married-couple family with two children. To make this adjustment, we start with the full $3,000 extension and put it in approximate 2001 dollars, using 3 percent as the annual inflation rate. With that adjustment, the $3,000 extension in 2007 is equivalent to about a $2,500 extension in 2001.

The impact of this change is only on households with earnings greater than $13,090, the income at which the phase-out range began in 2001. Since the phase-out rate of 21.06 percent is unchanged, the benefit schedule line shifts out parallel, beginning at the new phase-out income of $15,590. Benefits are increased by $526.50 (equal to the 21.06% phase-out rate × $2,500) at all incomes between $15,590 and $32,121 (the income at which all EITC benefits were lost under the old schedule). The change in the schedule also provides a benefit between $0 and $526.50 to households with income between $13,090 and $15,590, and between $32,121 and $34,621.

This reform makes a modest dent in the marriage penalty of EITC recipient households who would otherwise be on the phase-out range. For households with two children, it reduces the marriage penalty by the $526.50 additional EITC benefits. For married-couple households with one child, the schedule change is worth $399.50 (0.1598 × $2,500). It provides no EITC marriage penalty relief for married-couple households with children and total family earnings of less than $13,090.

In Chapter 8, when we discuss possible reforms of the EITC program, we show that the marriage penalty can be addressed in other ways as well, including, for example, by adjusting the phase-out rate and adjusting the benefit formula for larger families. The proposal we make provides substantially more marriage penalty relief than is offered in tax act of 2001.

DOES THE EITC AFFECT MARRIAGE?

These EITC bonuses and penalties could plausibly affect an individual's decision about marriage and divorce. The standard economic approach to marriage treats individuals as making a decision about their marital status based on the comparison of the utility or well-being they can expect if married and if single. That utility depends, in part, on the income they would have in each situation. Thus, if the EITC alters household income if married relative to household income if single—which, as we've seen, it often does—it may make marriage more or less attractive relative to being single.

Just as in the case of labor supply, the impact of the EITC penalties and bonuses on family structure can be examined in two ways, either via some form of natural experiment comparing groups with larger or smaller EITC marriage penalties/bonuses or by direct modeling of the impact of economic incentives, including the changing structure of the EITC on the probability of marriage. The effects could operate on both marriage and divorce, so one could, just as is done in the AFDC literature, examine either an individual's current marital status or his/her transitions into or out of marriage.

There is a rather limited amount of work in this area; it is quite understudied relative to labor supply. The only work on EITC marriage effects within a natural experiment framework is by Ellwood (2000), who examined changes in marital status between 1986 and 1998 for identifiable groups of women whose marriage penalty has been changing relative to one another. To do this, he classified women by the quartile of their predicted wage rate and then computed an expected or average marriage penalty in each quartile for a woman with two children who married a childless man with median earnings.[12] He found that the marriage penalty fell over this time period by about 16 percent for women in the lowest wage quartile, although there is still, on net, a marriage penalty. In contrast, the marriage penalty rose almost 40 percent for a woman in the second quartile and by 50 percent for a woman in the third quartile. For women in the top quartile, the change is much smaller. These findings are generally consistent with the pattern of EITC marriage bonuses and penalties shown in Table 4.2, although the penalties computed by Ellwood incorporate the impact of changes in not only the EITC program, but also taxes and transfers (especially AFDC). Ultimately, Elwood compared changes in marriage behavior across quartiles of women on the basis of the changing marriage penalties they face. He has also performed a comparable analysis among cohabiting couples with children.

Eissa and Hoynes (2000) and Dickert-Conlin and Houser (2000) presented and estimated economic models of marriage that incorporate the effects of the EITC. The approaches are broadly similar, although the details differ significantly. Eissa and Hoynes examined the probability that a woman is married as a function of, among other things, the tax incentives she faces. For each currently married woman in their sample, they computed the taxes she would face in her current marital status (i.e., married) and the taxes she would face if she were, instead, single. They did the same for each single woman in the sample, again computing taxes in the current marital status (single) and if she were married. Since a woman is either married or single at a point in time, but not both, they must estimate the taxes she would have in the counterfactual marital status. For married women, they made fairly straightforward estimates, assuming, for example, that a woman retains custody of children and does not alter her labor supply and earnings. For single women, this estimation is more problematic, since they must, in effect, assign a marriage partner (and thus marriage income) to single women. They did this based on a woman's own characteristics; the procedure is undoubtedly imperfect, but serviceable, and follows procedures used by other researchers in parallel analyses.[13]

Finally, Eissa and Hoynes incorporated the EITC penalty or bonus as part of their tax calculations, estimated the impact of tax incentives on marriage, and then simulated the impact of the EITC on marriage as the product of the estimated effect of taxes on marital status and the estimated EITC marriage bonus or penalty. They did not, however, directly estimate the impact of the EITC. Instead, they assumed that the EITC affects marital status in the same way as other taxes and transfers.[14]

Dickert-Conlin and Houser examined the probability of being a single parent, rather than the probability of being married. Note that these terms are not just complements—single women without children are treated differently in the two approaches. Rather than estimate taxes, including the EITC, in both single and married status like Eissa and Hoynes, they used an exogenous measure of EITC benefits—the maximum federal and state EITC for family with two children. They did this for a perfectly sensible reason—to provide an exogenous measure of EITC benefits rather than a measure that depends on a household's chosen labor supply, which we already know is likely to be affected, at least moderately, by the EITC schedule. The result, however, is that their model doesn't capture the stylized EITC bonus and penalty cases—in fact, there are no penalties or bonuses at all in their model, just EITC benefits that do not vary by marital status. The only variation in EITC benefits is across individuals solely on the basis of the state EITC for which they might be eligible and over time as the EITC became more generous.[15]

The findings of this literature are summarized in Table 4.3. The following general conclusions emerge.

- The negative effects of the EITC on marriage are probably small, at most. No study found large effects, and most studies estimated marriage effects that are not statistically different from zero.

- Ellwood's natural experiment found evidence inconsistent with the hypothesis of a marriage effect. The proportion of women married decreased most for women in the lowest wage quartile, even though they had a relative decrease in their marriage tax. Eissa and Hoynes found that tax penalties are a weak disincentive for marriage, while tax bonuses provide a weak incentive. Their simulations imply that the EITC may have increased marriage rates among families with incomes less than $25,000,[16] although their findings about the impact of the EITC are indirect. Dickert-Conlin and Houser estimated effects of the EITC on marriage that are consistently statistically insignificant across a series of specifications.

- Ellwood provided some very tentative evidence that EITC penalties and bonuses may have affected the cohabitation/marriage

Table 4.3 The Effect of the EITC on Marital Status

Study	Data and method	Findings	Comment
Eissa and Hoynes (1999)	CPS, 1984–97. Panel data model of current marital status for women, ages 18–47. Marital status modeled as function of marriage tax cost, including EITC. Model includes individual controls and state and year fixed effects. EITC impact on marriage is simulated; derived from estimated effect of taxes on marital status and estimated EITC marriage bonus or penalty by income bracket.	Tax cost has negative and statistically significant effect on probability of marriage; estimate is consistent across alternative specifications. $1,000 increase in tax cost reduces probability of marriage by 1.3 percentage points. 1997 EITC increases marriage rate by 1 percentage point (+5%) for families with income <$15,000, reduces marriage rate slightly for families with income >$25,000. Change in EITC, 1984–97, increased marriage rate for families with income <$25,000, smaller decrease in marriage rate for families with income $25,000–$50,000.	No direct estimation of EITC impact on marriage. Model assumes that a dollar of EITC income affects behavior same as a dollar of other tax and transfer income. Fairly simple statistical specification. Useful, but not definitive.

(continued)

Table 4.3 (continued)

Study	Data and method	Findings	Comment
Dickert-Conlin and Houser (2000)	Survey of Income and Program Participation (SIPP); data for 1989–95. Sample of women ages 18–50. Examines probability of being a single female parent. EITC benefits measured by maximum federal and state EITC for family with two children. Model allows AFDC benefits and EITC benefits to have separate effects on marital status and also includes state fixed effects.	No net impact of EITC on probability of being single parent for white women or black women. This is consistent with either no effect or offsetting positive and negative effects. No statistically significant effects for subgroups who are more likely EITC recipients.	Treating EITC benefits as exogenous eliminates the marriage bonus and penalty as usually understood. Model imputes maximum EITC benefits to all families, irrespective of potential family earnings. State fixed-effect model leaves very little variation to identify EITC effect. This is consistent with large estimated standard errors.
Ellwood (2000)	PSID, 1986–96. Natural experiment— comparison of marriage rates for women by wage quartile over time as a function of change in marriage tax for hypothetical woman with two children marrying childless man with median earnings. Includes all tax/transfer changes, not just EITC	No impact on marriage. Overall marriage tax penalty fell for women in lowest wage quartile relative to women in second and third quartiles. Marriage rates fell, rather than increased, for women in lowest wage quartile relative to women in second and third quartiles. Possible impact on cohabitation. Tentative evidence that marriage increased among cohabiting couples who faced EITC marriage benefits compared to cohabiting couples who faced EITC penalties or neutrality.	Natural experiment not very precise. Estimated expected marriage penalty for woman by wage quartile may not be very representative. Not very compelling evidence. Cohabitation findings are worth further study and monitoring.

decision. In general, the trend is not supportive of an impact. Between the mid 1980s and late 1990s, cohabitation among couples for whom the EITC created a marriage bonus rose more than among couples for whom the EITC created a marriage penalty. This trend sharply changed in 1998, however, when cohabitation rates continued to increase among the latter group but fall among the former group.

- The weak estimated EITC effects on marriage are consistent with the much larger literature on AFDC benefits, which also typically find weak impacts on family structure.
- Research in this area is still very far from definitive. None of the existing studies clearly captures the research problem. This is a research area that could benefit from additional research, especially research that focuses on the specific incentives faced by particular segments on the population.

SUMMARY

The particular structure of the EITC program, coupled with the substantial increase in benefit levels, now generates substantial marriage bonuses and penalties. While the benefit formula is technically neutral with respect to marital status, the relatively high phase-out rate and the cap on child-related benefits at two children mean that many married couples bear significant marriage penalties. In extreme and, admittedly, somewhat contrived circumstances, these penalties can exceed $5,000—a significant amount for families earning less than the EITC maximum of about $32,000.

Studies of the actual impact of the EITC on marriage penalties are less helpful than they might be. It is difficult to place a reliable dollar figure on the net marriage bonuses and penalties, although it is clear than penalties outweigh bonuses. At the moment, it does not appear that marriage and divorce decisions are affected by the economic incentives created by the EITC bonuses and penalties, but this literature is relatively new and not definitive.

Notes

1. See Holtzblatt and Rebelein (2000) for further discussion of marriage penalties and bonuses.

2. $0.34 \times \$5,894 \times 2 = \$4,008$, which is the credit that would be received by a family with two children and a joint income of $11,788. At higher individual incomes, the combined single credits exceed the credit if married.

3. If single, each would receive the maximum year 2001 EITC of $4,008 for a total of $8,016. If married, their EITC would equal $1,251 $= \$4,008 - 0.2106 \times$ ($26,180 $-$ $13,090).

4. The alternative is to begin with a sample of single individuals and "marry" them, but this requires a method for assigning spouses to single persons. Because that is complex and arbitrary at best, most studies follow the "divorce" approach.

5. Ellwood ignored the impact of the EITC for workers without children. This would likely cause him to overstate slightly the benefits to previously childless workers who marry and have a child.

6. The primary purpose of these papers was clearly to measure total EITC dollar impacts. Information on the proportion of married couples with bonuses or penalties can be derived from their tables, but this information is not emphasized in the papers themselves.

7. They also presented a case involving the allocation of unearned income across the individuals.

8. For methods 2 and 3, we rely on Holtzblatt and Rebelein (1999).

9. Aggregate estimates were not presented by Ellwood. We calculate them from the figures reported in his paper, supplemented by estimates of the number of married couples.

10. The figures presented here for Holtzblatt and Rebelein differ from the net impacts presented in their papers. For example, Holtzblatt and Rebelein (2000) used method 1 to derive a net change in marriage penalties due to the EITC of $3.1 billion; the $3.7 billion figure we report includes the $0.59 billion decline in net marriage bonuses created by the EITC. Similarly, they reported a $9.9 billion net penalty using method 2, to which we add the $10.9 billion decline in bonuses shown in their table. Since a decline in bonuses is exactly equivalent to an increase in penalties, this is an appropriate adjustment. We treat the computation of bonuses in a parallel way.

11. These changes are currently slated to be eliminated in 2011, although few observers expect this to happen.

12. The expected penalty is the weighted average of the penalties if a single woman is working or not working, where the weights are the proportion of single women in each (predicted) wage quartile who work. $MP = p_E \times M_E + (1 - p_E) \times M_{NE}$, where MP is the expected or average marriage penalty, p_E is the probability of employment and M_E and M_{NE} are the average marriage penalty/bonus for women who are employed (E) and not employed (NE). Ellwood conceded that this is not an ideal measure, but he argued that it is adequate.

13. This approach has been used in the literature on the effect of AFDC benefits on family structure. See Hoffman and Duncan (1988) and Duncan and Hoffman (1990) for examples.

14. This assumption may be correct, but we still know relatively little about how individuals perceive the EITC.

15. In general, many of their models appear to have insufficient variation in EITC benefits to estimate its impact on marital status with any reasonable precision. This is especially true when they estimate state fixed-effect models, since those estimates rely on within-state variation in EITC benefits to identify the impact of the EITC.

16. Eissa and Hoynes (1999) reported an EITC marriage bonus for families with incomes through approximately $25,000. That income level seems extremely high; it seems much more likely that families at that income, which is well on the phase-out range, would have EITC marriage penalties or EITC marriage neutrality.

5
The EITC and Other
Antipoverty Programs

The 1990s saw major changes not only in the EITC but also in much of the rest of the federal safety net. The traditional U.S. welfare system was dramatically reformed and restructured in 1996. The primary cash transfer program for poor families since the mid-1930s, AFDC was eliminated and replaced (effective July 1, 1997) by a program called Temporary Assistance for Needy Families, usually referred to as TANF. While TANF is similar to AFDC in some ways, it imposed meaningful work requirements as well as specific strict time limits for receipt of assistance. Welfare rolls fell by over 50 percent between 1997 and early 2001, both as a result of the reform itself and the booming economy.

At approximately the time welfare reform began, the minimum wage was increased from $4.25 per hour to $4.75 in 1996 and then to $5.15 in 1997. Legislation to increase it to $6.15 per hour was passed by the Senate in 2000, but it did not become law. While it is unlikely that the Bush Administration will support an increase in the minimum wage, legislative efforts to increase it are, nevertheless, likely. Supporters of the minimum wage still often view it as primarily a mechanism to increase the income of low wage workers, and thus it often appears that the EITC and the minimum wage are policy substitutes.

In this chapter, we compare and contrast the EITC to these alternative policies, as well as to two other approaches, a negative income tax (NIT) and a wage subsidy. We argue that the EITC is far superior to the minimum wage both in terms of its targeting efficiency and its labor market impacts. We also show that the EITC is fundamentally different from the welfare system in terms of its reward structure and work incentives. The NIT actually has more in common with welfare than with the EITC, while a wage subsidy program runs into severe implementation problems.

THE MINIMUM WAGE

Minimum wage laws operate by substituting a mandated wage rate for a market-determined wage rate. If labor demand curves are downward-sloping and labor markets are reasonably competitive, as most economists certainly believe they are, then a minimum wage that is higher than the market equilibrium will reduce employment. This very basic idea is shown in Figure 5.1, which represents a simplified market for relatively unskilled workers, a group whose market wage in the absence of a minimum wage is quite low. The market equilibrium in the absence of a minimum wage is at wage w^* and employment E^*. The minimum wage is shown as w_m, with corresponding employment E_m.

With the minimum wage in place, employment declines from E^* to E_m. Unemployment may also increase, although that depends on the job search behavior of workers who are unable to find work.[1] The magnitude of the decline in employment from E^* to E_m depends on the difference between w_m and w^* and on the slope of the demand curve. When the minimum wage is relatively low, as it was in the 1980s and early 1990s, its impact on employment is naturally quite small; the expected impact on employment increases as the gap between the mini-

Figure 5.1 The Effect of a Minimum Wage on Employment in a Competitive Labor Market

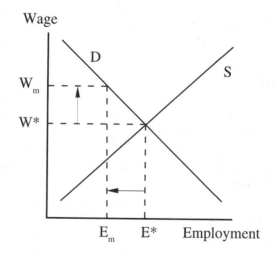

mum wage and the equilibrium wage increases. If the demand curve were steeper (more inelastic), the employment drop would be smaller; if it were flatter (more elastic) the decline would be greater. Only if the demand curve is vertical (completely inelastic) is there no decline in employment in a situation where $w_m > w^*$.

There are some alternative scenarios with more positive expected labor market impacts. If labor markets are monopsonistic, meaning that one employer completely dominates a particular labor market, then a minimum wage can, if it is not too high, actually increase both wages and employment. Virtually no economists, however, believe that many low wage labor markets are currently monopsonistic. Efficiency wage models in which higher wages elicit greater effort from workers are another possibility[2] although, again, there is no particularly compelling reason to either expect efficiency wages to be important in the low wage labor market. A recent survey of economists confirmed that in excess of 80 percent agreed with the statement, "The imposition of minimum wages reduces employment" (Alston, Kearl, and Vaughan 1992).

This predicted negative employment effect is clearly an important drawback of the minimum wage as an income-transfer program. Workers who are employed at the minimum wage benefit from the higher wage rate and may find their incomes increased, but those who cannot find employment clearly lose income. The EITC, in contrast, does not reduce employment or lower any worker's net income, because it does not interfere with labor market equilibrium. It does not reduce employment because it does not increase the market wage that firms must pay. It may affect the market equilibrium via its impact on labor supply, but the impact on the market wage will be very small and no worker will face involuntary unemployment at the new equilibrium.

Despite the straightforward theoretical predictions about the effect of a minimum wage on employment, empirical work has become unsettled in the past decade. Earlier estimates based on the time-series relationship between teenage employment rates and the value of the minimum wage suggested a relatively small negative impact. The received wisdom was that a 10 percent increase in the minimum wage would reduce employment approximately 1–3 percent (Brown 1988). This result is consistent with the idea that demand curves are downward-sloping but relatively inelastic. Deere, Murphy, and Welch.

(1995) found further support for a negative impact following the 1990 and 1991 increases in the federal minimum wage. They found that employment rates consistently fell more in demographic groups in which a higher proportion of workers were low wage workers affected by the minimum wage increase. Other research, primarily based on narrow natural experiments comparing specific states and/or industries, has failed to find the expected negative effects and, in some cases, has actually found a positive impact on employment. The most prominent such finding comes from Card and Krueger's (1994) analysis of the impact of an increase in the state minimum wage in New Jersey on employment in fast-food restaurants; other important contributions in the same vein include Card (1992a, 1992b) and Katz and Krueger (1992). Card and Krueger (1994) found that employment in New Jersey actually increased after the minimum wage increase, relative to a control sample of fast-food restaurants in Pennsylvania. An analysis of similar data by Neumark and Wascher (2000) found no such positive effect, while yet a further reanalysis by Card and Krueger (2000) concluded that "the increase in New Jersey's minimum wage probably had no effect on total employment in New Jersey's fast-food industry and possibly had a small positive effect" (p. 1,419).

While the impact of the New Jersey minimum wage on employment in the fast-food industry will probably never be fully resolved, we think that the weight of all the empirical evidence suggests that it is most probable that a minimum wage that is above the prevailing wage level in the low wage labor market decreases employment of less-skilled workers, as basic economic theory predicts. At the same time, the quantitative impact of a moderate increase in the minimum wage does not appear to be large.

No matter what the employment effects of a minimum wage are relative to the EITC, there is reasonably broad consensus that the minimum wage is more poorly targeted at the population of low and moderate income families. The reason is quite straightforward. The EITC is well targeted on these families, precisely because it uses total family income as the income concept for the determination of benefits and eventually phases out benefits as income increases. In contrast, the minimum wage increases the wages of low wage workers, irrespective of whether those individuals are attached to poor, moderate, or even high income families. The prototypical cases in point are employed teenagers from relatively affluent families: while the teen's wage rate may be low, the family's income is relatively high. Thus, to the extent that individuals like these are heavily represented among employed minimum wage workers, the minimum wage will have a weak equalizing effect on the distribution of income.

Some of the targeting differences between the two programs are obvious in comparing the distribution of the characteristics of the two recipient populations. Table 5.1 summarizes some of this information. We saw earlier that roughly 19 million households receive benefits from the EITC; approximately 4.4 million workers benefit from the minimum wage. The minimum wage population is much younger than the EITC recipient population (51 percent are less than age 24 versus just 7 percent for the EITC) and much less likely to be the head or spouse of a family. As a result, minimum wage workers are much more likely to have a middle class family income or even higher. More

Table 5.1 Recipient Population Characteristics, EITC and Minimum Wage

Population characteristic	Percentage of EITC population, 1996	Percentage of minimum wage population, 1997
Age		
16–19	1.0	30.4
20–24	6.3	20.6
>25	92.7	49.0
Family status		
Head or spouse	86.5	42.0
Child	0.0	35.1
Other relative	0.0	4.9
Not a family member[a]	13.5	18.0
Family income		
<$12,500	34.8	24.7
$12,500–$25,000	45.3	22.7
$25,000–$50,000	19.2	28.9
>$50,000	0.7	23.7

[a] In the EITC program, these are single individuals with no children.
SOURCE: The EITC information comes from the PSID for 1996; the minimum wage tabulations come from the 1997 CPS.

than half of minimum wage recipients have a family income greater than $25,000, including nearly a quarter with incomes greater than $50,000.   Only one-fifth of EITC recipients have a family income greater than $25,000 and only a tiny fraction have family income greater than $50,000.[3]

More direct evidence about the relative antipoverty efficiency of the minimum wage and the EITC comes from studies by Burkhauser, Couch, and Glenn (1996) and Neumark and Wascher (1999).   Burkhauser, Couch, and Glenn compared the distributional effects of the 1990 and 1991 increases in the minimum wage (from $3.35 to $4.25) with the increase in the EITC between 1989 and 1992.   Their key finding is summarized in Table 5.2, which is based on their analysis of data from the 1990 CPS.   Note that, for both the minimum wage and the EITC, the benefits are for the marginal increase in the program over this time period, so that, for example, the distribution of EITC benefits are not those for the program as a whole.   Also, they assumed that there are no changes in employment for the minimum wage analysis or in labor supply for the EITC.

The total benefits of the two changes were quite similar—$4.5 billion for the minimum wage and $4 billion for the EITC—but the EITC benefits are far more concentrated on poor and near-poor families. The EITC provided 42 percent of its benefits to families with an income-to-needs ratio of less than 1.25; the corresponding proportion for the minimum wage was half as large (21 percent).   In contrast, 60 percent

Table 5.2 Share of Total Benefits from Increase in the Minimum Wage and in EITC by Family Income-to-Needs Ratio, 1989–1992

Income-to-needs ratio	Minimum wage (%)	EITC (%)
<1.00 (poor)	15.6	25.0
1.00–1.25	5.3	17.1
1.26–1.50	7.3	15.4
1.50–2.00	11.7	22.8
2.00–3.00	22.2	14.4
>3.00	37.9	3.6
Total benefits	$4.5 billion	$4 billion

SOURCE: Burkhauser, Couch, and Glenn (1996, tables 5 and 7).

of the minimum wage benefits went to families with an income-to-needs ratio of greater than two and nearly 40 percent went to families with a ratio of greater than three. Only 18 percent of EITC benefits were received by families with an income-to-needs ratio that was greater than two.

The reason for the great difference in the distribution of benefits is precisely the point emphasized above: the EITC distributes benefits according to household income, while the minimum wage provides benefits on the basis of individual earnings, which are not necessarily strongly correlated with low household income. Indeed, this low correlation was stressed by Burkhauser, Couch, and Glenn. They noted that, in 1939, when the minimum wage was first established, 85 percent of all low wage workers were attached to poor households; among persons heading a household, 94 percent of low wage workers were poor. This reflected the very low labor force participation of secondary earners, including married women and teens. Over time, however, as the labor force participation of these workers has increased steadily, the correlation between low wages and poverty status has steadily weakened. Burkhauser, Couch, and Glen reported that, by 1989, only 22 percent of all low wage workers and 37 percent of low wage heads of households were themselves a member of a poor family.[4]

Some additional information on the relative antipoverty effectiveness of the EITC and the minimum wage comes from Neumark and Wascher (1999), who used national data on households from 1985 to 1994 to examine movements across the poverty line (in both directions) and across other portions of the low income distribution. They focused on household earned income relative to the poverty line, rather than, as in the official poverty statistics, total household income (pre-tax, post cash-transfer) relative to the poverty line. Fundamentally, they were interested in whether household earnings increase, net of the labor supply effects of the EITC and/or the labor demand effects of the minimum wage. As they noted, this is a procedure that greatly favors the minimum wage relative to the EITC, since the direct impact of a higher minimum wage rate is included in earned income, while the income transfer of the EITC is not included. Put differently, in their study, the EITC can only increase earnings if it increases household labor supply, while the minimum wage can increase earnings even if it reduces employment, as long as the reduction in employment does not fully offset the increase in the minimum wage itself. Their analysis incorporated both federal and state EITC programs.

They found that the overall impact of the EITC on the earned-income poverty rate is reasonably small, accounting for about one-third of the transitions from below the poverty line to above it and having no effect on movements from about the line to below it. They estimated a stronger impact of the EITC on the probability that a poor family with children and with no adult worker becomes non-poor. They attributed this to an increase in the labor force participation of adult workers in families that faced the incentives of the phase-in range, a potential effect that we emphasized in our analysis of labor supply impacts. When they directly compared the effects of the EITC and the minimum wage on poverty transitions of families with children, they found that the EITC has its largest positive impact among the poorest families and among families just below the poverty line, while the minimum wage has its biggest impact among families just below the poverty line. Given the range of recent policy changes in the EITC and minimum wage, their estimates suggest a much larger impact of the EITC.

In light of all of the evidence presented here, it is hard to construct a strong argument, indeed almost any argument, favoring an increase in the minimum wage over an increase in the EITC. The EITC avoids the negative, although admittedly disputed, employment effects of the minimum wage, and it targets its benefits to poor, low, and moderate income households with far more precision than the minimum wage does. The truth is that for the poorest of workers and households—those who find themselves on the phase-in range of the EITC—the EITC operates like an increase in the minimum wage without the potentially troubling increase in the wage price of labor. For such a worker with two children, the effective minimum wage is not its statutory rate of $5.15, but rather $7.21, including the 40 percent credit subsidy. The only argument in favor of the minimum wage is that it is not a federal government expenditure because its costs are entirely borne by firms and consumers. In a time period of large federal deficits, this might be an argument worth considering.

THE WELFARE SYSTEM

The welfare system refers to a series of federal and state programs that provide cash assistance and in-kind benefits to low income families. For many years, the main cash assistance program for poor families was AFDC, which came to be widely known as just "welfare." Eventually, AFDC itself was abolished as part of the Personal Responsibility and Work Opportunity Reconciliation Act of 1996 and TANF was substituted in its place. TANF is essentially similar in structure to AFDC, but it is not a legal entitlement as AFDC was, and it imposes strict time limits on lifetime usage as well as such other requirements as each state may choose to impose.[5] Other major programs that are part of the safety net and that are still in place include food stamps, Medicaid, and public housing.

Almost all of these programs, especially and most importantly TANF and food stamps, share a common benefit structure. Benefits are at their maximum for households with no income of their own at all and then are rapidly phased out as household income increases. Currently, the phase-out rate (usually called a benefit reduction rate in this context) is 67 percent for the first three months of work, increasing to 100 percent thereafter. With a 67 percent phase-out rate, an individual's net take-home wage is just one-third of its monetary value; with a 100 percent phase-out, the net take-home wage is zero. The case is actually worse than indicated just above because any welfare recipients earning income would lose not only some portion of their TANF benefits, but also their food stamps at a phase-out rate of 30 percent and possibly benefits from other programs as well.

The net result of the TANF schedule (and of AFDC before it) is to provide very strong work disincentives to welfare recipients. Adults receiving assistance from either AFDC or TANF find themselves in a situation in which they have both a very sharply lower net wage rate and more income than previously. This is precisely the situation that confronts workers in the EITC along the phase-out range, except that in the case of the EITC the impacts are larger (because the wage and income magnitudes are larger) and they are focused on workers on the margins of the labor market rather than with the somewhat higher incomes of the phase-out range. The result is that household income is barely increased by work, unless it is at a wage well above that typically available to welfare families. It is often simply not rational to work in such a situation, and, indeed, very few AFDC/TANF recipients worked regularly during the past few decades of the program.

The philosophical difference between the two programs is enormous. EITC rewards work, at least through the phase-in and stationary ranges, with a substantial wage subsidy. In contrast, TANF penalizes work with a substantial wage tax that falls most heavily on the poorest families. While the EITC does impose a wage tax in the phase-out range, that tax is far smaller than in TANF, and it falls on workers who already have at least a moderate income. Finally, it is important to understand one more feature of the two programs. While EITC benefits have increased substantially in the 1990s, they are still, in general, far short of benefits available under TANF in most states. The maximum EITC benefit in 2001 is just over $4,000 a year. The median TANF plus food stamp benefit for a family of three in 1999 was over $700 per month, or about $8,400 a year.

The sharp difference between the TANF and EITC benefit schedules is shown in Figure 5.2. The familiar EITC benefit structure (phase-in, flat, phase-out) is shown for a family with two children; TANF benefits are shown for a maximum benefit of $5,000 per year and a phase-out rate of 67 percent, figures close to the median. Benefits for TANF are greatest at zero earnings, a point at which EITC benefits are zero. TANF benefits begin to phase out immediately[6] and rapidly, while EITC benefits increase for the first $10,000 of earnings. EITC benefits are at their greatest along the stationary range of the

Figure 5.2 Comparing Benefits—EITC and TANF

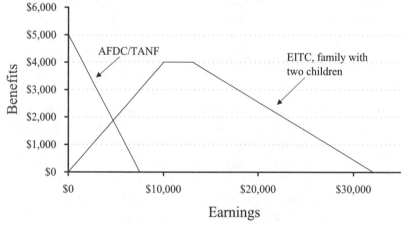

program and then phase out, but at roughly one-fourth the rate of the TANF program.

The EITC is an important part of welfare reform. It is now absolutely clear that the welfare system as we knew it for 60 years has come to an end. Unrestricted cash assistance to able-bodied, low income individuals and their families is no longer a viable policy option, and there is little public support for that approach. As former welfare recipients are moved into the labor market, often with few skills and at low market wages, the benefit schedule of the EITC has become an increasingly important wage supplement. For this group in particular, an increase in the minimum wage poses some genuine employment risks.

OTHER APPROACHES

The Negative Income Tax

When welfare reform was first widely considered, more than three decades ago, most proposals involved what came to be known as a negative income tax, or NIT for short. As proposed, the NIT would operate through the tax system to provide cash benefits to low income households. An NIT system could be understood as a simple extension of the conventional positive income tax system to incomes sufficiently low that the "taxpayer" would receive cash from, rather than pay cash to, the IRS. Such low income taxpayers would, in effect, pay "negative taxes," which accounted for the name of the proposal.

An NIT does share some important features with the EITC. Like the EITC, the amount of benefits depends on income in an NIT program. And like the EITC, the NIT operated through the tax system rather than through a welfare bureaucracy. So how does an EITC differ from an NIT?

The benefit schedule of an NIT plan is essentially identical to that of AFDC and TANF in that it provides maximum benefits to nonworking households and then rapidly reduces those benefits as household income increases. Thus, the NIT does not contain the crucial phase-in region that distinguishes the EITC from traditional welfare programs.

The NIT is essentially a traditional welfare program except for its administration via the tax system.

Wage Subsidy

A wage subsidy program pays an individual a fraction of the gap between his or her wage and some target wage. For example, an individual might receive a credit equal to 50 percent of the gap between his wage and $9. If the individual's wage were $6, the credit per hour would be $1.50 (50 percent of the $3 gap); if the wage were $7, the credit per hour would be $1.00 (50 percent of the $2 gap). More generally, the wage subsidy formula is $S = \alpha(W_T - W)$, where W_T is the target wage and α is the proportion of the wage gap that is covered. The wage subsidy formula can be rewritten as $S = G - \alpha W$, where $G = \alpha W_T$. In this form, a wage subsidy program bears some resemblance to both welfare and an NIT in the sense that there is a guarantee that is immediately phased out. Typically, however, a wage subsidy program applies only to workers and is based on the hourly wage rate.

Along the phase-out range, the EITC shares the basic benefit structure of a wage subsidy program. Along that region, EITC benefits are given by the formula $C = C_m - p_o(Y - Y_b)$, where C_m is the maximum credit, p_o is the phase-out rate, Y is family income, and Y_b is the beginning of the phase-out region. A comparison of the formulas for the two programs identifies the important distinction. A wage subsidy is based on an individual's wage and ignores the earnings or other income of other family members, whereas the EITC is based on a household's total income. If a wage subsidy applied to all low wage individuals, it would be subject to the same criticism as the minimum wage law: its benefits would be poorly targeted because low wage workers in middle income families would benefit as well as low wage workers in poor families. The targeting problem can be mitigated by limiting wage subsidy eligibility to the principal earner (i.e., the individual who earned the most money during the previous calendar quarter), but the advantage of the EITC is that it handles the targeting problem simply and automatically.

Under a wage subsidy, working more hours is always encouraged because the subsidy per hour remains fixed regardless of how many hours the person works. On the other hand, working harder or better in order to receive a higher wage is discouraged because the subsidy per hour always decreases as the wage increases towards the target wage. By contrast, in its phase-in range the EITC encourages an individual both to work more hours and to obtain a higher wage. Along the phase-out range, the EITC has the same negative incentives as the wage subsidy, although as a practical matter, the benefit reduction rate is typically lower in the EITC than in any proposed wage subsidy programs.

Finally, there is a serious practical implementation problem with any wage subsidy program. Because it is difficult to measure wages and work hours independently, the wage subsidy program is subject to manipulation. Suppose an employer and employee agree on annual compensation of $18,000. Although the employee actually works 2,000 hours, implying a wage of $9, suppose the employer and employee agree to report a wage of $8 and hours of 2,250 ($8 $\times$ 2,250 = $18,000). If the wage subsidy "target" is $9, the employee is not entitled to any wage subsidy. But, by reporting a wage of $8, the employee can obtain a subsidy. If the wage subsidy "fraction of the gap" is 50%, then the employee would obtain a subsidy of $0.50 per hour by reporting $8; by reporting 2,250 hours, the employee would obtain a subsidy for the year of $1,125. Because it is difficult for auditors to determine actual hours worked, especially in small firms, many employers and employees might be tempted understate the wage and overstate hours worked. Monitoring wages and hours is far more difficult than monitoring their product—earnings. One important advantage of the EITC in this respect is precisely that it piggybacks on the tax system in which accurate reporting of income is established and where sanctions for inaccurate reporting are already in place.

SUMMARY

A survey of policy alternatives strongly supports the EITC and the unique way it is structured. By any reasonable standard, it dominates an increase in the minimum wage as a more effective and more efficient way to transfer income to the target population and one that avoids the potential negative impacts on employment. The same issues of target inefficiency also plague wage subsidy programs, and these programs are further beset by reporting problems. The approach of traditional welfare, whether in the form of AFDC, TANF, or the NIT has been soundly rejected by the political sphere.

It is well worth emphasizing that the EITC is not a solution for all low income households, and it is not a transfer policy panacea. Households who are poor because of lack of earnings due to health, lack of skills, other impairments, or even macroeconomic distress are clearly not in a position to benefit from the EITC. Some safety net is essential, whether in the form of targeted programs such as Supplemental Security Income or broad programs such as food stamps.

Notes

1. Only workers without jobs who have made a specific effort to find work in the past month are classified as unemployed. Most studies of the impact of the minimum wage have emphasized changes in employment not unemployment because there is no ambiguity about predicted changes in employment.
2. See Yellen (1984) for a summary of efficiency wage models.
3. These high income families qualify for EITC because they have low earned income but substantial nontaxable income, probably transfer income of some kind.
4. For the purposes of this study, low wage workers are workers with a wage less than 50 percent of the average private-sector wage. This is roughly the level of the minimum wage, although there has been some variation over time in this ratio.
5. From the budgetary standpoint of the states, however, TANF is quite different than AFDC. AFDC was a matching grant, meaning that the federal government shared in program costs at some fixed rate. TANF is a block grant; states get a lump sum but the federal government does not share in additional program costs. There are also enormous differences between AFDC and TANF in terms of work requirements and eligibility.
6. In practice, there is often a small "income disregard" so that benefits do not actually phase out immediately.

6
The Efficiency Cost of the EITC

As we noted in Chapter 1 EITC recipients received a total of nearly $30 billion in tax credits in the year 2000, which enabled the recipients to increase their consumption and thus increase their well being. Of course, this $30 billion came from total tax revenues and was thus paid by households who were ineligible for the EITC, typically because their income was too high. These families are worse off on account of the EITC; their after-tax income is lower and, thus, their consumption and well-being will fall. At first glance, it might seem that these tax-payers lose exactly as much as the recipients gain because the dollar amount paid by taxpayers equals (ignoring a small administrative cost) the dollar amount received by recipients, so that taxpayers must reduce their consumption by the same amount that recipients can increase their consumption.

Economists have long emphasized, however, that the dollars trans-ferred or received only partially measure the change in economic well-being of taxpayers or recipients. Any tax/transfer program changes the incentives on both taxpayers and recipients and, in so doing, causes distortions of economic behavior. This is potentially true of the EITC as well.

There are two possible ways these distortions could occur in the EITC. First, as we saw in Chapter 3, the benefit structure of the EITC creates substantial changes in the net (after-transfer) wage rate and in family income via its phase-in and phase-out rates, thereby altering labor supply incentives. For example, individuals in households whose income and earnings (without the EITC) place them along the phase-out range of the EITC are simultaneously richer and face a lower after-tax wage rate. As we explained in Chapter 3, these incentives will cause them to reduce the number of hours they work, thereby reducing earnings and increasing the EITC they receive. Second, and equally important, the higher taxes necessarily imposed on taxpayers to finance the EITC will affect their net wage and income, potentially altering their labor supply incentives. The resulting changes in labor supply behavior in themselves affect economic well-being over and above the direct dollar magnitudes. The taxpayers may be worse off than the dollar value of the taxes they pay.

Economists have devised methods of estimating the dollar value of the behavioral changes to taxpayers and recipients. Economists refer to these additional costs as the efficiency cost, deadweight loss, or "excess burden" of a tax; we use the term efficiency cost in this chapter. When the dollar value of these behavioral changes is counted, it often turns out that the total dollar loss to taxpayers from a tax/transfer program exceeds the total dollar gain to recipients. If the loss to taxpayers exceeds the gain to recipients by 50 percent, economists say that the efficiency cost of the tax/transfer program is 50 percent. If the efficiency cost is 50 percent, taxpayers lose $1.50 for each $1 of benefit to recipients. For a graphical exposition of the efficiency cost of the EITC, see Appendix C.

It is crucial to emphasize that the "efficiency cost" of the EITC ignores the benefit that citizens derive from making EITC transfers to recipients they regard as worthy of assistance because they work. Many nonrecipient taxpayers, as citizens, clearly believe that the EITC contributes to making a better, fairer society. If a citizen regards this benefit as large, then that citizen should support an EITC expansion even if it entails a large efficiency cost. For example, consider two citizens with differing personal views of the benefit of expanding the EITC. For citizen X, the benefit is small so that X would oppose an expansion if the efficiency cost exceeds 50 percent (i.e., raising the economic well-being of a recipient by $1.00 entails reducing the well being of a taxpayer more than $1.50). By contrast, for citizen Y, the benefit is large so that Y would support an expansion as long as the efficiency cost is less than 400 percent (i.e., raising the well-being of a recipient by $1.00 entails reducing the well-being of a taxpayer less than $5.00). Thus, an estimate of the EITC efficiency cost is useful information for each citizen's decision making, but it does not determine what the decision should be.

Economists have shown that what matters for the efficiency cost of a tax/transfer program is the "marginal tax rate" it imposes on individuals. Suppose an individual's net income would increase $75 if he earned another $100 in income. Then, the individual's marginal tax rate is 25 percent. Obviously, a taxpayer in a 25 percent income tax bracket tax faces a marginal tax rate of 25 percent from the income tax, but it must also be recognized that a transfer recipient subject to a benefit phase-out also faces a marginal tax rate. If the recipient's transfer income would be cut $25 if the recipient earned another $100 of income, then the recipient faces a marginal tax rate of 25 percent because his net income would increase only $75 if he earned another $100. Thus, a tax/transfer program generally changes the marginal tax rate faced by recipients as well as taxpayers, and the efficiency cost of the tax/transfer program is affected by its impact on recipients as well as taxpayers.

In measuring the efficiency cost of expanding a particular tax/transfer program, it is crucial to consider the other tax and transfer programs already in the economy as well as the initial level of the program to be expanded. As a general proposition, economists have shown that the efficiency cost of an increase in the marginal tax rate facing an individual increases with the square of the tax rate. Thus, if the EITC increases the marginal tax rate facing an individual by Δt percentage points, the efficiency cost will be greater as the initial marginal tax rate rises. Thus, a study of the efficiency cost of an EITC expansion should take account of its interaction with other tax and transfer programs already in the economy.

Because the marginal tax rate is what matters for efficiency cost, it is crucial to specify the exact details of the expansion of the EITC and, in particular, how it will affect the marginal tax rates faced by individuals. For example, the current phase-in rate for a family of four is 40 percent, the phase-in range ends at $10,020 of earnings, the phase-out begins at $13,090, the phase-out rate is 21.06 percent, and the phase-out ends at $32,121. One way to expand the EITC would be to raise the phase-in rate above 40 percent. Another way would be to keep the phase-in rate of 40 percent but raise the endpoint of the phase-in range above $10,020. If such changes were made, a choice must then also be made concerning the EITC phase-out. If the beginning and endpoint of the EITC phase-out range are to remain unchanged, then the EITC phase-out rate must be raised. Alternatively, if the endpoint of the EITC phase-out range is raised enough, the phase-out rate can be kept at 21.06 percent. If the endpoint is raised even further, the phase-out rate can be cut below 21.06 percent. The exact details of an EITC expansion would affect the efficiency cost of the expansion.

There have been three important studies of the efficiency cost of an EITC expansion, and the three studies reach strikingly different estimates. Triest (1994) estimated the efficiency cost to be only 16 percent, so that for each $1 of benefit to recipients, taxpayers lose $1.16. At the other extreme, Browning (1995) estimated the efficiency cost to be 303 percent, so that for each $1 of benefit to recipients, taxpayers lose $4.03. Finally Liebman (2001) provided an intermediate estimate (closer to Triest's than to Browning's), of 88 percent so that, for each $1 of benefit to recipients, taxpayers lose $1.88. We begin with Triest's study and then consider relevant articles by Heckman (1993) and Moffitt and Wilhelm (2000). We then turn to Browning's study and, finally, consider Liebman's study.

Before presenting the details of our analysis, we will preview our basic conclusion. Based on our review of the labor supply literature, we believe that Triest's assumption about labor supply elasticities is much closer to the mark than Browning's. The evidence presented in Chapter 3 about the labor supply impacts of the EITC is also consistent with the smaller elasticities that Triest used. If labor supply elasticities were as large as those used by Browning, then the EITC would generate larger labor supply effects than are consistently observed. Liebman's study utilized a plausible microsimulation model calibrated to microdata from the 1999 CPS that carefully distinguishes the diverse effects of the EITC on different recipients and potential recipients and weights the diverse effects according to each type of recipient's share of the recipient population. In particular, Liebman properly emphasized, in contrast to Browning, the impact on previously nonworking potential recipients who choose to go to work as a result of the EITC. As a consequence, we conclude that the efficiency cost of an EITC expansion, especially if it is done the way we recommend in Chapter 8, will be much less than Browning's estimate and will probably be in the range between the estimates of Liebman and Triest.

TRIEST'S STUDY OF AN EITC EXPANSION

Triest (1994) simulated an EITC expansion financed by an increase in income tax rates. He used data for 1987 when the tax rates of the U.S. income tax were 0 percent, 11 percent, 15 percent, 28 percent, 35 percent, and 38.5 percent; the EITC phase-in rate was 14 percent for the first $6,080 of earnings, for a maximum credit of $851; and, beginning at earnings of $6,920, the phase-out rate was 10 percent so the credit was reduced to zero at an AGI of $15,432. He simulated an EITC expansion financed by a 1-percentage-point increase in the 15 percent and 28 percent tax rates (to 16 percent and 29 percent). It is important to note the key features of Triest's EITC expansion: the EITC phase-in and phase-out rates remained at 14 percent and 10 percent, but both ranges were increased.

Triest described his simulation methodology—and used the PSID data set for 1987. He imputed a budget constraint for consumption and leisure for every sample member, assumed a particular functional form for labor supply which implied a functional form for the underlying preferences, calibrated the labor supply functions, and simulated the EITC expansion. He limited his sample to heads of households and spouses between the ages of 20 and 60. In the budget constraint of individuals he included food stamps, welfare (AFDC), income tax, the employee (but not the employer) share of the payroll tax, and the EITC. Heads and spouses are assumed to have desired hours that depend on the wage, the marginal tax, and other income.[1] For married couples, he assumed sequential labor supply decision making, so that a husband chooses his hours ignoring his wife's hours, and a wife decides hours assuming her husband's hours are fixed.[2] For nonworkers, he imputed a wage based on a regression. He used the labor supply elasticities he estimated econometrically in Triest (1990), where he found low labor supply elasticities for males or females who are already working.

Table 6.1 shows Triest's simulation results. The four lowest income deciles (below an income of $14,183) receive an increase in transfers, whereas the six highest pay higher taxes. The lowest decile works a bit more, while all the other deciles work a bit less. The "mean equivalent gain" is the lump-sum transfer that would result in the same change in well-being as the reform simulated. Note that the mean equivalent gain has a pattern similar to the tax column, but the amounts are not identical because each transfer must also compensate for the distortion in behavior. When the mean equivalent gain is expressed as a percentage of after-tax-and-transfer income (last column), the percentage gain is over 4 percent for the two lowest deciles, 2 percent for

Table 6.1 The Efficiency Cost of an EITC Expansion

Decile	Change in taxes ($)	Change in hours worked	Equivalent gain ($)	Percent
1	− 340	1.8	351	4.6
2	− 693	− 0.6	673	4.8
3	− 405	− 4.3	354	1.9
4	− 104	− 6.0	50	0.2
5	114	− 4.4	− 140	− 0.5
6	188	− 4.8	− 212	− 0.7
7	241	− 4.0	− 264	− 0.8
8	282	− 2.8	− 307	− 0.8
9	338	− 1.7	− 355	− 0.8
10	377	− 0.7	− 377	− 0.5
All	0	− 2.8	− 23	− 0.1
Efficiency cost		16%		
Increase in phase-in range		$7,321		

SOURCE: Triest (1994) Table 5a.

the third, 0 percent for the fourth, and the loss is less than 1 percent for each of the six highest deciles.

The efficiency cost is the percentage by which the losses to taxpayers exceed the gains to recipients. Here, it equals the sum of the mean equivalent losses over the deciles that lose, divided by the mean equivalent gains over the deciles that gain, minus 1 (expressed as a percentage). The efficiency cost of the EITC expansion represented in this table is only 16 percent. Thus, the welfare losses of the higher income deciles are just 16 percent greater than the welfare gains of the lower income deciles.

Triest noted that the efficiency cost would be larger if only the top marginal tax rates (35 percent and 38.5 percent) were raised to finance the EITC expansion, but pointed out that technical problems reduce his confidence in these higher estimates. Triest also considered three other labor-supply parameter sets and computed the efficiency cost for each set. The efficiency costs for these simulations are 4 percent, 44 percent, and 118 percent. Finally, Triest substituted a demogrant for the EITC, to achieve redistribution, once again using his preferred labor-supply elasticity (from Triest 1990), and once again raising the 15 percent and 28 percent tax rates by a percentage point. He found an efficiency cost of 27 percent, somewhat higher than the 16 percent he found for the EITC, but much lower than Browning and Johnson's (1984) efficiency cost estimate of 249 percent for a demogrant. Thus, the reason Triest found a low efficiency cost is not because he analyzed an EITC rather than a demogrant; he found a low efficiency cost for both.

Triest concluded that:

> In this paper I have investigated the efficiency cost of several possible progressivity-increasing tax reforms. Based on the labor supply parameters I consider to be most reasonable, it appears possible to devise progressivity-increasing tax reforms that have a quite small degree of "leakage" in redistributing after-tax economic welfare from upper-income to lower-income families. The efficiency cost of using an expansion of the earned income credit—financed by 1-percentage-point increases in the 15 percent and 28 percent federal marginal tax rates—to transfer $1 of economic welfare from upper-income families to lower-income families is only $0.16. (p. 167–168)

Labor supply estimates are crucial for Triest's results. His preferred parameter set is based on his 1990 econometric study which found low wage and income elasticities for males and working females. The male uncompensated wage elasticity ranges from 0.03 for the lowest income decile to 0.10 for the highest, and the male income elasticity is 0.00 for all deciles. Because the income elasticity is 0.00, the compensated wage elasticity equals the uncompensated wage elasticity, so the male compensated wage elasticity also ranges from 0.03 for the lowest income decile to 0.10 for the highest; thus, the average male compensated wage elasticity is 0.07. The estimates for females used data only on those with positive hours of work. The female uncompensated wage elasticity ranges from 0.16 for the second lowest income decile to 0.33 for the highest, and the female income elasticity ranges from −0.02 to −0.07. Thus, the female compensated wage elasticity ranges from approximately 0.18 for the lowest income decile to approximately 0.40 for the highest,[3] and the average female compensated wage elasticity is approximately 0.29. Since male workers outnumber female workers, Treist gave a two-thirds weight to males and a one-third weight to females and calculated the average compensated wage elasticity as approximately 0.14. Later, we will see that Browning assumed an average compensated wage elasticity that is roughly twice as large (0.30).

Triest's labor supply estimates contrast with Hausman (1981) who estimated a large negative income effect for married men and a zero uncompensated wage effect, implying a large positive compensated (substitution) effect. Because the efficiency cost depends on the magnitude of the substitution effect, Hausman's result implies a large efficiency cost from income taxation. Triest argued that more recent work on the response of male labor supply to income taxation has generally found very small income and substitution effects. In his own econometric work (Triest 1990), where he estimated a specification very similar to that of Hausman (1981), he found an income elasticity of zero (in contrast to Hausman's large negative income elasticity) therefore implying a very small substitution effect. Triest further argued that MaCurdy, Green, and Paarsch (1990) also found that male labor supply is largely unresponsive to economic incentives and that Burtless (1987) reported low responsiveness in income maintenance experiments. Summarizing both econometric and income maintenance experiment studies, Triest concluded:

> Overall, the bulk of the evidence on male labor supply suggests that there are only minor incentive effects. Although it is important to take any incentive effects into account in analyzing possible tax- or transfer-program changes, one needs to view with some skepticism any efficiency cost calculations that are based on large male labor supply elasticities. (p. 141)

Triest said that, although female labor supply has been thought to be more elastic, this view has changed somewhat recently. In Triest's view, Mroz (1987) persuasively critiqued the techniques used in earlier female labor supply studies and, using better technique, found that economic factors such as wage rates, taxes, and nonlabor incomes have only a small impact on the labor supply behavior of *already-working* married women. Triest emphasized that Mroz's results are consistent with the view that economic factors may have a large impact on the decision to participate in the labor force. Triest estimated a model of female labor supply and found low responsiveness for already-working women.[4] He said that the participation decision is more sensitive to economic incentives than is hours of work (given participation) because of the existence of fixed costs associated with working. He assumed that women face fixed monetary costs of working which vary with family size and the number of young children, and he expressed his belief that his incorporation of fixed costs into the simulation results in a realistic model of the participation decision, even in scenarios with low assumed wage and income elasticities for already-working women. Burtless (1987) reported low responsiveness of female labor supply in income maintenance experiments. Triest concluded:

> Overall, recent work on female labor supply has called into question the assumption that women's hours of work are highly responsive to economic incentives. In simulating the efficiency cost of progressivity, using low to moderate wage and income elasticities seems most reasonable. (p. 142–143)

Other Labor Supply Estimates

Triest's use of low labor supply elasticities for EITC recipients who already work received support from Heckman's (1993) review of empirical work. Heckman said that it is crucial to distinguish between a person's decision about whether to participate in the labor force (to work or not to work) and the person's decision, once working, about how many hours to work. He wrote:

> These distinctions are empirically important. Participation (or employment) decisions generally manifest greater responsiveness to wage and income variation than do hours-of-work equations for workers. The 1960's characterization of married-female labor supply as much more wage- and income-elastic than male labor supply arose, in part, because participation elasticities for women were being compared with hours-of-work elasticities for men. (p. 117)

Heckman reported that several studies show that, given participation, both males and females show very little responsiveness of hours worked to wages or income. He said Mroz's (1987) influential study found small elasticities for married women, close to those found for males by MaCurdy, Green, and Paarsch (1990). A major lesson of the past 20 years is that the strongest empirical effects of wages and nonlabor income on labor supply are to be found on the decision of whether to work at all.

Heckman also provided support for Triest's use of low elasticities for the more affluent taxpayers who will finance any EITC expansion. Recall that Triest took issue with Hausman's (1981) finding of a large negative income elasticity and a large positive substitution effect for male taxpayers, and so did Heckman. He noted that Kosters (1967), Mroz (1987), and MaCurdy, Green, and Paarsch (1990) all found low labor supply elasticities:

> In the period between Kosters (1967) and MaCurdy et al. (1990), economists were entertained by the spectacle of anomalously large estimates of income effects and compensated substitution effects for male hours of work produced from functional-form-dependent estimation schemes designed to estimate the effect of taxes on labor supply (see the survey by Jerry Hausman [1985]) . . . These schemes have now fallen into disrepute. The econometric procedures used to produce the estimates were econometrically and economically inconsistent in part because they did not properly correct for missing wage data for nonworkers (see Heckman, 1983). Competent analysts have been unable to replicate the earlier findings even using the same data (see MaCurdy et al. 1990). When these models are re-estimated using more robust schemes, weak wage and income effects of taxes are found for males in numerous countries. (p. 118)

Further support for Triest's low elasticity for affluent taxpayers is provided by Moffitt and Wilhelm (2000):

> A long-standing issue in the effects of taxation on individual behavior concerns whether labor supply, most commonly measured by hours of work, responds to taxation. We have examined whether high income men—the rich—so respond. High-income taxpayers are often thought to have more opportunities to respond to tax law changes and to have a greater incentive to do so because of their high marginal tax rates. Our analysis of changes in the hours of work of such men between 1983 and 1989, in response to the marginal tax rate reductions legislated in the 1986 Tax Reform Act, finds essentially no evidence of any such response. (p. 221)

Finally, empirical studies of the labor supply impact of the EITC usually find relatively small effects on hours worked (e.g., Eissa and

Liebman 1996). Most of the studies do not estimate income and substitution effects or labor supply elasticities; the natural experiment approach adopted by most researchers provides an estimate of net program impact, rather than the underlying behavioral parameters. Nevertheless, the small estimated effects are clearly consistent with relatively low labor supply hours elasticities. If elasticities were larger, then the substantial EITC increases in the 1990s would undoubtedly have generated much larger impacts than have been observed.

BROWNING'S STUDY OF AN EITC EXPANSION

Edgar Browning (1995) also analyzed the efficiency cost of an EITC expansion. He assumed the expansion is accomplished by raising the phase-in rate and the phase-out rate but holding constant the endpoint of the phase-in range and the beginning and endpoint of the phase-out range. By contrast, Triest assumed that the expansion is accomplished by raising the endpoints of the phase-in and phase-out ranges but holding constant the phase-in and phase-out rates. We will return to the significance of this difference at the end of this section.

Browning emphasized that most EITC recipients are on the phase-out range. Citing Hoffman and Seidman (1990), he said that only about one-fourth of recipients are in the phase-in range. Citing Scholz (1994), he estimated that only 5 percent of the earnings of EITC recipients are from households in the phase-in range. Because of this, the EITC is similar to welfare or a negative income tax for most recipients: it confronts them with a phase-out rate—a positive marginal tax rate. In Chapter 2, we showed that approximately two-thirds of EITC recipient households in 1996 had incomes that placed them on the phase-out region of the EITC.

To estimate the impact of the EITC on individuals in the phase-out range, Browning needed an elasticity that applies to hours—the adjustment of hours for someone already working—not labor force participation. Recall that Heckman's interpretation of the empirical literature is that the hours elasticity is near zero for both males and females, in contrast to the participation elasticity, which is positive. But, Browning did not distinguish between these two elasticities when he surveyed the empirical literature:

> As will become apparent, it is the magnitude of the compensated
> wage elasticity that is crucial. In previous work, I have used a
> value of 0.3 for an economy-wide average value for this elasticity,
> intended to represent a weighted-average value for different demo-
> graphic groups. (p. 30)

He reported that, in Pencavel's (1986) survey of empirical research
for men (30 estimates), the average value of the compensated wage
elasticity for men is 0.12; and, in Killingsworth and Heckman's (1986)
survey for women (70 estimates after dropping the five highest and five
lowest), the average value of the compensated wage elasticity for
women is 0.75. The weighted average of these two averages for men
and women (with a one-third weight for women, approximately equal
to their share of total earnings) is 0.33. He concluded (p. 30) that, "In
view of this literature, a value of 0.3 for the average compensated wage
elasticity seems reasonable."

Thus, Browning took an average elasticity from studies that include participation as well as hours elasticities. Heckman's paper implied that Browning therefore used an elasticity that is too large for
analysis of the adjustment of hours on the phase-out range.

Browning estimated that the EITC actually reduces the disposable
income of families in the upper end of the phase-out range; their reduction in gross earnings is greater than the credit they receive:[5]

> The striking implication of these estimates is that families over a
> wide range of incomes will have lower disposable money incomes
> as a result of the EITC . . . This suggests there is a real possibility
> that the EITC will reduce the disposable money incomes of a ma-
> jority of families in the phase-out range . . . These results depend
> critically on how much the EITC causes earnings to decline . . .
> The results are very sensitive to the assumed value of the compen-
> sated wage elasticity . . . Halving or doubling of that elasticity
> would significantly alter the results. (p. 32)

Browning acknowledged that the well-being of recipients depends
not only on the impact of the EITC on disposable income but also on
leisure. He said there are two equivalent measures of the impact on
recipients' well-being: 1) the increase in their disposable income plus
the dollar value of the increase in their leisure and 2) the budgetary
cost minus the loss to recipients from distorting their labor supply in
response to the phase-out rate. Applying his elasticity to the second

measure, he estimated that each additional $1.00 of budgetary cost results in a distortion cost to recipients of $0.54 and, hence, a net benefit to the recipient of only $0.46. He commented that, since he estimated that recipients' disposable income on average is nearly unchanged (because their reduction in gross earnings offsets their EITC credit), this net benefit is entirely due to an increase in their leisure.

Browning then inferred the efficiency cost of an EITC expansion:

> It should also be noted that a figure of 46 cents for the marginal benefit per dollar of budgetary cost does not mean that the cost to taxpayers of providing a transfer worth 46 cents to recipients is one dollar. To acquire the funds to finance the transfers, the government must increase taxes on upper income families, and these taxes have distorting effects also, implying that the true cost on taxpayers is greater than the amount of revenue involved . . . I have elsewhere (Browning, 1987) estimated the marginal welfare cost (again, evaluating labor supply effects alone) of raising additional tax revenue through the federal income tax to be in the range of 45.8 to 85.2 percent of the marginal dollar of revenue. (These estimates were developed using the same compensated labor supply elasticity, 0.3, employed here.) Using the higher of these figures [footnote: These estimates of marginal welfare cost for the federal income tax were developed on the assumption of a proportional increase in marginal tax rates for all taxpayers. In the case of the EITC, only those taxpayers with incomes above $27,000 can finance the net benefits provided by the EITC, and this implies a more progressive change in the federal income tax, and hence, a higher marginal welfare cost. For that reason, I use the higher figure estimated in my earlier paper], this implies that it costs upper income taxpayers $1.85 to provide a transfer worth $0.46 to EITC recipients, or about $4.03 per one dollar of benefit. (p. 36)

Hence, Browning's estimate of the efficiency cost was 303 percent. This is even higher than the Browning and Johnson (1984) efficiency cost estimate of 249 percent for a demogrant ($3.49 loss to taxpayers per dollar of benefit to recipients). Browning showed how the estimate varies with the compensated wage elasticity. If the elasticity is 0.15 (instead of 0.3), the net benefit per dollar of budgetary cost is $0.58 (instead of $0.46); if it is 0.45, the net benefit per dollar is $0.38.

Browning's figure of $0.85 as the efficiency cost per dollar of tax reve-
nue for high income taxpayers is based on the elasticity of 0.3. Suppose that with half the elasticity there is half the efficiency cost, $0.42.
Then, it costs upper income taxpayers $1.42 to provide a transfer worth
$0.58, or about $2.45 per dollar of benefit. This estimate is still much
higher than Triest's $1.16 per dollar of benefit. Thus, Browning's low-
est efficiency cost estimate is 145 percent whereas Triest's estimated
efficiency cost is only 16 percent.

Browning emphasized that one reason the efficiency cost of an
EITC expansion is this high is the initial level of taxes and transfers in
the economy. Browning included the entire payroll tax (employer plus
employee) and state taxes in his combined initial marginal tax rate,
thereby generating a combined marginal tax rate of 65.1 percent for a
family of four in the EITC phase-out range with food stamps (which
has a phase-out rate of 24 percent) but no income taxes, or 59.6 percent
for a family of four in the EITC phase-out range without food stamps
but facing federal and state income taxes.

Browning directly addressed Triest's study:

> In sharp contrast to the findings in this paper, Triest finds that
> an expansion in the EITC has a very small efficiency cost. There
> appear to be at least three reasons for this difference. First, Triest
> uses labor supply elasticities that are significantly lower than I
> employ, at least in his preferred simulations. In his base case, the
> weighted-average compensated wage elasticity is about 0.11.
>
> Second, his estimates of preexisting marginal tax rates are
> lower than mine. For the bottom four deciles of the income distri-
> bution, the average marginal tax rate before the simulated expan-
> sion in the EITC is about 25 percent. This low figure results, at
> least in part, from his failure to include the employer portion of
> the social security payroll tax, state income taxes, or sales and
> excise taxes in his estimates of marginal tax rates. Of course, the
> smaller the initial marginal tax rate, the smaller is the marginal
> welfare cost of increasing it.
>
> The third major difference in the Triest study is the way he
> simulates an expansion in the EITC. Because this raises an impor-
> tant general issue, it is worthwhile examining in some detail.
> Triest envisions expanding the range of incomes over which *un-
> changed* phase-in and phase-out marginal tax rates apply ... Note
> that the additional redistribution accomplished by this change in

the EITC is likely to have low welfare costs, at least disregarding the taxes that finance it. (p. 39–40)

Figure 6.1, derived from Browning, shows the difference between Browning's and Triest's EITC expansions. The initial EITC schedule is $0ABY_3$. Browning's expansion yields $0CDY_3$. Triest's expansion yields $0FY_4$. Browning suggested that Triest's expansion is likely to have a smaller efficiency cost, but that Browning's expansion is more likely to be enacted.

It is not obvious, however, which method of expansion should have a larger aggregate efficiency cost. Because Browning has a higher phase-out rate than Triest, Triest has a lower efficiency cost for persons between Y_2 and Y_3. Between Y_3 and Y_4, however, Triest has a higher efficiency cost because Browning has phased out the EITC by Y_3 while Triest is still phasing it out until Y_4. Also, Browning has a lower efficiency cost for persons between 0 and Y_1 because his higher phase-in rate offsets more of the positive marginal tax rate from welfare, food stamps, and regular taxes.

Browning contended that his EITC expansion is more likely to be enacted for two reasons. First, historically, expansions have in fact

Figure 6.1 Triest's vs. Browning's EITC Expansion

Credit

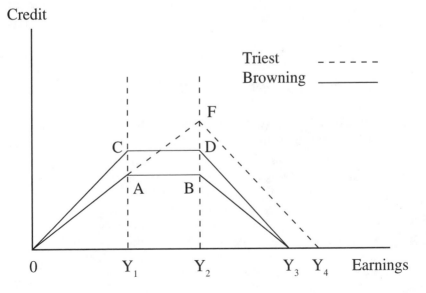

raised both phase-in and phase-out rates. Second, his expansion is better targeted: it raises the incomes of the lowest earners while Triest's does not.

Browning summarized his differences with Triest:

There are four major factors that interact to determine the efficiency cost of redistribution. Three of these are the level of initial marginal tax rates, the compensated wage elasticity of labor supply, and the type of policy change being evaluated [footnote: The fourth is the initial inequality in labor earnings: the more equally distributed are labor earnings, the higher is the marginal welfare cost of redistribution. Since lifetime incomes are more equally distributed than annual incomes, efficiency costs are higher when evaluated from a long-run perspective.] Triest has made assumptions regarding all three of these factors that differ from mine and lead to lower marginal welfare costs. I think the assumptions I use are better, but the important point is to understand that these assumptions are critical in determining the welfare effects of redistributive policies. (p. 41)

Finally, Browning said even his high efficiency cost estimate understates the efficiency cost of an EITC expansion because he confined his analysis to the distortion in labor supply. Additional efficiency cost will be generated from distortion in saving, human capital investment, diversion of income into nontaxable forms (other than leisure), administrative and compliance costs, and possible effects on marital and fertility decisions.

LIEBMAN'S STUDY OF THE EITC

Liebman (2001) gave a clear explanation of efficiency cost of transfer programs in his introduction:

A fundamental issue for any transfer program is whether it increases the well-being of its recipients by enough to outweigh the reduction in well-being that it causes for the higher-income taxpayers from whom the revenue for the program is raised. In general, the cost of providing one dollar's worth of utility gain to a transfer recipient can be substantially more than a dollar. This disparity occurs for two reasons. First, raising the revenue for the program involves deadweight loss; therefore, taxpayers lose more than a dollar's worth of utility for every dollar raised. Second, because the program alters the incentives facing recipients, the value of the transfer to recipients is less than if the same transfer were paid as a lump sum; therefore, beneficiaries gain less than a dollar's worth of utility for every dollar they receive. These two sources of leakage imply that society may have to value a dollar given to a transfer recipient at several times the value of a dollar in the hands of the typical taxpayer in order to justify using distortionary tax and transfer systems to redistribute income. (p. 196)

Liebman then contended that there are some special complications for applying this reasoning to the EITC:

While this basic logic applies to the EITC, the design of the EITC provides several exceptions to these general principles that makes it interesting to study. First, it is not always the case that a dollar spent on the EITC produces less than a dollar's worth of utility gain to beneficiaries. Because the credit is available only to workers, the EITC offsets some of the distortions created by the rest of the welfare and tax systems, and taxpayers who leave welfare to claim the EITC can increase their well-being at the same time as government expenditures decline. Therefore, for some beneficiaries, the cost of providing a dollar's worth of utility is actually less than a dollar. Moreover, for some two-earner couples and for some EITC recipients receiving the maximum credit, the EITC is effectively a lump-sum transfer that does not produce any deadweight loss. (p. 197)

The impact therefore depends on how many households are in each situation in relation to the EITC. Liebman used a microsimulation model calibrated to microdata from the 1999 CPS to incorporate this quantitative information. From his simulations he drew these conclusions:

The research underlying this chapter has two basic results. First, in contrast with the findings of Browning (1995), I find that the overall efficiency cost of transferring income through the EITC is fairly low. While Browning found that it cost $4.03 to provide one dollar's worth of utility gain to recipients in the phase-out region and almost $2.00 to provide one dollar's worth of utility to recipients in the phase-in and constant region, I find that it typically costs less than $2.00. An important reason for my lower results is that I take into account the impact of the EITC on the labor force participation of single parents. Recent research suggests that the EITC causes a large number of welfare recipients to enter the labor force. When the savings from reduced welfare spending are taken into account, the EITC appears to be a much more efficient way to accomplish income redistribution than when they are ignored. In addition, a significant portion of the labor supply responsiveness of married couples is likely to be due to secondary earners leaving the labor force. My simulations indicate that much of this responsiveness is due to the income effect of the EITC rather than the substitution effect. Therefore, for these households, the EITC is effectively a lump-sum transfer. (p. 197)

Liebman carefully distinguished the diverse effect of the EITC on different types of recipients:

There are five basic scenarios that illustrate the ways in which the labor supply behavior of an unmarried taxpayer could be affected by the introduction of an Earned Income Tax Credit. First, a taxpayer might have had earnings greater than the EITC breakeven point if there were no EITC, but reduces his or her earnings in order to receive the EITC. Second, a taxpayer might have had income in the EITC phase-out region even in the absence of the EITC, but because both the income and substitution effects of the EITC encourage the taxpayer to reduce her earnings, he or she moves to a lower level of earnings. Third, a taxpayer with earnings in the constant region might reduce his or her earnings due to the negative income effect from the EITC. Fourth, a taxpayer with earnings in the phase-in range might alter her earnings in either direction since the positive substitution effect and the negative income effect make the net impact on labor supply ambiguous. Finally, a taxpayer who would not have had any annual earnings in the absence of the EITC might decide to participate because the EITC increases the average return to working. Such a taxpayer could enter the labor force at any level of earnings eligible for the EITC. In all of these cases the taxpayers receiving the EITC have higher utility than they did before the EITC was introduced. (p. 198)

It is this last category, the person who is induced by the EITC to enter the labor force, that plays an important role in reducing Liebman's estimate of the efficiency cost well below Browning's, as Liebman emphasized in his conclusion:

The results indicate that the efficiency cost of transferring income through the EITC is substantially lower than previous studies have found. It costs upper income taxpayers only $1.88 to provide a transfer worth $1.00 to EITC recipients. The main reason for the difference among head of household filers, is that this study takes into account the positive impact of the EITC on labor force participation of single parents and the savings on welfare spending that this labor supply response brings about. Among married filers, it appears that a substantial amount of the labor supply response to the EITC is likely to be due to secondary earnings leaving the labor force. The simulations indicate that this responsiveness is primarily due to the income rather than the substitution effects of the credit and therefore that the EITC is effectively a lump-sum transfer for these households. (p. 226)

CONCLUDING COMMENTS

Triest's (1994), Browning's (1995), and Liebman's (2001) studies of the efficiency cost of an EITC expansion are extremely useful. Browning is helpful in clearly delineating how he and Triest reach such strikingly different results. Based on our review of the labor supply literature in Chapter 3, we believe that Triest's assumption of a low labor supply response by recipients on the phase-out range and by taxpayers who will finance the expansion is much closer to the mark than Browning's, and this alone would tend to bring the efficiency cost much closer to Triest's 16 percent than to Browning's 303 percent. In Chapter 8, in contrast to Browning's expansion which *raised* the phase-out rate, and even Triest's which held it constant, we propose an EITC expansion that *reduces* the phase-out rate. This difference would also reduce the efficiency cost of the EITC. Finally, Liebman's study emphasized, in contrast to Browning's, the positive impact on labor force participation of the EITC: as its originators hoped, empirical evidence indicates that the EITC induces a significant number of single parents to enter the labor force and work. This is an important reason why Liebman found an efficiency cost of only 88 percent, in contrast to Browning's 303 percent.

It is important to reiterate the basic point we made at the beginning of this chapter concerning the role of an estimate of the EITC efficiency cost in a citizen's decision making. An estimate of the EITC efficiency cost is useful information, but it does not determine what the decision should be. For example, consider a citizen who believes the EITC has a very high benefit for society, and is willing to support an expansion as long its effiiciency cost is less than 400 percent (each $1.00 gain to recipients reduces the consumption of taxpayers less than $5.00). Such a citizen should support an EITC expansion even if Browning's estimate of 303 percent is correct. At the other extreme, consider a citizen who has a modest regard for the benefit of the EITC for society, and would oppose an expansion even if its efficiency cost is 0 percent (each $1.00 gain to recipients reduces the consumption of taxpayers $1.00). Such a citizen should oppose an EITC expansion even if Triest's estimate of 16 percent is correct. This said, clearly more citizens should and will support an EITC expansion if they believe its efficiency cost is low. Provided the EITC expansion is done as we recommend in Chapter 8, it seems likely in our judgment that the efficiency cost of an EITC expansion will in fact be relatively low—much closer to Triest's estimate than to Browning's, and probably close to Liebman's estimate of 88 percent.

Notes

1. More specifically, desired hours $h = \gamma + \alpha w + \beta y$, where w is the net wage and y is virtual income. The net wage equals the wage minus the combined marginal tax rate due to tax and transfer programs to which the person is subject; virtual income is the vertical intercept that results if the relevant segment of the individual's budget line is extended to the axis.
2. A husband's earnings are excluded from a wife's virtual income to avoid double counting.
3. The relationship between a person's uncompensated wage elasticity ϵ_u and compensated wage elasticity ϵ_c is given by $\epsilon_u = \epsilon_\alpha + (E + Y)\mu$, where μ is the income elasticity, E is labor earnings, and Y is nonlabor income. If we assume that a wife gets to use half her husband's earnings, then her Y is half her husband's earnings; if that wife's earnings are roughly half her husband's, then her E/Y equals 1, so that $\epsilon_u = \epsilon_c + \mu$.
4. Triest provided some detail on his estimate of female labor supply, "Including data on nonparticipants in the estimation resulted in uncompensated wage elasticities (evaluated at the sample means of women with positive hours of work) of approximately 0.9, and virtual income elasticities of about -0.3 . . . When I estimated the same specification but used only data on women with positive hours of work (with an appropriate statistical adjustment), the uncompensated wage

elasticity fell to approximately 0.27 and the virtual income elasticity fell to about −0.16. This decrease in the magnitude of the wage and income elasticities when one moves from a censored (including observations with zero hours of work) to a truncated (excluding such observations) specification is consistent with Mroz's (1987) work. Mroz similarly finds that wage and income elasticities drop in magnitude when switching from a censored to a truncated tobit specification (in a model without taxes). Moreover, he finds that the elasticities drop by an even larger amount when one switches from a truncated tobit specification to a more general self-selection correction. Mroz is able to reject both the censored and truncated tobit specifications in favor of the more general specification. This implies that even the relatively small elasticities I estimated using the truncated specification may be too high. However, it is important to recall that Mroz's results apply only to working women." (p. 142)

5. Browning assumed an income elasticity of −0.20. He said his results are not very sensitive to his assumption about the income elasticity.

7
EITC Compliance Issues

During the 1990s, a controversy developed over the EITC "error rate." According to several IRS studies, roughly 25 percent of EITC payments were technically in error—that is, roughly 25 percent of EITC payments did not comply with at least one of the EITC technical requirements under a strict and precise interpretation of EITC provisions concerning the definition of a "qualifying child," the rules for filing status, and the AGI tiebreaker rule for determining eligibility. What inferences should be drawn from the 25 percent EITC error rate, and what are the appropriate responses?

In this chapter we review the details of the EITC error rate problem. Before plunging into these details, which are complex but hopefully interesting, we want to state our main conclusions. First, the literature suggests that a substantial part of the EITC error rate is due to the confusion of recipients concerning the complex provisions and rules of the EITC. No evidence has been provided to demonstrate that a substantial part of the error rate is due to intentional fraud. Second, most technically "erroneous" EITC payments go to households with a head who works but earns modest income. Third, there is no evidence that the EITC error rate exceeds the error rate resulting from other provisions of the personal and corporate income tax. Fourth, promising efforts are being made to reduce the error rate by simplifying some of the complex and confusing EITC provisions.

THE EITC ERROR RATE

Ventry (2000) provided a brief history of the EITC error rate. The problem burst onto the political radar screen with the 1990 release of the IRS's Taxpayer Compliance Measurement Program (TCMP) study of the 1985 tax year. This study discovered an EITC "over-claim rate"—defined as the dollar amount claimed in error divided by the total dollar amount claimed—of 39.1 percent. A follow-up TCMP study of the 1988 tax year, released in 1992, detected an over-claim rate of 35.4 percent. In 1994 and 1995, the IRS conducted two more studies of EITC noncompliance for the years 1993 and 1994, finding an over-claim rate of 26.1 percent for 1993 and 25.8 percent for 1994. Although not all dollars claimed were actually paid by the IRS, most claimed dollars were in fact paid. Needless to say, these studies attracted attention in Congress and provoked a reaction.

As a consequence, an effort to reduce noncompliance was started in 1990 and it gradually escalated in intensity over the ensuing decade. In 1990, the Treasury recognized that many EITC over-claims were due to errors about qualifying child criteria and filing status, and it therefore presented a proposal to Congress (which was subsequently enacted) that simplified the qualifying child criteria and filing status and made it easier for the IRS to verify EITC eligibility based on information reporting. The IRS was given the authority to match names and taxpayer identification numbers (TINs) on tax returns to individual Social Security numbers (SSNs), initially exempting but eventually including SSNs of qualifying children under the age of one. Using its administrative authority, the IRS began to reject electronic returns with missing, invalid, or in some cases duplicate SSNs. The welfare reform act of 1996 provided the IRS with authority to treat the failure to provide a valid SSN as a mathematical or clerical error. Using the math error procedures, the IRS can deny or reduce the credit before a refund is paid. The IRS was given the power to impose penalties on persons who abused the EITC. The Taxpayer Relief Act (TRA) of 1997 imposed a due diligence requirement for paid preparers. It gave the IRS authority to recover excess refund payments or unpaid taxes by garnishing a percentage of unemployment and means-tested benefits, and it contained provisions that disqualified abusive filers for various lengths of time depending on the infraction.

Liebman (2000) discussed several sources of error that might well have resulted from confusion among persons claiming the EITC. The TCMP studies of the 1985 and 1988 tax years found that an important source of error was failure to meet the "support test," a test that was eliminated for the EITC by Congress in 1990 because it was judged confusing and inappropriate. Prior to 1990, the taxpayer had to provide at least half of the total financial support for the child to be eligible for the EITC, where total support included financial assistance from all sources *including* government transfer payments such as food stamps and welfare. This support test must still be met to claim a dependent exemption under the federal personal income tax, but consider the case of a single parent working part time whose children live with her year-round. This parent might well claim the EITC without realizing that, if she received government transfer payments (food stamps, welfare, etc.) greater than her own earnings, she failed the EITC support test and was ineligible for the EITC. The support test was eliminated for the EITC in 1990 and was replaced with a residency test and an AGI tiebreaker.

These two tests are also subject to confusion. Under the residency test, the child must live with the taxpayer at least half the year. If a child spends substantial time residing with each of two separated parents (as is often the case), each parent may be inclined to believe that child resides with him or her "roughly half" the time; hence, each files for the EITC. Of course, if a parent claims a child who seldom resides with him, the error is probably intentional. Under the AGI tiebreaker rule, if a child can potentially be claimed by two taxpayers who reside together (e.g., the child's parent and grandparent), only the person with the higher AGI is eligible to take the credit. It seems likely that many parents would assume, incorrectly, that they can automatically claim the credit.

McCubbin (2000) provided further details on the EITC compliance problem. She noted that the IRS has not conducted a comprehensive study of taxpayer compliance since 1988, postponing indefinitely a TCMP study planned for tax year 1994 in order to avoid budgetary cost and imposing a burden on taxpayers who are studied. However, the IRS's Criminal Investigations Division (CID) performed a more limited study (IRS 1997) of the tax returns of about 2000 randomly selected taxpayers who filed EITC claims for the tax year 1994. She noted that the EITC errors identified in that study include both intentional noncompliance and unintentional reporting mistakes, and the two types of errors are not readily distinguishable in the data. The study found an over-claim rate of 25.8 percent, but these error rates are for amounts claimed rather than amounts paid. Moreover, the Treasury Department estimated that IRS enforcement procedures in effect during the 1995 filing season would have reduced the error rate about 2 percentage points and, if the new enforcement procedures first in effect during the 1997 filing season had been in effect in 1995, the error rate would have been reduced another 3 percentage points. Thus, the error rate for amounts paid would have been about 20 percent.

McCubbin explained the confusion that arises because a child may entitle a parent to the EITC but not a dependent exemption or to a dependent exemption but not the EITC. Consider a single working parent who must figure out whether she can claim a child for the EITC and whether she can claim a child as a dependent for the personal exemption. With the EITC, there is a residency test but no support test—the child must live with the taxpayer for at least half the year, but the taxpayer need not provide half of the total financial support of the child. The EITC qualifying child need not be the taxpayer's dependent. To claim the EITC, however, the taxpayer must have the highest AGI of all taxpayers who may claim the child. By contrast, to claim the dependent exemption, the taxpayer must generally provide over half of the support for the child. A welfare recipient who provides less than half of the total support (including welfare) of the child may not claim a dependent exemption for the child but may still claim the EITC. On the other hand, a noncustodial parent may be allowed to claim a dependent exemption for a child that he or she supports, but a noncustodial parent may not claim the EITC.

Not surprisingly, over half of the total amount over-claimed was due to an error concerning the qualifying child criteria involving either the residency or AGI tiebreaker requirement. Of these, the most important was an error concerning the residency requirement; the audit ascertained that the child lived with the taxpayer less than half the year. If a parent claims a child who hardly ever resides with him, this error is no doubt intentional. But, if a child frequently sleeps over at his residence, the father may assume, incorrectly, that he satisfies the residency requirement. Also important was an error concerning the AGI tiebreaker; the audit ascertained that the child should have been claimed by someone else with a higher AGI (in some cases, the taxpayer's parent; in other cases, the child's father to whom the taxpayer is not married).

Another important source of error for the 1994 tax year was filing status. Nearly one-third of the total amount over-claimed was due to the misreporting of filing status; married people filed as heads of households and, as a consequence, received larger EITC credits. Consider the situation of a mother still technically married but whose husband has long since left. She might think she can file as a head of household and claim the EITC. It seems likely that confusion may be the source of much of this filing status error.

Although some have asserted that the EITC has a high error rate because it is refundable, the CID data refute this assertion. The EITC over-claim rate among EITC claimants with no income tax or self-employment tax liability (before taking the EITC into account), who would have received the entire EITC in the form of a refund, was 12.7 percent. The over-claim rate among EITC claimants with some income or self-employment tax liability, who therefore would have received less than the entire EITC as a refund, was 37.7 percent. Surprisingly, the error rate for claimants receiving the entire EITC as a refund was, for some reason, much smaller than the error rate for all other EITC claimants.

Some have speculated that the availability of "refund anticipation loans" may raise the error rate, but this also seems doubtful. The over-claim rate among filers who applied for loans (26.6 percent) is similar to the rate among filers who did not (24.0 percent).

According to McCubbin (2000), the error rate is also not affected by whether the taxpayer uses a tax preparer: "The CID data show virtually no difference in the error rates of taxpayers who used paid preparers and those who prepared their own returns."

One possible source of intentional error in the 1994 tax year was a loophole that has since been plugged. In 1994 the taxpayer had to provide a taxpayer ID number, typically the SSN, for each child claimed *except* children under the age of one. This exception opened the possibility of listing children said to be under age one without fearing that the IRS would cross-check SSNs.

Some have speculated that the EITC would cause persons with low earnings on the phase-in range to overstate their earnings in order to obtain a larger credit and persons with higher earnings on the phase-out range to understate their earnings in order to obtain a larger credit. Interestingly, the CID study found that income underreporting to limit the phase out of the credit was not a large source of error, and income overreporting in the phase-in range in order to raise the credit was extremely rare.

McCubbin reviewed the efforts begun in the second half of the 1990s to reduce the EITC error rate. The welfare reform act of 1996 required all EITC claimants to provide valid SSNs for themselves and *all* of their children; prior to the tax year 1996, SSNs were not required for children under age one, and taxpayers who could not obtain an SSN because they were undocumented workers could still claim the EITC. The 1996 act enabled the IRS to treat the failure to provide a valid SSN as a "mathematical or clerical error," by which the IRS can deny or reduce the credit before any tax refund is paid and without auditing the tax return.

The Taxpayer Relief Act of 1997 established new penalties for taxpayers claiming the EITC improperly. If a taxpayer makes an EITC error that is determined to be the result of "negligence or intentional disregard" of the EITC provisions, the taxpayer cannot claim the EITC for the next 2 years; if the error is the result of "fraud," the taxpayer cannot claim the EITC for the next 10 years. If a taxpayer's credit is disallowed or reduced (except due to a mathematical or clerical error), the taxpayer must undergo "recertification" by providing additional information to the IRS the next time the taxpayer attempts to claim an EITC benefit.

The 1997 act contained new penalties for tax preparers filing EITC claims improperly. The CID data showed that there were big differences in the error rate by the type of paid preparer, with error rates much lower among returns prepared by lawyers, CPAs, enrolled agents, or large national tax preparation organizations. This result gave rise to the paid preparer due diligence requirements in the 1997 act. To avoid a penalty, a preparer with an EITC error must show he utilized "due diligence" by documenting that he obtained certain information from the taxpayer before filing the EITC claim. Because the burden of proof of due diligence is placed on the preparer, and because the IRS can impose fines without an audit, the provision makes it cheaper for the IRS to penalize preparers. The provision informs preparers about the EITC eligibility criteria by specifying precisely what information is necessary to evaluate a taxpayer's claim.

The 1997 act gave the IRS new sources of information that should be useful. The IRS will have access to the Federal Case Registry of Child Support Orders, which should enable the IRS to identify noncustodial parents who generally fail the EITC residency test. The Social Security Administration will be required to obtain the SSNs of parents who apply for a SSN for a child; this information will help the IRS identify persons likely to fail the EITC relationship test.

The Balanced Budget Act of 1997 provided more funding for EITC compliance efforts. The IRS has used these funds to develop new forms and regulations; change the computer programs to automatically deny the EITC to taxpayers with SSN problems; update or develop databases; improve the clarity of EITC forms, notices, and publications; increase the availability of taxpayer assistance; and audit more EITC returns. The IRS estimates that, for every dollar spent on these efforts in 1998 and 1999, roughly 10 dollars were saved for the EITC program.

Is the error rate by taxpayers claiming the EITC higher than the error rate by taxpayers not claiming the EITC? McCubbin commented:

> The errors made by EITC claimants (including misreporting filing status, misreporting family and household characteristics, and under-reporting income) can also be made by taxpayers who do not claim the EITC. Without comparable data on taxpayers who do not claim the EITC, it is impossible to fully understand the extent to which EITC overclaims are the result of the EITC itself, and the extent to which they are part of a more general compliance problem. The absence of broader compliance data also makes it difficult to evaluate the importance of the EITC compliance problem relative to other tax compliance problems, and to efficiently allocate IRS enforcement resources.

Greenstein and Shapiro (1998) of the Center on Budget and Policy Priorities made five basic points in their evaluation of the EITC compliance problem. First, the error rate, though still high, is significantly less than a decade ago. Second, most of the errors were due to confusion rather than intention. Third, the fact that the EITC is refundable is not the source of its relatively high error rate. Fourth, some other provisions of the tax code have higher error rates. Fifth, and most importantly, new compliance measures that have been enacted in the past few years should reduce the error rate in coming years. Consider each point in turn.

Greenstein and Shapiro noted that the error rate in the 1980s was about 35 percent according to IRS studies. But, the IRS study of tax year 1994 released in April 1997 (IRS 1997) estimated that 20.7 percent of EITC benefits were paid in error (the over-claim rate was 25.8 percent), thereby indicating a significant decline in the error rate.

Moreover, the true error rate was probably less than 20.7 for the following reason. According to the study, nearly one-fifth of the errors occurred when a parent claimed a child for EITC purposes but, according to the AGI tiebreaker rule, another relative in the household (such as a grandparent) should have claimed the child instead. The loss to the Treasury in these cases is the amount by which the EITC amount paid to the parent exceeds the amount that should have been paid to the grandparent. The IRS study, however, did not collect the data needed to determine the amount the grandparent should have received in such cases and improperly classified the entire amount paid to the parent in these cases as being in error.

It seems likely that the errors were often unintentional. The IRS study found relatively few EITC errors to have resulted from actions by families to hide incomes. Instead, most EITC errors were related to the living arrangements of families and the complex rules the tax code establishes with regard to family relationships, tax filing status, and the tax treatment of children in divorced, separated, and multi-generational families and families where the caretaker is someone other than the parent.

Greenstein and Shapiro stated that refundability is not the source of the EITC's relatively high error rate:

> The study contains one other significant finding—it indicates EITC errors are not due primarily to the EITC's refundable nature. The study found the error rate among working families that have incomes too low to have a pre-EITC income tax liability (and consequently receive their full EITC payment in the form of a refund check) was only one-third as high as the error rate among families that do have an income tax liability before the EITC is applied. (p. 10)

Some other provisions of the tax code have higher error rates:

> Data from the Internal Revenue Service and the General Accounting Office also show that a number of other provisions of the tax code have higher error rates than the EITC does and lose larger amounts of revenue. The errors in these other provisions, however, have not been the subject of much legislative scrutiny. (p. 2)

They also provided further details on the error rates of these other provisions:

The EITC error rate exceeds the average error rate for the income tax as a whole, which is approximately 15 percent. Many elements of the income tax, however, have higher error rates than the EITC does. For example, the Internal Revenue Service has reported that 29 percent to 30 percent of business income is not reported on tax returns. The IRS also estimates that sole proprietors who formally operate businesses other than farms fail to report 31 percent to 32 percent of their business income. Similarly, some 31 percent to 32 percent of farm income and 27 percent to 28 percent of income from the sales of business property go unreported.

Data from the GAO and the IRS indicate that EITC losses account for less than 5 percent of the total losses in the individual and corporate income tax. The focus on EITC errors seems disproportionate to its share of the total losses due to errors.

Finally, they emphasized that compliance measures enacted after 1994 should reduce the EITC error rate. For example, filers have been required to provide SSNs of all children, regardless of age, since 1997. And, only since 1997 has the IRS been able to deny claims based on doubt about the validity of SSNs and thereby shift the burden of proof to the filer to show that the SSN is valid.

It is also only since 1997 that the IRS has used the Federal Child Support Case Registry database, established by the Welfare Reform Act of 1996. Once this database is fully developed, the IRS should be able to use it to ascertain whether a parent is noncustodial and therefore ineligible for the EITC credit. And, since 1998, a parent seeking a SSN for a child must also provide the SSN of the child's parents as well.

The 1997 budget act authorized funds for EITC compliance. The compliance effort has the following elements. First, the IRS will stop returns with missing or invalid SSNs. Second, more EITC returns will be inspected. Third, the IRS has sent out warnings to filers who claimed a child for the EITC when that same child was claimed by another filer.

Finally, we turn to the most recent IRS examination of the EITC error rate, the IRS Study released in September 2000 (U.S. Treasury 2000a) of EITC noncompliance in the tax year 1997. The study found an over-claim rate of 30.6 percent, several points higher than the study of the tax year 1994 (25.8 percent), and an overpayment rate of 25.6

percent, also several points higher than the study of the tax year 1994 (20.7 percent). The study begins with this executive summary: "Of the estimated $30.3 billion in EITC claims made by taxpayers who filed returns in 1998 for Tax Year 1997, it is estimated that $7.8 billion (25.6 percent) should not have been paid."

The main sources of the errors were the familiar ones: claiming a child who was not a qualifying child, claiming a qualifying child who was also the qualifying child of someone else with a higher AGI, and filing as single or head of household when the correct filing status was married-filing-separately. The study does not necessarily mean that the pre-1997 efforts had no effect because it is quite possible that the error rate would have been even higher without these efforts. Whatever the effectiveness of the pre-1997 efforts, however, an EITC overpayment error rate of about 25 percent remains.

As the IRS report itself emphasizes, important new compliance measures have been implemented since the 1997 tax year. Consequently, it is still too early to tell whether these new compliance measures will prove effective in cutting the error rate significantly.

NEW INITIATIVES TO REDUCE THE EITC ERROR RATE

The Treasury (U.S. Treasury 2000b) responded to the report in two ways. First, it pointed out that measures have been implemented since the 1997 tax year. Second, it proposed a set of new compliance initiatives.

Since 1997, the following four measures have begun to be implemented.

- The development of new data to detect errors. Beginning in 2001, the IRS will use a new data set that combines the Federal Case Registry of Child Support Orders (which has information on child custody arrangements), social security records, and tax records.

- Establishment of new procedures to prevent erroneous refunds. The IRS has expanded its use of "mathematical error" procedures so that it can deny certain types of questionable EITC claims during processing, thereby avoiding the need for an audit; for example, the IRS now uses its mathematical error authority to deny EITC claims if their children do not meet the credit's age qualifications, they do not reside with their children, they are under 25 or over 64, or they were denied the credit in a previous year and did not follow recertification requirements enacted in 1997.

- Paid preparer initiative. The IRS now tries to reach tax return preparers who have recently prepared at least 100 EITC returns, providing direct instruction from IRS agents and informing them of their new due diligence responsibilities.

- Simplifying the tax return. Since 1999, the tax return now contains a clever simple step-by-step test of EITC eligibility, under which the taxpayer is shown a picture of a stop sign whenever she answers a question that rules out EITC eligibility.

The Treasury proposed new compliance initiatives in September 2000. These will be discussed in more detail in Chapter 8. Here we simply list the eight Treasury proposals: 1) immediately notify taxpayers who appear to be nonqualifying parents, 2) improve compliance among paid preparers, 3) expand the use of IRS authority to deny questionable claims, 4) enhance the use of the dependent database, 5) simplify the rule for married but separated taxpayers, 6) simplify the AGI tiebreaker rule for parents in low income households, 7) simplify the definition of earned income, and 8) simplify the definition of dependent child.

As part of its comprehensive three-volume study on tax code simplification, the Joint Committee on Taxation (2001) recommended adopting a uniform definition of "qualifying child" for determining eligibility for the EITC, the dependency exemption, the CTC, the dependent care credit, and head of household filing status. It also urged changing the EITC tie-breaker rule to make sure that a parent can claim the child (even if a grandparent in the same residence has a higher income).

Finally, the tax act of 2001 adopted several measures to reduce the EITC error rate. It modified the tie-breaker rule and simplified the definition of "qualifying child." It authorized the IRS, beginning in 2004, to use math error authority to deny the EITC if the Federal Case Registry of Child Support Orders indicates that the taxpayer is the noncustodial parent of the child. It replaced "modified" AGI with AGI and excluded nontaxable employee compensation from the definition of earned income (for EITC purposes).

CONCLUSIONS

Several IRS studies have detected an EITC "error rate" of about 25 percent—that is, roughly 25 percent of EITC payments did not comply with at least one of the technical requirements under a strict interpretation of EITC provisions concerning the definition of a qualifying child, the rules for filing status, and the AGI tiebreaker rule for determining eligibility.

Based on the analyses reported in this chapter, we arrive at four main conclusions concerning the EITC error rate. First, it seems likely that the EITC error rate is due mainly to the confusion of recipients concerning the complex provisions and rules of the EITC and that only a small fraction of the error rate is the result of intentional fraud. Second, most recipients of technically "erroneous" EITC payments are parents who work but earn modest income. Third, the EITC error rate may be comparable to the error rate resulting from other complex provisions of the personal and corporate income tax. Fourth, promising efforts are under way to reduce the error rate by simplifying some of the complex and confusing EITC provisions. In Chapter 8 we will recommend additional measures to reduce the EITC error rate.

8
Reforming the EITC

In this chapter, we propose a reform of the EITC that preserves its successful features but addresses the major concerns that have been identified throughout this book. Our reform is simple, focused, and feasible. It aims at addressing three weaknesses of the 2001 EITC program—work disincentives along the phase-out range, the marriage penalty, and the still below-poverty line income of families with three children. The reform consists of three elements: reducing the phase-out rate, providing a more generous schedule for married couples, and providing an additional credit for a third child. Because the weaknesses are interrelated, these three changes can contribute to improving all of the problems.

We analyze what would have happened if our reform had been implemented in the year 2001. We provide estimates of the cost and impact of our proposal using data from the PSID. The tax act of 2001 did not reform the EITC program for the year 2001 (although it did change the child tax credit for 2001, and we have incorporated this change into our analysis). The act did, however, adopt a more generous schedule for married couples beginning in the year 2002. After quantifying what would have happened in 2001 had our reform been fully implemented in that year, we compare our reform with other proposals and then with the reform adopted in the 2001 tax act providing a more generous schedule for married couples beginning in 2002. Finally, we present recommendations to improve compliance.

A PROPOSED REFORM OF THE EITC

Problems in the 2001 EITC Program

On balance, it is clear that the EITC is a highly effective program that meets its primary objectives well. Nevertheless, there are some problems that have been identified and ought to be addressed; these problems can, we will show, be addressed relatively easily.

First, although the EITC provides positive work incentives for many households, especially those on the phase-in range, it may discourage individuals in households that have reached the phase-out range from working additional hours. Even more important, it may decrease labor force participation altogether among secondary workers in some of these households. The empirical evidence on this shows a consistent negative impact of moderate size. We believe this warrants reform that reduces the phase-out rate.

Second, and related to this, is concern about the efficiency cost created by the EITC. Any income-transfer program, including the EITC, causes some distortion in the behavior of taxpayers and recipients, resulting in an "efficiency cost" so that the recipients gain less than the taxpayers lose. Although we think that the efficiency cost is small in light of the labor supply literature, a reform that might reduce even this small efficiency cost is, nevertheless, worthwhile.

Third, we believe that as a matter of fairness and as a matter of economic opportunity, it is important to reduce the marginal tax rate faced by low and moderate income households. Currently, in the range where the EITC phase-out overlaps with the income tax, the combined marginal tax rate is 31.06 percent (where the income tax rate is 10 percent) and 36.06 percent (where the income tax rate is 15 percent). Even if there were no response of labor supply and no efficiency cost from this marginal tax rate, we believe it is unfair to place these individuals in a situation where they do not gain more than $64 to $69 from earning another hundred dollars. It curtails their opportunity to advance themselves by additional effort and earnings.

Fourth, because the 2001 EITC has the same schedule regardless of marital status, the 2001 EITC imposes substantial financial penalties on many marriages, and it may also discourage some unmarried persons from getting married (as a consequence of the tax act of 2001, there is a more generous schedule for married couples beginning in 2002). Research clearly shows that these marriage penalties apply to many families and that they are often large. There is relatively little information about whether these penalties actually reduce marriage rates although, to date, no study has found anything but small impacts. But, once again, even if the reduction turns out to be small, we believe it is unfair to impose such large marriage penalties.

Fifth, despite the expansions of the EITC in the 1990s, the EITC still does not assure that a family of four (two parents, two children) with one full-time, year-round, low wage worker will reach the official poverty threshold. We believe that ought to be a goal of the EITC.

Finally, the EITC does not currently provide any additional credit for a third child. Because the EITC is restricted to working families, it is our view that some additional EITC assistance for a third child is warranted for such families.

It is important to understand that these problems are not independent. Solving one problem contributes to solving the others. The relatively high phase-out rate that provides a work disincentive for households on the phase-out range of the EITC is also responsible for much of the efficiency cost of the program and, in addition, it indirectly contributes to the marriage penalty and the continuing poverty status of a family of four. A reduction in the phase-out rate will address all of those problems. Similarly, an adjustment that reduces the marriage penalty directly will also help lift a family of four out of poverty. An additional credit for families with three or more children not only helps reduce poverty among these families, but it also alleviates the marriage penalty associated with marriage among single parents with children. Thus, this interaction among the EITC problems that we have identified enables us to address them through a reform that is relatively simple.

A Specific Proposal to Reform the EITC

We propose the following three changes in the EITC program:

- Reduce the current EITC phase-out rate for a family with two or more children from 21.06 percent to 15.98 percent (the current phase-out rate for a family with one child), a reduction of 5.08 percentage points. This reduction raises the reward to additional work for persons on the phase-out range, reduces the efficiency cost and the marriage penalty, and helps lift larger families above the poverty line by allowing them to retain a larger proportion of their EITC while they are still below the poverty income level. Because the EITC phases out more slowly, the EITC maximum income increases and more families receive an EITC benefit.

- Establish a more generous EITC schedule for married couples. We propose to do this by keeping the same phase-in rate but giving married couples a larger phase-in income range than single heads of households. The use of different tax schedules for married couples and heads of households is well established under the federal personal income tax. We propose to increase the income at which the phase-in range ends by $2,000 for a married couple with children and by $1,000 for a married couple with no children. This change further alleviates the marriage penalty of the EITC and also helps lift larger families above the poverty line. It also raises the EITC phase-out income so that more families receive an EITC benefit. The tax act of 2001 adopted a more generous schedule for married couples beginning in 2002. We will compare our schedule with the one adopted in the act later.

- Provide a more generous rate schedule for families with three or more children. Specifically, we propose to increase the phase-in rate for a family with three or more children from its current value of 40 percent to 42 percent and raise the income at which the phase-in range ends for these families. With this reform, the phase-in rates increase with the number of children from 34 percent to 40 percent to 42 percent, so the increment for the third child (2 percent), is one-third of the increment for the second child (6 percent). Symmetrically, the increase in the phase-in range for the third child ($960) is one-third of the increase for the second child ($2,880) so that the phase-in range for a married couple with one child ends at $9,140; with two children, at $12,020 ($2,880 more); and with three children, at $12,980 ($960 more). This raises the EITC phase-out income so that more families receive an EITC benefit.

These three changes—a reduction in the phase-out rate for larger families, an increase in the credit for married couples, and a more generous schedule for families with three or more children—are sufficient to address all of the major problem areas of the 2001 EITC. They do not eliminate these problems, but they do make substantial progress in that direction.

Table 8.1 presents the current 2001 EITC schedule in its top block and the EITC as if our reform had been fully implemented in 2001 in

Table 8.1 Current and Proposed EITC Benefit Schedule, 2001

Family and marital status	Phase-in rate (%)	Income at which phase-in ends ($)	Maximum credit ($)	Income at which phase-out begins ($)	Phase-out rate (%)	Income at which phase-out ends ($)
Current EITC Schedule (2001)						
No children	7.65	4,760	364	5,950	7.65	10,710
One child	34.0	7,140	2,428	13,090	15.98	28,281
Two or more children	40.0	10,020	4,008	13,090	21.06	32,121
Proposed EITC Schedule (2001)						
No children						
Single	7.65	4,760	364	5,950	7.65	10,710
Married	7.65	**5,760**	**441**	5,950	7.65	**11,710**
One child						
Single	34.0	7,140	2,428	13,090	15.98	28,281
Married	34.0	**9,140**	**3,108**	13,090	15.98	**32,537**
Two children						
Single	40.0	10,020	4,008	13,090	**15.98**	**38,171**
Married	40.0	**12,020**	**4,808**	13,090	**15.98**	**43,178**
Three or more children						
Single	**42.0**	**10,980**	**4,612**	13,090	**15.98**	**41,949**
Married	**42.0**	**12,980**	**5,452**	13,090	**15.98**	**47,205**

NOTE: Entries in bold are changes from current schedule.

the bottom block.   The bold entries in the bottom block indicate changes from the corresponding numbers in the top block.   It is evident that our reform raises the EITC phase-out income for most families and therefore increases the number of families that will receive an EITC benefit. As discussed below, we estimate that our reform would raise the cost of the EITC program by $13.9 billion in 2001 (from $30.6 billion to $44.5 billion), or by 45 percent.

Our comparison of the current 2001 EITC program and our proposed reform is based on the numerical parameters of the EITC program and the tax system for the year 2001.   Throughout this comparison, we use the word "current" to refer to the 2001 EITC program. When we compare our reform with the current EITC, the comparison is for the year 2001.

Our proposed reforms for married-couple families are illustrated in Figures 8.1A–D, which show EITC benefits by family income under the 2001 EITC program and under our proposal (if it had been implemented in 2001). These figures show that, for each family size, our

Figure 8.1 Current and Proposed EITC Benefits for 2001
A. Married Couple, No Children

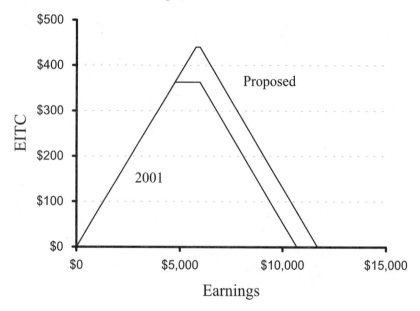

B. Married Couple, One Child

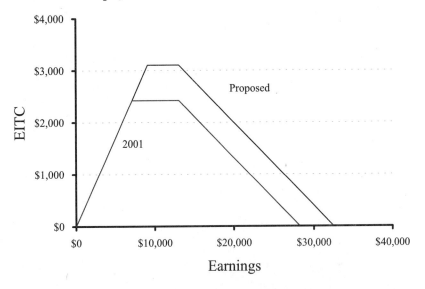

Earnings

reform provides a larger benefit for all families on the current EITC flat and phase-out ranges and a new benefit for all families with an income between the current EITC phase-out income and our new higher EITC phase-out income. Thus, our reform raises the EITC benefit for *all* families with income above the current EITC phase-in range but below our new EITC phase-out income (which exceeds the current EITC phase-out income). It is important to emphasize the obvious point that families between the old and the new, higher, phase-out income levels benefit from our reform, because we will see below that our reform raises the marginal tax rate faced by these families, and this fact may mislead some readers into thinking that our reform hurts these families.

For families on the phase-in range, our reform provides the same EITC benefit as the current EITC if the family has two children or less but a larger benefit if the family has three or more children. As indicated in Table 8.1, our benefit is 42.0 percent of earnings for families with three or more children instead of the current 40.0 percent Our reform and the current EITC coincide over the current EITC phase-in range for those with one, two, or no children. In the case of a married

C. Married Couple, Two Children

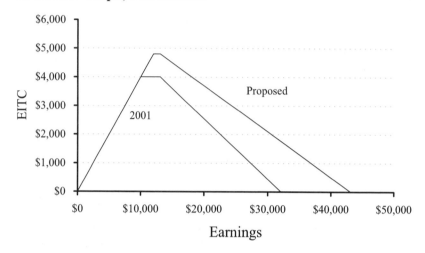

couple with 3 or more children our benefit is intended to appear slightly larger in the phase-in range.

We now present a set of figures to clarify how our reform affects a married couple with two children. In Chapter 1, five figures (1.2–1.6) were presented to illustrate the features of the current EITC for such a family; here, we present five corresponding figures (8.2–8.6) to contrast our proposed EITC with the current EITC for a family of four. This family of four with two children is affected by the first two components of our reform, the reduction in the phase-out rate and the more generous schedule for married couples. The third component of our reform, the more generous schedule for a family with three or more children, obviously has no effect on a family with two children.

Figure 8.2 shows a simplified version of the proposed EITC and the current EITC that makes it easier for nonspecialists to remember the key magnitudes. Each schedule is simplified by using round numbers and percentages and by omitting the flat range connecting the phase-in and phase-out ranges. The phase-in rate is 40 percent in both schedules. The phase-in range is extended to $12,000 for the proposed EITC (versus $10,000 for the current EITC), so the maximum EITC benefit is $4,800 for the proposed EITC (versus $4,000 for the current EITC). The phase-out rate is 16 percent for the proposed EITC (versus

D. Married Couple, Three or More Children

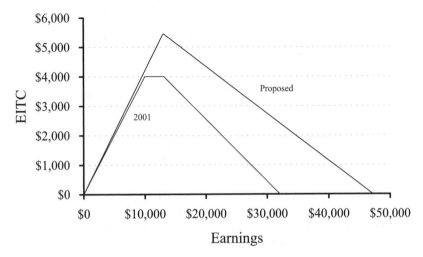

Figure 8.2 Simplified Proposed and Current EITC Schedules, Family of Four with Two Children

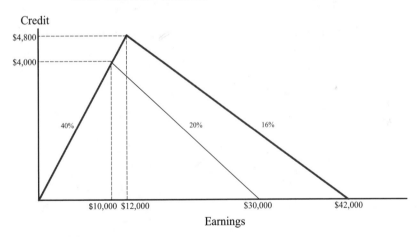

Note: Simplified proposed schedule in bold.

20 percent for the current EITC), so the proposed EITC phases out at $42,000 (versus $30,000 for the current EITC). It is clear from Figure 8.2 that our proposal improves the well-being of *all* families with two children with incomes between $10,000 and $42,000 (for families with earnings less than $10,000, our proposal provides the same benefit—40 percent of earnings). All families with income between $10,000 and $42,000 receive a larger EITC payment under our proposal than under the current EITC schedule.

Figure 8.3 shows the proposed EITC and the current EITC with the exact numbers for 2001. The phase-in rate is 40 percent under both schedules, but the phase-in ends at $12,020 for the proposed EITC (versus $10,020 for the current EITC) so the maximum credit is $4,808 (versus $4,008 for the current EITC). The phase-out begins at $13,090 under both schedules, but the phase-out rate is 15.98 percent for the proposed EITC (versus 21.06 for the current EITC). Because the maximum credit is $4,808, it takes $30,088 of additional income (because $4,808/0.1598 = $30,088) to completely phase out the credit. Thus, when income reaches $43,178, the credit is zero ($13,090 + $30,088 = $43,178).

It is clear from Figure 8.3 that our proposal improves the well-being of all families with incomes between $10,020 and $43,178 (for

Figure 8.3 Proposed and Current EITC Schedules, Family of Four with Two Children (2001)

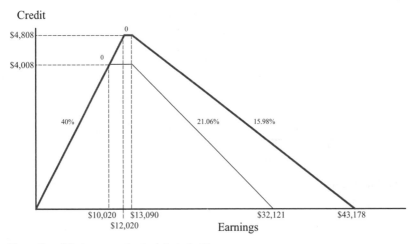

Note: Simplified proposed schedule in bold.

families with earnings less than $10,020, our proposal provides the same benefit—40 percent of earnings—as the current EITC schedule). All families between $10,020 and $43,178 receive a larger EITC payment under our proposal than under the current EITC schedule. Consider, for example, families with incomes between $32,121 (the income at which the credit phases out to $0 under the current EITC schedule) and $43,178 (the income at which the credit phases out to $0 under our proposed reform). These families are clearly better off: they receive an EITC payment under our proposal but receive none under the current EITC schedule. It is important to emphasize that these particular families gain from our reform because we will see below that our proposal raises the marginal tax rate these families face (by 15.98 percentage points), and this fact may mislead some readers into thinking that these families are hurt by our reform.

For 2001, the current EITC and proposed EITC schedules are as follows (where C is the credit, E is labor earnings, and Y is income from both labor and capital), with bold type indicating a difference from the corresponding number in the current EITC:

Current EITC (2001)

$C = 0.40E$	if $E \leq \$10,020$.
$C = \$4,008$	if $\$10,020 \leq E$ and $Y \leq \$13,090$.
$C = \$4,008 - 0.2106(Y - \$13,090)$	if $\$10,020 \leq E$ and $\$13,090 \leq Y \leq \$32,121$.
$C = 0$	if $Y \geq \$32,121$.

Proposed EITC (2001)

$C = 0.40E$	if $E \leq \textbf{\$12,020}$.
$C = \textbf{\$4,808}$	if $\textbf{\$12,020} \leq E$ and $Y \leq \$13,090$.
$C = \textbf{\$4,808} - \textbf{0.1598}(Y - \$13,090)$	if $\$10,020 \leq E$ and $\$13,090 \leq Y \leq \textbf{\$43,178}$.
$C = 0$	if $Y \geq \textbf{\$43,178}$.

Figure 8.4 shows the marginal tax rates generated solely by our proposed EITC and, for comparison, by the current EITC. In the phase-in range, the EITC recipient faces a negative marginal tax rate equal to -40 percent (or equivalently, a marginal subsidy rate of 40 percent), the same as the current EITC. In the phase-out range, the marginal tax rate is 15.98 percent (versus 21.06 percent for the current EITC). Thus, in the phase-out range up to the current EITC phase-out income ($32,121), our proposed EITC reduces the marginal tax rate by 5.08 percentage points (21.06 − 15.98). However, from $32,121 to

Figure 8.4 Proposed and Current EITC Marginal Tax Rates, Family of Four with Two Children (2001)

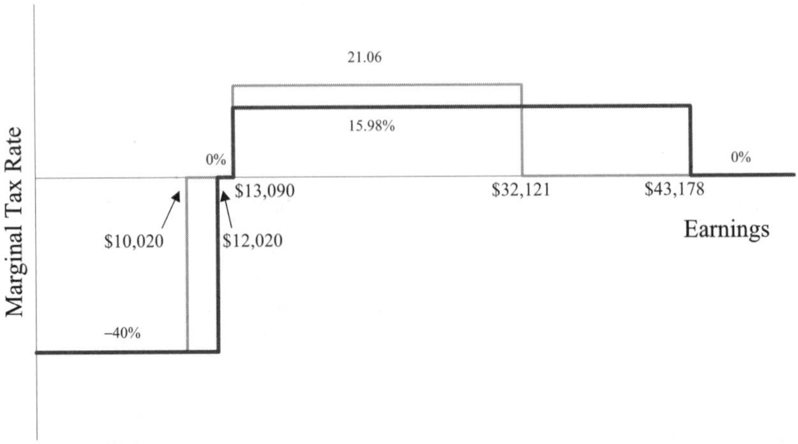

Note: Simplified proposed schedule in bold.

$43,178, our proposed EITC imposes a higher marginal tax rate (15.98 versus 0 percent), even though these families are helped by our reform because they receive an EITC for the first time.

What Our EITC Reform Accomplishes

Our EITC reform addresses each of the problem areas that we have identified in the current EITC.

Labor Supply

The labor supply impacts of our reform are, in fact, complex and depend on exactly where along the EITC schedule a household is currently located, whether we are examining the impact on hours of work or on labor force participation, and whether we focus on primary or secondary workers. Any reform, like ours, that changes both phase-in and phase-out rates for some recipients may generate both income and/ or substitution effects that, in theory, yield an indeterminate effect.

We have relied on the key findings of the empirical literature on the labor supply effects of the EITC (see Chapter 3) in designing this reform. That literature suggests that labor force participation decisions are far more responsive to changes in the EITC than are changes in hours of work among current workers. This finding is consistent across studies and, indeed, is consistent with the non-EITC literature on labor supply impacts. On that basis, we expect our reform to have the following effects on labor supply.

- The lower phase-out rate for larger families is likely to improve work incentives for primary workers in families currently located along the EITC phase-out range. We expect a substantial positive impact on the labor force participation of second earners in married-couple families. Since the reform also increases the credit that most of these families will receive, it actually generates conflicting income and substitution effects that leave the labor supply impact in doubt. The empirical literature, however, strongly supports the hypothesis that labor supply effects will be positive.

- Work incentives will also be improved for current nonworkers in married-couple families who are currently on the phase-in or stationary range. Under our reform, these workers will face either a higher phase-in rate (families with three or more children) or a higher phase-in income level (all married couples). In either case, the returns to work will be improved.

- Work incentives will be negative for workers in families who are made newly eligible by the extension of the income at which the EITC phases out. For married couples with two children, these are households with incomes between $32,121 and $43,178. Workers in households like these will face precisely the combination of negative income and substitution effects of a standard means-tested transfer program. They will have a lower net wage (courtesy of the phase-out rate) and a higher income at their current hours of work (courtesy of the credit itself).

Efficiency Cost

Recall that in Chapter 6 on the efficiency cost of an EITC expansion, we noted the difference between the EITC expansion analyzed by Browning (1995) and the EITC expansion analyzed by Triest (1994). Browning's expansion raised the phase-out rate whereas Triest's kept the phase-out rate constant. Our expansion reduces the phase-out rate. For those currently on the EITC phase-out range, this reduction in the phase-out rate tends to achieve a lower efficiency cost than do the changes introduced by Browning and Triest. On the other hand, our expansion tends to raise the efficiency cost for those above the current EITC phase-out range but who now are eligible for the EITC.

Fairness and Economic Opportunity

Even if there were no response of labor supply and no reduction in the efficiency cost, our reform enables most low income workers to gain more than they currently do whenever they earn an additional $100. Thus, our reform promotes economic opportunity.

Marriage Penalty

Our reform also provides substantial relief to married-couple families who currently bear a large EITC marriage penalty. As discussed more fully in Chapter 4, there are some situations of EITC marriage bonuses, typically involving a childless low income wage earner who marries a nonworker with children. There are far more situations of EITC penalties, however, involving marriages between two wage earners; if both earners have children, the penalties can be exceptionally large. The results from Table 4.1 are repeated here in Table 8.2 in the column entitled "Current law." As shown, there is a large bonus in the first situation, a small bonus in the second, and penalties that range up to $6,765 in the last four situations. The column entitled "Proposed" shows the EITC penalty or bonus these families would receive under our proposed reform. The changes reflect the impact of all of the proposed changes, including the lower phase-out rate, the more generous schedule for married couples, and the new schedule for families with three or more children.

It is evident from the table that our proposal significantly reduces the EITC marriage penalty. Although our reform does not eliminate the penalty, it reduces it by $1,200 to $2,100 for families in rows 3–5. This amounts to three-quarters of the penalty for the family in row 3 and about one-third for the other two families. Virtually all married couples would benefit from our proposal, especially those with two or more children. Note that the high income family in the last row would get no marriage tax relief from our proposal.

Reducing Poverty in Larger Families

Consider a family with two children where one of the two parents works 40 hours a week for 50 weeks a year at an hourly wage of $6.50,

Table 8.2 EITC Marriage Bonus or Penalty Under the Current and Proposed EITC Benefit Schedules

	EITC Marriage bonus (+) or penalty (−) ($)		
Situation	Current law (2001)	Proposed	Net change
Childless full-time minimum wage worker marries nonworker with two children	+3,977	+4,089	+112
Worker with $5,000 earnings and one child marries worker with $5,000 earnings and one child	+600	+600	0
Childless full-time minimum wage worker marries full-time minimum wage worker with two children	−1,613	−431	+1,182
Full-time minimum wage worker with two children marries full-time minimum wage worker with two children	−5,590	−3,764	+1,826
Worker with two children earning EITC maximum marries worker with two children earning EITC maximum	−6,765	−4,756	+2,009
Worker with two children earning $20,000 marries worker earning $50,000	−2,553	−2,553	0

NOTES: Minimum wage worker @ $5.15/hour × 2,000 hours.
EITC earnings maximum in 2001 = $13,090.

thereby earning $13,000.[1] Under the current EITC schedule, this family would fall on the plateau region of the EITC and thus receive the maximum earned income credit, $4,008, raising its income to $17,008. As we explained in Chapter 2, the income from the EITC does not affect this family's official poverty status, because the official definition of poverty is based on pre-tax income and the EITC is considered a tax rebate. Even if we include the income from the EITC in the family's income (as the Census Bureau does for some alternative definitions of poverty), however, this family would still be considered poor. In 2001, official poverty threshold for a family of four was about $17,776,[2] so the family would be $768 under the poverty threshold.

If, however, the end of the phase-in range is raised $2,000 to $12,020 (with the same 40 percent phase-in rate), the family's credit would be $800 higher, for a total of $4,808. This would increase the family's income to $17,808, just exceeding the poverty threshold of $17,776. This is exactly the adjustment that we already instituted when we introduced a more generous schedule for married couples. Hence, that adjustment has removed the family from poverty as well as reduced the marriage penalty.

Our reform substantially aids all low-income married couple families with children. For example, a married couple with one child and one wage earner working at the federal minimum wage ($5.15 per hour in 2001) for 2,000 hours would have an earned income of $10,300 and would currently receive a credit of $2,428. The poverty threshold for this family is $13,874, leaving it $1,146 short. In our proposal, this family would benefit from a higher applicable phase-in range and would receive a credit of $3,108, an increase of $680. This increase nearly removes this family from poverty. If the worker can earn $5.40 per hour for 2,000 hours or work 2,100 hours at the minimum wage, the EITC increase in our proposal will be enough to lift the family out of poverty.

For families with three or more children, our reform offers a $1,444 increase in the maximum credit. Because the poverty standard for a families of five is nearly $21,000, such a family with a single low-wage earner will still be well below the poverty level, even with the larger EITC benefit. Even full-time work above the minimum wage at $6.50 an hour plus the maximum EITC would still leave this family $2,550 below the poverty line.

Simulating the Impact of the Proposed EITC

In Table 8.3, we show our estimates of the impact of our reform proposal for the EITC in 2001. As before, our estimates are based on nationally representative data on households from the PSID. That data (analyzed in Chapter 2) is for 1996; here, we have simply rescaled it to 2001 dollars using the CPI. The EITC program in 2001 is identical in real terms to the EITC in 1996; income thresholds for the three parts of the EITC schedule have been adjusted for inflation, but the phase-in and phase-out rates are identical. Thus, our estimates for the current

Table 8.3 Estimated Impact of the Proposed EITC Reform

	Current EITC (2001)	Proposed EITC (2001)
Percent of households eligible	13.1%	16.0%
Total credits[a]	$30.6 billion	$44.5 billion
Average credit per EITC household	$1,496	$1,773
Total credits,[a] poor households	$13.9 billion	$16.2 billion
Total credits,[a] near-poor households[b]	$9.8 billion	$13.9 billion
Average credit, poor households	$1,639	$1,901
Average credit, near-poor households[b]	$1,860	$2,540
EITC households by income-needs ratio		
<1.0	41.3%	34.0%
1.0–1.5	25.8%	21.8%
1.5–2.0	21.0%	23.7%
>2.0	11.8%	20.5%
EITC dollars by household income-needs ratio		
<1.0	45.3%	36.4%
1.0–1.5	32.1%	31.2%
1.5–2.0	15.4%	22.3%
>2.0	7.2%	10.1%

[a] All total dollar figures are calibrated based on IRS estimates for 2001.
[b] Near-poor households have total income between poverty line and 150 percent of poverty line.

2001 EITC program are identical to the 1996 estimates we presented in Chapter 2. When we compute the impact of our reform proposal, we proceed just as we did in that chapter, by computing the EITC benefits a household would be eligible for, given its earnings, income, age, number of children, and family structure.

The estimates of the reform proposal we present are dependent on several assumptions. First, we do not incorporate behavioral responses either via labor supply or marriage. Existing estimates, which are drawn primarily from natural experiment analyses, do not allow us to estimate the impact of reforms other than the ones analyzed in the experiment. We have already indicated the general direction of likely labor supply responses. Below, we quantify the changes in the marginal tax rates that EITC recipients would face as a result of the reform and offer some general ideas about how our estimates might differ, given plausible labor supply responses.

Second, we again assume that all eligible households receive EITC benefits and that no ineligible households do. Given our data, there is no other way to proceed. We deviate from this practice in one respect, however, primarily for ease of interpretation. Whenever we cite figures related to total program expenditures or for total credits accruing to a particular group, we have used the official estimate for 2001 as a baseline (U.S. Committee on Ways and Means 2000) and calibrated estimates as a multiple of that. Our own estimates of expenditures are somewhat lower than these because our estimate of the recipient population, which is limited to eligible households, is smaller than the IRS estimate and our estimate of the average credit received by recipients is also somewhat lower. Readers may well wish to interpret the costs of the reform in relative, not absolute terms. We think our estimates are certainly in the ballpark and are highly useful, especially on a comparative basis. At the same time, we do not wish to attribute an inappropriate level of precision to them.

Table 8.3 shows our estimates of the current EITC and the corresponding estimates for our proposal. As seen in the first row, our proposed EITC reforms would increase the number of EITC recipients from 13.1 percent to 16.0 percent of the population (about a 22 percent increase). It would increase the total cost of the EITC program from $30.6 billion to $44.5 billion, or $13.9 billion, an increase of 45 percent. The average credit for recipient families would increase from $1,496 to nearly $1,773, an increase of 18.5 percent.

The impact of our reform on different income-needs groups is complex. On the one hand, total spending on poor and near-poor families would increase substantially. Total EITC credits for poor families would increase from $13.9 billion to $16.2 billion and the average credit would increase from $1,639 to $1,901 (16 percent). Near-poor families (no more than 50 percent above the poverty line) would gain even more—$4.1 billion in total and $680 on average. At the same time, the share of EITC recipients who are poor or near-poor falls as does the share of EITC dollars going to these families. This is a consequence of the lower phase-out rates that are essential to reduce marriage penalties and improve work incentives along the phase-out range. The lower phase-out rate enables families with somewhat higher incomes to receive benefits. Note, however, that while the representation of households with an income-needs ratio (family income divided by the official poverty standard) greater than two increases by almost 9 percentage points (from 11.8 percent to 20.5 percent), their share of EITC benefits increases by less than 3 percentage points (7.2 percent to 10.1 percent).

As Table 8.1 and Figures 8.1A–D make clear, any reform that involves higher credits and/or lower phase-out rates necessarily extends the income range for eligibility, thereby drawing into the recipient pool families with higher incomes. Additional analyses, not included in Table 8.3, shed light on the new recipients and the marginal expenditures of our reform. We estimate that these new recipients will comprise 18 percent of the new EITC population. Because of the way we have designed the reforms, more than half of these households have two children and another 30 percent have three or more. About one-third have an income-needs ratio between 1.5 and 2.0 and another 55 percent have an income-needs ratio between 2 and 3. Nearly 90 percent of those newly eligible are married.

The marginal expenditures are much more focused on the poor and especially the near-poor. In all, the new recipient households—18 percent of the total recipient population—get only 8.2 percent of total spending and about one-quarter of new spending. The rest of the additional spending is received by current recipients as higher credits. Nearly half of the additional expenditures goes to poor and near-poor households and only one-sixth goes to households with an income-needs ratio greater than 2.0. Ninety percent of new spending goes to families with two or more children.

Marginal Tax Rates

Table 8.4 examines the changes in marginal tax rates that our reform will create. The numerical values of our proposed EITC (given in Table 8.1) imply that an EITC-recipient household, depending on its size and earnings, will experience one of eight possible changes in its marginal tax rate due to our reform. The eight possible changes are

Table 8.4 Changes in EITC Marginal Tax Rate Due to EITC Reform

Change in EITC marginal tax rate (%)	Percent of EITC recipient population
0	45.9
−5.08	29.1
15.98	17.8
−2.0	5.5
−42	0.9
−40	0.4
7.65	0.4
−34	0.1

listed in the left column of Table 8.4. The corresponding entry in the right column shows our estimate, using PSID data, of the percentage of recipient households that will experience that particular change in its marginal tax rate. By "recipient households" we mean all households that will receive an EITC benefit under our proposed EITC. One possible "change," shown in row 1, is 0 percent, or no change; we estimate that 45.9 percent of recipient households will experience no change. Other than no change, the two changes affecting the largest number of recipients are shown in row 2 (affecting 29.1 percent of recipients) and row 3 (affecting 17.8 percent). The other changes affect only a small percentage of recipients.

Row 2 shows that 29.1 percent of households experience a reduction of 5.08 percentage points in their marginal tax rate. These are households on the current phase-out range with two or more children who used to face a phase-out rate of 21.06 percent but who will now face a phase-out rate of only 15.98 percent. This cut of 5.08 percentage points in the marginal tax rate for nearly a third of EITC recipients is an important accomplishment of our proposed reform.

Row 3 shows that the next largest group of recipients (17.8 percent) experiences an increase of 15.98 percentage points in their marginal tax rate. These are households with income too high to receive any benefit under the current EITC but not too high to receive some benefit under our proposed EITC. Under our reform, they are on the phase-out range and face a 15.98 percent marginal tax rate. An increase in the marginal tax rate for some workers is an inevitable feature of any reform that increases benefits and/or decreases phase-out rates. As we noted above, there may be negative labor supply consequences of this, although the research literature suggests that impacts on hours of work will be relatively small.

If there are labor supply responses, they will change a family's earned income and thus its credit. On the basis of the full pattern of income and substitution effects and the existing empirical literature, we can make some informed guesses about what is likely to happen and how it will affect program costs. Labor supply will probably increase for workers in larger families currently on the phase-out range. This increase will reduce the credit they receive because family earnings will increase. Labor supply will also probably increase for current nonworkers in married-couple families who are currently on the phase-in or stationary range because they will face either a higher phase-in rate or a higher phase-in income level. For these workers, the increase in labor supply will likely increase their credit. Finally, labor supply may fall for the newly eligible workers who face higher marginal tax rates as well as higher family income. That change will reduce family income and thus increase the credit that they will be eligible to receive. It is difficult to predict whether total EITC program costs will increase or decrease as a result of these labor supply responses. Our best estimate is that costs might increase slightly relative to the static estimates shown in Table 8.3.

Reform Variations

It is useful to isolate particular components of our EITC reform in order to assess the contribution of each component. We do this by beginning with the full reform and then removing a single component, leaving the rest of our reform package in place. The changes we examine are summarized in Table 8.5. In row 1 of the table, we remove only the reduction in the phase-out rate for families with two or more children. In row 2, we remove only the more generous schedule for married couples, retaining all other provisions. Finally, in row 3, we remove only the additional credit for a third child. The exact details of these variations on our reform are given in Appendix D.

Table 8.6 compares our full reform (column 1) with the three variations (columns 2–4). As the first row shows, the reduction in the

Table 8.5 Comparison of Three Alternative EITC Reform Plans

EITC reform alternative	Phase-in rate	Income at which phase-in range ends	Maximum credit	Phase-out rate
1) Full reform plan without reduction in phase-out rate for families with two or more children	Same	Same	Same	Retain at current rate of 21.06% for families with two or more children
2) Full reform plan without separate married-couple benefit schedule	Same	Retain at current level (No increment for married couples)	Reduced for married couples	Same
3) Full reform plan without third child benefit	Retain at current level (no increment for third child)	Same	Reduced for families with three or more children	Same

Table 8.6 Estimated Impact of Full Proposed EITC Reform and Three Alternatives

	Full reform	Without reduction in phase-out rate	Without separate married-couple schedule	Without third child benefit
Percent of households eligible	16.0%	14.4%	14.5%	15.7%
Total credits[a]	$44.5 billion	$38.1 billion	$37.6 billion	$41.7 billion
Average credit per EITC household	$1,773	$1,705	$1,657	$1,699
Total credits,[a] poor households	$16.2 billion	$15.8 billion	$15.1 billion	$15.4 billion
Total credits,[a] near-poor households[b]	$13.9 billion	$12.5 billion	$11.9 billion	$13.0 billion
EITC households by income-needs ratio				
<1.0	34.0%	37.8%	37.3%	34.7%
1.0–1.5	21.8%	24.1%	23.4%	22.2%
1.5–2.0	23.7%	24.0%	24.4%	23.8%
>2.0	20.5%	14.0%	14.9%	19.3%
EITC dollars by household income-needs ratio				
<1.0	36.4%	41.5%	40.1%	36.8%
1.0–1.5	31.2%	32.8%	31.7%	31.4%
1.5–2.0	22.3%	18.3%	19.9%	21.9%
>2.0	10.1%	7.3%	8.3%	9.9%

[a] All total dollar figures are calibrated based on IRS estimate for 2001.
[b] Near-poor households have total income between poverty line and 150 percent of poverty line.

phase-out rate and the separate married-couple schedule are each responsible for about half of the 3-percentage-point increase in the proportion of households who would be eligible for the EITC. The third child benefit adds just 0.3 percentage point. Total expenditures follow the same pattern, with the third child benefit responsible for just $2.8 billion (one-fifth of the total increase) and the other two reforms each accounting for $6.5 billion.

The full reform provides more than $30 billion in total credits to poor and near-poor households. The three alternatives range from $1.5 billion to $3 billion less. The separate married-couple schedule is particularly effective at channeling additional income to both poor and near-poor households. Finally, the distribution of households and EITC dollars by household income-needs ratio varies considerably across the plans. With all three reforms in place, the EITC population shifts toward slightly better-off households relative to the three alternatives. This is especially clear in the proportion of households with income more than twice the poverty line; these households comprise one-fifth of EITC recipients in our proposal and less than 15 percent in two of the others. Again, we emphasize that this is a natural consequence of the higher benefits we propose for married couples in conjunction with the lower phase-out rate for larger families. But, as the last row shows, the difference across alternatives in the share of dollars to the better-off families is much more modest. The reduction in the phase-out rate has the largest impact in increasing the share these families receive.

OUR PROPOSED EITC, THE CHILD TAX CREDIT, AND THE INCOME TAX

Under our proposed EITC, a working family of four with two children receives an EITC if its income is less than $43,178. If the family's earnings are above $10,000, it also receives a child tax credit (CTC). At the same time, if its earnings are above $19,200, it faces an income tax rate of 10 percent until its income reaches $31,200, at which point the tax rate jumps to 15 percent; this schedule determines its *tax-before-credits* (TBC), that is, its tax before deducting the two credits. The household's net payment to the government therefore equals TBC

– CTC – EITC. If this amount is negative, it means the household receives a net payment from the government equal to EITC + CTC – TBC. Thus, the family's net receipt from or payment to the government, and the combined marginal tax rate it faces, depends on the interaction of the EITC, CTC, and TBC. In this section we analyze this interaction.

Figure 8.5 shows our proposed EITC, the CTC, and the TBC for a household with a husband, wife, and two children in 2001 and with no other sources of income other than earned income. It also shows the sum of the two credits EITC + CTC. The EITC schedule is the same as in Figure 8.3.

The TBC is zero until $19,200 because of the standard deduction, $7,600, and four personal exemptions ($2,900 each) totaling $11,600 ($7,600 + $11,600 = $19,200). The tax act of 2001 set a tax rate of 10 percent on the first $12,000 of taxable income ($12,000 of income above $19,200); when income reaches $31,200, the tax rate jumps to 15 percent.

The tax act of 2001 made the CTC refundable, so there are now two important refundable tax credits implemented through the federal personal income tax: the EITC and the CTC. The CTC equals 10 percent of the excess of earnings over $10,000, plus the amount needed

Figure 8.5 Proposed EITC, CTC, and TBC Schedules, Family of Four with Two Children (2001)

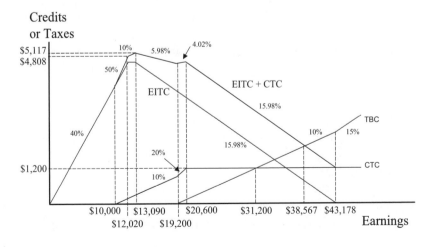

to cancel the TBC (CTC = 0.10 × [earnings − $10,000] + TBC), up to a limit of $1,200 (2 × $600 per child). As shown in Figure 8.5, the CTC begins at earnings of $10,000 and phases in at a 10 percent rate until earnings reach $19,200 (where the TBC schedule begins with the new first-bracket rate of 10 percent) and the CTC reaches $920. The phase-in rate then jumps to 20 percent (the additional 10 percent is due to the 10 percent needed to cancel the new first-bracket tax rate under the TBC) until income reaches $20,600 and the CTC reaches $1,200 (because the CTC = 0.10 × [earnings − $10,000] + TBC = 0.10 × [$20,600 − $10,000] + 0.10 × [$20,600 − $19,200] = $1,060 + $140 = $1,200). Thereafter, the CTC remains constant at $1,200 until the family's income is very high, after which it phases out (not shown in the figure).

The EITC + CTC schedule is also shown in Figure 8.5. From $0 to $10,000 (where the CTC begins), it coincides with the EITC schedule with a phase-in rate of 40 percent. Over the range from $10,000 to $12,020, it has a phase-in rate of 50 percent (40 + 10). From $12,020 to $13,090 (where the EITC phase-out begins), its phase-in rate is 10 percent, due entirely to the CTC (because the EITC is constant over this range). At $13,090, EITC + CTC is at its maximum value of $5,117 (an EITC of $4,808 and a CTC of $309). From $13,090 to $19,200, the EITC + CTC phase-down rate is 5.98 percent (15.98 − 10); from $19,200 to $20,600, its phase-in rate is 4.02 percent (20 − 15.98); from $20,600 to $43,178 (where the EITC phases out to zero), its phase-out rate is 15.98 percent (15.98 − 0); at $43,178, EITC + CTC reaches $1,200 and then remains constant (until a high income), after which it phases out (not shown).

If EITC + CTC is greater than TBC, the household receives a net payment from the government. This is the case until income reaches $37,378.[3] Thus, a household must earn more than $37,378 before its TBC exceeds EITC + CTC.

Figure 8.6 shows the marginal tax rate facing the family as a consequence of the interaction of the EITC, CTC, and TBC. From $0 to $10,000, the marginal tax rate equals −40 percent (due to the EITC alone); from $10,000 to $12,020, −50 percent (due to the EITC and CTC phase-in rates of 40 percent and 10 percent); from $12,020 to $13,090, −10 percent (due to the CTC alone); from $13,090 to $19,200, 5.98 percent (because the EITC phases out at 15.98 percent

Figure 8.6 Marginal Tax Rates, Family of Four with Two Children (2001)

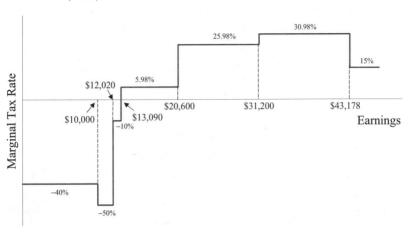

but the CTC phases in at 10 percent); from $19,200 to $20,600, 5.98 percent (the income tax rate is 10 percent and the EITC phase-out rate is 15.98 percent, but the CTC phase-in rate is 20 percent, so 10 + 15.98 − 20 = 5.98); from $20,600 to $31,200, 25.98 percent (the income tax rate is 10 percent, the EITC phase-out rate is 15.98, and the CTC is constant); from $31,200 to $43,178, 30.98 percent (the EITC phase-out rate of 15.98 percent plus the income tax rate of 15 percent); and above $43,178, 15 percent (due to the income tax alone).

In Figure 8.6, at $31,200 the marginal tax rate jumps 5 percentage points, from 25.98 percent to 30.98 percent, because the income tax rate jumps from 10 percent to 15 percent. The marginal tax rate remains 30.98 percent until the EITC phases out to zero at $43,178; thereafter, the marginal tax rate drops to equal the income tax rate of 15 percent. We therefore make the following proposal:

> Postpone the jump in the income tax rate until the EITC fully phases out—that is, extend the first-bracket of the income tax to the income at which the EITC phases out, *provided* the revenue loss is made up by raising high-bracket income tax rates appropriately.

Instead of increasing the income tax rate from 10 percent to 15 percent at $31,200, as under the 2001 tax schedules, extend the first bracket of the TBC schedule to $43,178. The first-bracket rate of 10 percent, instead of applying to the first $12,000 of taxable income (taxable income equals income minus $19,200), would apply to the first $23,978 of taxable income ($43,178 − $19,200 = $23,978). The effect of this proposal is shown in Figures 8.7 and 8.8. In Figure 8.7, the TBC line keeps its slope of 10 percent until $43,178 (instead of jumping to 15 percent at $31,200, as it does in Figure 8.5). As a result, EITC + CTC would be greater than TBC until income reaches $38,567.[4] In Figure 8.8, the marginal tax rate would remain 25.98 percent from $20,600 to $43,178 (instead of jumping to 30.98 at $31,200 and remaining at this value until $43,178).

The aim of our proposal is to reduce the marginal tax rate on, and improve the well-being of, households between $31,200 and $43,178. We oppose losing income tax revenue by cutting income taxes for households above $43,178. To avoid such a revenue loss, higher bracket rates must be simultaneously raised in order to maintain total income tax revenue. An essential component of our proposal is the raising of these higher bracket rates. Of course, this implies that those in higher brackets will bear a higher tax burden and higher marginal tax rates than they do currently. In our view, this loss is worth incurring to improve the well-being of, and hold down the marginal tax rate on, households between $31,200 and $43,178.

Figure 8.7 Proposed EITC, CTC, and Proposed TBC, Family of Four with Two Children (2001)

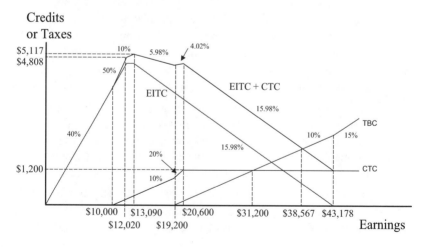

**Figure 8.8 Proposed Marginal Tax Rate, Family of Four with Two
Children (2001)**

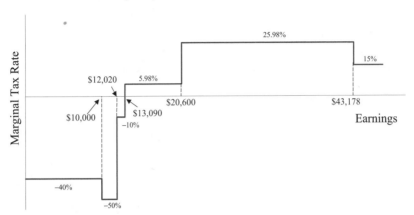

SHOULD THE EITC AND THE CHILD TAX CREDIT BE COMBINED?

The CTC, originally enacted in 1997, became refundable with the tax act of 2001. Does it make sense to have two refundable credits, the EITC and the CTC, or would it be better to combine the two credits into a single refundable credit? To answer this question, it is useful to review the history of the CTC.

Prior to the tax act of 2001, the CTC allowed households to reduce their taxes by $500 per child, but not below zero (except for families with three or more children meeting certain complex criteria) so that the CTC, in contrast to the EITC, did not result in a net payment from the government to the household. Before the 2001 tax act, the TBC schedule began with a 15 percent tax rate at $19,200, and because the CTC was nonrefundable, it in effect phased in at the same 15 percent rate beginning at $19,200, thereby exactly canceling the TBC until the CTC reached $1,000, at which point it remained constant.

The 2001 act cut the income tax rate to 10 percent on the first $12,000 of taxable income, raised the CTC to $600 per child in 2001 (over the next few years it will be raised to $1,000 per child), and made it partially refundable: a household earning more than $10,000 can claim a refundable child credit equal to 10 percent of its earnings above

$10,000, plus the TBC, up to a limit of $1,200 (2 × $600). For example, consider a family of four with two children, with $19,200 in earnings. Because it can claim a standard deduction of $7,600 and four personal exemptions totaling $11,600, it has exactly zero taxable income, so its TBC is zero. But, under the 2001 act, it can claim a CTC equal to 10 percent of $9,200 ($19,200 − $10,000), or $920, so it would receive a net payment from the government of $920 for the CTC plus $2,721 for the EITC,[5] or a total of $3,641. The CTC is called "partially refundable" because, if it were fully refundable, this household would receive a net payment of $1,200 ($600 per child) instead of only $920.

As it stood at the beginning of 2001 prior to the tax act, the CTC was projected to have a total cost in 2001 of $19.9 billion (U.S. Committee on Ways and Means 2000, p. 782), roughly two-thirds of the estimated cost of the EITC ($30.7 billion). Of course, all EITC benefits went to families with income below the end of the EITC phase-out range ($32,121 for a family of four), whereas CTC benefits went to most families but excluded low income families who did not reach the income tax threshold ($19,200 for a family of four) and high income families (the CTC phase-out began at $110,000 of income).

Given the conservative and Republican support during the 2000 election campaign for expanding the CTC, in early 2001 several advocates of assistance to low income working families decided to push for making the CTC partially refundable, rather than pushing solely for EITC expansion. For example, Sawhill and Thomas (2001), while also advocating an EITC expansion, wrote:

> *CTC Expansion and Refundability.* We adopt President Bush's proposal to double the Child Tax Credit by providing families with $1,000— rather than $500— per child. We also make the credit partially refundable for families who do not earn enough to owe taxes, but whose annual earnings are at least high enough to correspond with full-time, minimum-wage work. We take full-time employment to be defined as working 30 hours a week, 50 weeks a year. At an hourly wage rate of $5.15, this works out to be a little less than $8,000 annually. We therefore use a phase-in threshold of $8,000. Beginning at this threshold, we phase in benefits at a rate of 15% of earnings until they reach a maximum of $1,000 per child. Thus, a two-child family earning $19,000 a

year receives a credit of $1,650 [.15 × ($19,000 − $8,000)]. This particular structure was chosen because it encourages full-time work, helps to offset the high marginal tax rates associated with the loss of means-tested benefits in this income range, and merges smoothly with the bottom rate of the income tax system. (p. 5)

The tax act of 2001 followed their design but with modifications. First, the phase-in threshold is $10,000 (instead of $8,000). Second, the phase-in rate for 2001 is 10 percent (it will be raised to 15 percent beginning in 2005). Third, the maximum credit for 2001 is $600 per child, $1,200 for a family with two children (this maximum will be raised in 2005 and will eventually reach $1,000 per child in 2010). Fourth, the CTC equals 10 percent of income above $10,000, *plus the TBC* (up to a limit of $1,200).

In early 2001, it was not obvious that it would be politically possible to make the CTC partially refundable. Nonrefundability was a central reason many conservatives and Republicans supported enacting the CTC in 1997 and expanding it in 2001.[6] With an evenly divided Senate, however, the final negotiations over the tax bill required conservatives and the Bush Administration to compromise in order to obtain the necessary support of moderates to pass their tax cut. And several moderates (for example, Senator Snowe of Maine, a moderate Republican) strongly supported making the CTC partially refundable.

Having recounted this history of the CTC, we now ask: should the EITC and the CTC be combined? Our first point is that there is no urgency because the EITC and the CTC interact reasonably. Look back at Figures 1.5 and 1.6. In Figure 1.5, the EITC + CTC schedule has a reasonable shape: the initial phase-in rate is 40 percent, then 10 percent (except for a tiny invisible range from $10,000 to $10,020 where it is 50 percent); the initial phase-out range is 11.06 percent, then 21.06 percent (except for a short range, from $19,200 to $20,600 where it is 1.06 percent). In Figure 1.6, the marginal tax rate resulting from the EITC, the CTC, and the TBC, is also reasonable.

Now look at Figures 8.7 and 8.8, which result from our proposed EITC, our proposed extension of the 10 percent income tax range until the EITC phases out to zero, and the current CTC. The range where both are phasing in is no longer tiny so, from $10,000 to $12,020, the combined phase-in rate is 50 percent. Admittedly, there is no good reason to jump the combined phase-in rate from 40 percent to 50 percent at $10,000, but it is not clear that the jump is harmful. Similarly, there is no good reason for the change at $19,200, where a phase-out rate of 5.98 percent suddenly becomes a phase-in rate of 4.02 percent until income reaches $20,600. The change probably does little harm, however. Thus, despite these aesthetic imperfections between $10,000 and $12,020, and between $19,200 and $20,600, the EITC + CTC schedule is reasonable in Figure 8.7, and so is the marginal tax rate schedule in Figure 8.8. Thus, there is no urgency for combining the two credits: they are interacting reasonably.

Given the recent political history of the two credits, advocates of assistance to low income working families ("targeted assistance") may prefer to have the two credits remain separate. Although conservatives were primary originators of the EITC in the 1970s (as we saw in Chapter 1), and many conservatives today remain supportive, some have become opponents of any further EITC expansion. By contrast, conservatives today are strong supporters of CTC expansion.

It has been argued that combining the CTC and the EITC would reduce tax complexity, but there is some simplicity that derives from the fact that middle and high income families know they should ignore the EITC but pay attention to the CTC. Of course, for the sake of households eligible for both, every effort should be made to harmonize the definition of qualifying child.

Advocates of targeted assistance should always prefer an EITC expansion to a CTC expansion because the EITC is much more efficient: the EITC spends all its revenue on families below its phase-out income, whereas the CTC spends a large portion of its revenue on families above the EITC phase-out income. But, if there is to be a CTC expansion, advocates of targeted assistance should work politically to maintain the partial refundability of the CTC that was achieved in the 2001 tax act so that low income families derive some benefit. For example, under the 2001 tax act, the CTC is scheduled to gradually increase from $600 per child to $1,000 per child. If this expansion occurs, then partial refundability will secure some benefit for low income families.

We therefore focus on the efficient method of increasing assistance to low income working families—an expansion of the EITC—taking the CTC as separate and given, but supporting its partial refundability.

SHOULD THE EITC, THE CTC, AND THE DEPENDENT EXEMPTION BE COMBINED?

There are three important elements in the federal income tax that affect the tax treatment of families with children: the dependent exemption, the CTC, and the EITC. The EITC targets its benefit to low income working families, whereas the other two do not. The simplest and most transparent way to assist low income working families is to expand the EITC, and this is what we have proposed. There is an alternative approach, however, that is less direct and less transparent: integrate the EITC, CTC, and dependent exemption in a way that ends up channeling more money to low income working families. In this section we consider this alternative approach.

Cherry and Sawicky (2000, 2001) proposed a refundable "simplified family credit" (SFC) to replace the EITC, CTC, and dependent exemption. Like the EITC, a household must have labor earnings to receive the credit. The phase-in rate is 50 percent, and the phase-in range, hence the maximum benefit, increases with the number of children. The threshold for the beginning of the phase-down range also increases with the number of children. The phase-down rate is 5 percent. The credit phases down but not out. For example (using figures for 1999), for a family with two children, the credit would reach a maximum of $4,500 when the family's earnings reach $9,000 (the phase-in rate is 50 percent). The phase-down would begin at $15,000 and end at $53,000, when the credit would reach $2,600 (the phase-down rate is 5 percent); it would remain constant at $2,600 for further increases in income. More generally, they phase down the credit until the credit equals $1,300 times the number of children.

How does this proposal compare with ours? We maintain the current phase-in rates of 34 percent for a family with one child and 40 percent for a family with two children, but we propose raising the phase-in rate to 42 percent for a family with three or more children. They set a phase-in rate of 50 percent regardless of family size. Our maximum benefit is similar to theirs for families up to three children, but they raise the benefit with each additional child whereas we do not. Our phase-out rate is 15.98 percent, and we completely phase out the credit at $43,178 (in 2001) for a married couple with two children (though there is a benefit from the dependent exemption). Their phase-down rate is only 5 percent and their phase-down ends (at an income of $53,000 for a family with two children) when the credit reaches $2,600.

The most striking feature of their plan is the low phase-down rate of 5 percent, implying a marginal tax rate of only 5 percent. We could do the same thing with the EITC alone, however. Without touching the dependent exemption or CTC, we could phase-down the EITC at a rate of 5 percent instead of 15.98 percent. Of course, then our EITC would phase out at a much higher income, thereby providing benefits to many middle and even moderately high income families. The obvious problem with doing this is that it would enormously multiply the budgetary cost of the EITC. To raise the money to pay for credits to all these additional families, tax rates must be raised substantially. Thus, the good news for marginal tax rates would be the lower phase-down rate; the bad news would be the higher tax rate needed to pay the much higher budgetary cost.

To take a simple example, suppose tax rates are raised solely on households with an income above the end of the new high phase-down range. Then households on the phase-down range would have a lower marginal tax rate, but all households above the end of the phase-down range would have a higher marginal tax rate. Moreover, if more money is being transferred to households below the end of the new high phase-down range, the additional money must obviously come from households above the end of the range. Although we are sympathetic to this rearrangement of marginal tax rates and of income, we doubt that it is politically feasible. In our judgment, our proposed EITC expansion, which entails a 45 percent increase in the cost of the EITC program, is sufficiently politically challenging.

Ellwood and Liebman (2001) considered several proposals involving the interaction of the EITC, CTC, and dependent exemption. They explained their motivation as follows:

> The combination of the highly targeted and refundable Earned Income Tax Credit (EITC) and the non-refundable credits and exemptions creates a situation where the tax benefits from children are much higher for low and high income parents than for middle income parents. Middle income parents, who earn too much to qualify for much EITC and too little to gain much benefit from the other tax-linked benefits might be said to face a kind of "mid-

dle-class parent penalty" relative to their poorer and richer counterparts. This middle class parent penalty not only raises issues of fairness; it also generates marginal tax rates and marriage penalties for moderate income families that are as high or higher than those facing more well to do taxpayers. (p. 2)

They considered several options for reducing the "middle class parent penalty" by providing greater support for middle income families. They described their most ambitious option as follows:

> The simplest and most complete way to end the middle class parent penalty would be to eliminate the exemption and child tax credit, and simply not allow the EITC to phase out at all until family income reaches $110,000 and then phase it down to $1000 per child. (p. 29)

This option is very similar to Cherry and Sawicky's Simplified Family Credit (SFC), but phases down at a much higher income than the SFC. Unfortunately, Ellwood and Liebman estimated the cost of this plan to be $53.0 billion. By contrast, the cost of our proposed EITC expansion is only $13.9 billion, so their proposal's cost is nearly four times greater than ours. Their plan would therefore require a significant increase in marginal tax rates on high income households and a substantial transfer of income from these households to the middle income families they want to help. As we said in our review of Cherry and Sawicky's plan, we are sympathetic to this rearranging of marginal tax rates and income, but we doubt that it is politically feasible at this time. Finally, they offer a less ambitious plan for half the cost ($27.5 billion), but still double the cost of our plan ($13.9 billion).

To summarize: there is no magic available. The more ambitious a plan is in transferring income to low and moderate income working families, the greater is its budgetary cost and, hence, the greater is its increase in marginal tax rates on the affluent and the greater is the redistribution of income from the affluent. We are sympathetic with plans more ambitious than ours, but we believe ours is sufficiently ambitious (involving a 45 percent increase in the cost of the EITC program) to make a significant improvement. Because our proposed reform does not involve terminating either the dependent exemption or the CTC, and because it is not as ambitious about redistributing income, we believe it may have a better chance politically.

COMPARISON WITH OTHER EITC REFORM PROPOSALS

Others have also proposed modifying the EITC parameters. Choosing among modifications involves trade-offs so there is no unambiguously superior EITC parameter reform, including our own. Each is more attractive in some respects and less attractive in others. To illuminate the trade-offs, it will suffice to compare our proposal (presented in Table 8.1) to two others: 1) the Clinton Administration plan (U.S. Treasury 2000c) and 2) the Sawhill/Thomas plan.

The Clinton Administration offered an EITC proposal for the year 2000 as part of its budget proposal (essentially the same proposal was made during the 2000 presidential campaign by the Democratic candidates for president and vice president, Gore and Lieberman, in their campaign blueprint, *Prosperity for America's Families,* p. 104–105). The Clinton plan has the same three objectives as ours: reducing the phase-out rate, reducing the marriage penalty, and providing additional assistance for a third child.

Here is the description of the proposal in the Clinton budget document:

> For taxpayers with three or more children, the credit rate would increase from 40 percent to 45 percent . . . For married couples, the beginning point of the EITC phase-out range would be increased by $1,450 in 2000 and 2001 . . . All of these dollar amounts would be indexed in subsequent years. The EITC phase-out rate would be reduced from 21.06 percent to 19.06 percent for taxpayers with two or more children. (p. 12–13)

Let us consider their provisions in turn. Like ours, the Clinton plan provides additional assistance for a third child. It raised the phase-in rate from 40 to 45 percent, whereas we raise it only to 42 percent. We also increase the phase-in range by $2,000, from $10,020 to $12,020, while it does not increase the phase-in range. Thus, under the Clinton proposal, the maximum credit for a family with three or more children would increase (in 2001) from $4,008 (40 percent of $10,020) to $4,509 (45 percent of $10,020), or by $501; under our plan, the maximum credit for a family with three or more children increases from $4,008 to $5,048 (42 percent of $12,020), or by $1,040. The Clinton plan provides 5 percentage points of additional incentive to work up to $10,020, ours only 2 percentage points, but ours keeps the 2 percentage points going until $12,020, whereas the Clinton plan does not.

Like ours, the Clinton plan reduces the marriage penalty by making the EITC more generous for married couples than for single persons. It does this by raising the starting point for the phasing out the EITC for married couples (by $1,450) but not for single persons. We do it by raising the endpoint of the phase-in range for married couples (by $2,000) but not for single persons. The Clinton plan reduces the marriage penalty on couples with earnings above the starting point of the EITC phase-out range. Ours reduces the marriage penalty on couples with earnings above the current endpoint of the EITC phase-in range. The magnitude of the marriage penalty reductions differ depending on the earnings of the couple.

Like ours, the Clinton plan reduces the phase-out rate. It reduces it 2 percentage points. We reduce it 5.08 percentage points (from 21.06 percent to 15.98 percent). Since our phase-out rate is lower, ours implies larger EITC benefits for more people on a more extended EITC phase-out range, and therefore a larger budgetary cost.

Next we turn to a proposal offered in early 2001 by two researchers at the Brookings Institution, Isabel Sawhill and Adam Thomas. They wrote:

> *EITC Plateau Extension.* We make two changes to the Earned Income Tax Credit benefits for families with children. First, we begin phasing out EITC benefits $3,000 "later" than is the case under current law. Thus, while benefits currently begin to be phased out at an income level of $13,090 for families with children, we do not begin the phase-out until a family reaches $16,090 in income. Second, we raise these phase-out thresholds by an additional $5,000 for two-parent families with children. (p. 5)

Like ours, their proposal clearly addresses one of our three objectives: reducing the marriage penalty. They do it by beginning the EITC phase-out later for married couples than for single persons. We do it by extending the phase-in range for married couples but not single persons. Their plan reduces the marriage penalty only for couples earning more than the phase-out threshold for a single person ($16,090 under their proposal). Ours reduces the marriage penalty for couples earning more than the phase-in limit for single persons ($10,020).

Unlike ours, their proposal does not reduce the phase-out rate. It does, however, make the phase-out begin at a higher income so that families above the old phase-out threshold and below the new threshold enjoy a large reduction in their marginal tax rate. Thus, their plan achieves a large reduction in the marginal tax rate below the new phase-out threshold but no reduction above it, whereas ours achieves a reduction in the marginal tax rate for all families with two or more children above the old phase-out threshold. Unlike ours, their proposal does not condition additional assistance on a third child; they postpone the phase-out threshold by $3,000 for families with children regardless of the number of children. Thus, their proposal assists families equally, whereas ours adjusts assistance according to family size.

To summarize, our reform has much in common with other plans that also propose modifying the EITC parameters in order to reduce the marginal tax rate, reduce the marriage penalty, and provide more assistance especially to larger families. There are a variety of ways to adjust the EITC parameters to try to achieve these objectives, and each set of adjustments does better in some respects and not as well in others.

THE EITC REFORM ADOPTED IN THE 2001 TAX ACT

The Economic Growth and Tax Relief Act of 2001 included a modification of the EITC benefit formula for married couples, intended to reduce the EITC marriage tax. When fully effective in 2008, the income at which the phase-out of EITC benefits begins will be increased by $3,000, after which it will be adjusted for inflation each year.[7] Figure 8.9 shows how this change, when fully phased in, compares both to the EITC in 2001 and the reforms we have proposed for a married-couple family with two children. To put the 2008 change into 2001 dollars, we assume an annual inflation rate of 3 percent between now and 2008. With that, the $3,000 income extension of the beginning of the phase-out range in 2008 is equivalent to about a $2,500 extension in 2001.

As the figure shows, the impact of this change is only on households with earnings greater than $13,090, the income at which the phase-out range began in 2001. Since the phase-out rate of 21.06 per-

**Figure 8.9   Comparison of Current, Modified, and Proposed EITC,
Married Couple with Two Children, 2001**

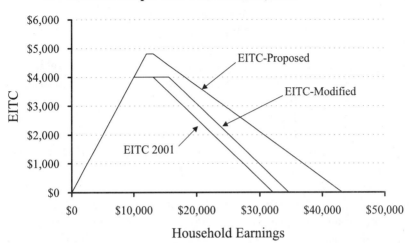

cent is unchanged, the benefit schedule line shifts out parallel, beginning at the new phase-out income of $15,590. Benefits are increased
by $526.50 (equal to the 21.06 percent phase-out rate × $2,500) at all
incomes between $15,590 and $32,121 (the income at which all EITC
benefits were lost under the old schedule). The change in the schedule
also provides smaller benefits to newly eligible households with income between $32,092 and $34,592 and to married couples with one
child.[8] Married-couple households with total earnings that place them
on the current phase-in or stationary range of the EITC receive no
additional benefits under this provision.

The impact for the EITC of the married household schedule change
in the 2001 tax act is quite modest compared to what we propose.
Using the same procedures that we used in constructing Table 8.2, we
can simulate what the EITC program would look like had the 2008
married household schedule change been in place in 2001. We estimate
that the change would increase the proportion of eligible households
from the current 13.1 percent to 13.8 percent; our proposal increases it
to 16.0 percent. It would raise the average EITC by less than 4 percent
($55), compared with an increase of 18.5 percent ($277) in our proposal. Total annual EITC spending would rise by just $3 billion, com-

pared with $14 billion in our proposal. Less than $0.5 billion of additional credits would go to poor families and only $1.2 billion to near-poor families. In our proposal, these families would gain a total of $6.4 billion additional credits—four times as much.

In terms of the marriage penalty of the EITC, the 2001 tax act provides much less relief than our proposal. As shown in Table 8.2, our proposal offered marriage penalty relief for the illustrative cases of from nearly $1,200 to over $2,000. The 2001 tax act provides relief equal to $526.50 for all of these cases—roughly one-half to one-quarter of the relief provided in our proposal. Across the full sample of married-couple households currently eligible for the EITC, the 2001 tax act would provide an average EITC increase of $325, compared with $950 in ours.

The reason the marriage penalty reduction is so much greater in our proposal than in the tax act of 2001 is that, as we explained earlier, all of the changes we propose affect the marriage penalty. Thus, the reduction in the phase-out rate from 21.06 percent to 15.98 percent makes a very important contribution to the reduction in the marriage penalty. Additionally, our proposal is more generous because it extends the phase-in range for married couples, thereby increasing the maximum credit that can be received, and it provides additional benefits to larger families. Our proposal helps additional married-couple families—those on the 2001 stationary range with family earnings between $10,020 and $13,090 and also those with earnings above the new end of the phase-out range.

We conclude that the Economic Growth and Tax Relief Act of 2001 makes a modest contribution to ameliorating the marriage penalty in the EITC, but very substantial marriage penalties would remain and much more could be done. We believe that the our proposal is still valuable despite the reform adopted in the 2001 act.

IMPROVING EITC COMPLIANCE

The EITC has an "error rate" of roughly 25 percent—that is, about 25 percent of EITC payments do not conform to a strict interpretation of its complex provisions for eligibility. As we stated in Chapter 7, the literature suggests that a substantial part of the EITC error rate is due to the confusion of recipients concerning the complex provisions and rules of the EITC. No evidence has been provided to demonstrate that a substantial part of the error rate is due to intentional fraud. The confusion, in turn, is caused by the complexity of the provisions concerning "qualifying child" and filing status. In this section we describe recommendations that have been made by the U.S. Treasury for reducing this complexity in order to reduce the EITC error rate. We also offer a suggestion that would clarify the EITC on the 1040 tax return.

Reducing the Error Rate

During the past decade, some essential steps were taken to improve EITC compliance, such as requiring social security numbers for all children and parents claiming the EITC. Since 1997, the last tax year subject to an IRS study of EITC compliance (released in September 2000), a number of new promising compliance measures (described in Chapter 7) have been introduced, but it is too early to tell how effective they have been in reducing the error rate. For example, beginning in 1999, the tax return contains a simple step-by-step test of EITC eligibility, under which the taxpayer is shown a picture of a stop sign whenever she answers a question that rules out EITC eligibility.

It seems likely, however, that further measures need to be implemented that directly address two major sources of EITC error: the rules concerning "qualifying child" and filing status. In September 2000, the U.S. Treasury issued a new compliance proposal—a set of initiatives that would address these and other sources of EITC errors (U.S. Treasury 2000b). We will discuss the Treasury proposal, and then note which elements were adopted in the tax act of 2001.

Treasury Compliance Proposal

The Treasury compliance proposal contained both administrative and legislative initiatives. We will first look at several of the new administrative initiatives. The first is to immediately notify taxpayers who appear to be nonqualifying parents. This initiative is aimed at the largest source of EITC errors: taxpayers claiming children who fail to meet the EITC residency test. As we noted earlier, the IRS is developing a new database containing information on custody agreements from the Federal Case Registry of Child Support Orders and other administrative data. This database will be the most reliable source that the IRS has to identify EITC claims with residency errors. Late in 2000, the IRS sent notices to noncustodial parents who claimed the EITC on their 1999 tax returns, explaining the EITC residency rule and alerting taxpayers that they might not be eligible for the credit for tax year 2000. The notice advised taxpayers how to correct any errors on their recent returns involving the EITC.

The second administrative initiative is to improve compliance among paid tax preparers. Because paid preparers file about 60 percent of all EITC returns, the IRS has begun implementing EITC education and enforcement programs aimed at tax return preparers. In the fall of 1999, the IRS visited thousands of paid preparers who had prepared at least 100 EITC returns during the previous filing season. In these visits, IRS Revenue Agents provided instruction on EITC rules and reminded preparers that they are required to exercise due diligence in preparing EITC claims. In addition, fines were issued to preparers who had not met their due diligence responsibilities. In 2000, the IRS expanded the number of preparers it visited and also revisited a subset of the previous year's participants to see if they had improved the quality of their preparation, and it imposed penalties where warranted.

The third administrative initiative is to expand the use of IRS authority to deny questionable claims. In 1998, Congress provided the IRS with expanded authority to deny certain questionable EITC claims during the initial processing of returns without the need for an audit. Since 1998, the IRS has expanded its use of this process to automatically deny questionable claims. In 2000, the IRS attempted to deny the EITC unless both the taxpayer and the spouse provided valid social security numbers.

As we stated previously, the Treasury compliance proposal also contains several new legislative initiatives. The first is to enhance the use of the IRS's new dependent database (noted above). The legislation would permit the IRS to use mathematical error authority to deny EITC claims if the Federal Case Registry indicates that the taxpayer is the noncustodial parent of the child claimed on the tax return. This authority would permit the IRS to deny the claims during the initial processing of the returns, before refunds are paid out, and without the need for an audit. Taxpayers could still obtain the EITC by responding to the mathematical error notice and providing evidence of their eligibility for the credit.

The second legislative initiative is to simplify the EITC rules for married taxpayers who no longer reside with their spouses. Under current law, a married taxpayer must generally file jointly with his or her spouse in order to receive the EITC. If a married taxpayer does not file jointly with his or her spouse, the taxpayer may receive the EITC only if the taxpayer lived apart from the spouse for the last half of the year and the taxpayer paid over half the costs of maintaining the home in which they and their dependent children resided. The household maintenance and dependency support tests prevent many low income separated taxpayers from qualifying for the EITC because they are often receiving help from family members or receiving state benefits through TANF. However, many individuals do not appear to understand the subtleties of these requirements or may not have been able to afford an attorney and obtain a legal separation from their estranged spouse, resulting in unintentional errors. Under the Treasury initiative, married taxpayers who file separate returns would be allowed to claim the EITC if they lived with their son, daughter, or stepchild for over six months during the year, and they lived apart from their spouse for the last six months of the year. The household maintenance and dependency support tests would not apply in determining eligibility for the EITC.

The third legislative initiative is to simplify the AGI tiebreaker rule for parents in low income households. Because many taxpayers live with their children in extended families, there is confusion about which adult in a household is supposed to claim the EITC. Under current law, if more than one person can claim the same child for the EITC, only the person with the highest modified AGI is allowed to claim the credit. The Treasury proposes that a parent be allowed to claim his or her child for EITC purposes even if they live with someone with higher income, as long as three conditions are met: 1) the taxpayer with the lower income is the parent of the child, 2) no other taxpayer claims the qualifying child for the EITC, and 3) the higher income taxpayer does not have income in excess of the maximum cut-off for the EITC for families with two or more children ($31,152 in tax year 2000). The

IRS Taxpayer Advocate and the American Bar Association have called for similar reforms of the AGI tiebreaker test.

Finally, the Treasury proposed two further simplifications. Under the first, the definition of "earned income" would be made the same for EITC purposes as for the rest of the individual income tax. Hence, nontaxable earned income (largely 401(k) plan contributions) would no longer be included in earned income when computing the EITC. Under the second, the definition of "dependent child" used for personal exemptions and child tax credits would conform more closely to the definition of child used for EITC purposes. A simple residency test, like the one currently used for EITC purposes, would replace the more complicated support test used to determine if a child is a dependent of the taxpayer.

Tax Act of 2001

The tax act of 2001 adopted several measures to reduce the EITC error rate. It modified the tie-breaker rule and simplified the definition of "qualifying child." It authorized the IRS, beginning in 2004, to use math error authority to deny the EITC if the Federal Case Registry of Child Support Orders indicates that the taxpayer is the noncustodial parent of the child. It replaced "modified" AGI with AGI, and excluded nontaxable employee compensation from the definition of earned income (for EITC purposes).

Clarifying the EITC on the 1040 and 1040A Tax Returns

Surprisingly, the EITC is included not in the tax credits section on the 1040 return but in a later section entitled "payments," where the taxpayer is instructed to add the EITC to federal income tax withheld and estimated payments. The EITC line directly follows the lines for tax withheld and estimated payments, seeming to imply that it is another payment from the taxpayer to the government. This instruction does lead to the correct answer about the proper check to be written by the household or the government, but including it in the "payments" section may confuse many taxpayers about the nature and purpose of the EITC.

The reason for this confusing treatment is that the EITC is a refundable tax credit. Thus, in the section for regular (nonrefundable) credits, it is necessary to ask the taxpayer to check whether total credits exceed tax liability before credits; if so, the taxpayer is not entitled to a check from the government for the difference, but is instructed to enter 0. With the refundable EITC, however, the taxpayer is entitled to a check for the difference, so it must be handled differently. The CTC, made refundable by the 2001 tax act, is also placed in the payments section.

We recommend that the *Payments* section be divided into two adjacent sections, the first entitled *Refundable Credits* and the second, *Payments*. The EITC and the CTC would be in the *Refundable Credits* section, and all payments from the taxpayer (or employer) to the government (withheld tax, estimated payments, etc.) would be in the *Payments* section. In the future, if any nonrefundable credit is made refundable, it can be relocated to the *Refundable Credits* section. The use of the section heading *Refundable Credit* would inform taxpayers that the EITC is indeed a credit, not a payment, but a credit that is somehow different from regular (nonrefundable) credits. By promoting citizen awareness that there are two kinds of tax credits—nonrefundable and refundable—it may stimulate discussion of whether particular credits should be left nonrefundable or be made refundable.

On the simpler 1040A return, the EITC and payments (such as tax withheld) are grouped in a section entitled *"Tax, Credits, and Payments,"* so the taxpayer does not automatically assume the EITC is a "payment." But, instead of following the regular tax credits, the EITC follows tax withheld and estimated payments, seeming to imply it is a payment rather than the credit. We recommend that the EITC (and the CTC) be relocated immediately following the regular tax credits, and before the payments, so that it is more likely that taxpayers will assume the EITC is a credit, not a payment.

SUMMARY

The EITC program operates very effectively and with substantial popular support. It achieves the important goal of providing substantial income assistance to low and moderate income working households, and it does so with relatively few negative effects. Nevertheless, our review identified some problems with the 2001 EITC—problems that are strongly interrelated. The changes we have proposed—reducing the phase-out rate, instituting a more generous benefit schedule for married couples, and increasing the benefit for families with three or more children—would make a substantial impact in mitigating these problems and do so at modest cost. Our proposed changes would reduce negative work incentives, reduce the efficiency cost of the EITC, improve fairness and economic opportunity, reduce the marriage penalty, and reduce poverty among larger working families. Our proposal is similar to several other recent proposals to modify EITC parameters and to the new schedule for married couples adopted in the tax act of 2001. Although recent proposals to integrate the EITC with the CTC and the dependent exemption are interesting and deserve serious consideration, we choose to offer recommendations that can be implemented through the EITC itself. The EITC change in the tax bill of 2001 provides modest marriage penalty relief for married-couple families, but it does not go nearly as far in that direction as the proposal we make.

Based on our review of several compliance studies, we conclude that the compliance problem is primarily the result of confusion resulting from the complexity of rules concerning "qualifying child" and filing status. We recommend most of the initiatives recently proposed by the U.S. Treasury (2000b) and other analysts for reducing this complexity, some of which were adopted in the tax act of 2001. Finally, for clarity, we recommend a change in the position of the EITC on the 1040 and 1040A tax returns so that it is clear to the taxpayer that the EITC is a refundable tax credit, rather than a "payment."

Notes

1. As of December 2001, the federal minimum wage was $5.15. In 2000, Congress considered, but did not pass, a proposal to raise it to $6.15.
2. In 1998 the poverty threshold for a family of four was $16,660 (U.S. Committee on Ways and Means 2000, p.1301). For 2001 we project a threshold 6.7 percent higher, or $17,776.
3. Let E^* be the income at which the household's net payment under the income tax is zero. We find E^* as follows. At $Y = 31,200$, TBC $= 0.1(31,200 - 19,200) = 1,200$; also, CTC $= 1,200$. But, EITC > 0 because it phases out to zero at 43,178. Thus, E^* must be greater than 31,200, so at E^*, TBC $= 1,200 + 0.15(E - 31,200)$. EITC $= 4,808 - 0.1598(E - 13,090)$. TBC equals CTC

+ EITC where $1,200 + 0.15(E - 31,200) = 1,200 + 4,808 - 0.1598(E - 13,090)$. Solving for E yields $E^* = 37,378$.

4. Let E^* be the income at which the household's net payment under the income tax is zero. We find E^* as follows. E^* is greater than $31,200$, so at E^*, TBC $= 0.1(E - 19,200)$. EITC $= 4,808 - 0.1598(E - 13,090)$. TBC equals CTC + EITC where $0.1(E - 19,200) = 1,200 + 4,808 - 0.1598(E - 13,090)$. Solving for E yields $E^* = 38,567$.

5. EITC $= 4008 - 0.2106(19,200 - 13,090) = 2,721$.

6. Technically, the CTC was already refundable in the case of certain families with three or more children meeting complex criteria, but in 2001, net payments to such families were only $0.8 billion out of the $19.9 billion total cost of the CTC.

7. The beginning and end of the phase-out range are increased by $1,000 for years 2002–2004 and $2,000 for years 2005–2007.

8. For married couple households with one child, EITC benefits increase by $399.50 $= 0.1598 \times \$2,500$.

9
The EITC in the
Twenty-first Century

In the first decade of the twenty-first century, it is almost impossible to imagine U.S. income-transfer policy without the EITC. Prior to the inception of the EITC in 1975, assistance for poor families was provided primarily through AFDC, food stamps, and Medicaid. Cash assistance for poor working families was literally non-existent. AFDC was already unpopular, and its negative labor supply incentives were already well-known among economists. Proposals to reform AFDC had been around for a decade. The most promising of these, the negative income tax, had even been field-tested in a series of famous experiments, but no genuine reform of AFDC would be forthcoming for nearly two decades.

In a remarkable sequence of events, the EITC, established with a very modest purpose and an equally limited budget, became a program that fit perfectly into the changing economic and political landscape of the 1990s and the 2000s. The designers of the EITC could hardly have guessed that the EITC would be expanded by both Republican and Democratic presidents, that the number of families benefitting from the program would have tripled in size within 25 years, or that EITC expenditures would have risen in real terms by almost 800 percent. It is unlikely that they expected the EITC to become such a politically popular program, with support across the broad ideological spectrum of American politics. They certainly couldn't have foreseen that the EITC would, by the end of the 1990s, become the largest cash transfer program for poor and near-poor workers and their families.

Nor could they have foreseen how central the EITC would become to the labor market realities of the 1990s and 2000s. When labor markets for less-skilled workers deteriorated substantially and earnings inequality rose in the 1980s and 1990s, the EITC was available to boost incomes of poor working families. When President Clinton sought in 1993 to make good on his pledge to "make work pay," he did not need to design a new program from scratch because the EITC could do precisely that, once it was suitably expanded. When President Clinton's pledge to "end welfare as we know it" resulted in a dismantling of entitlements for poor families and when many former AFDC recipients were pushed into self-support, the EITC was available to supplement the low earnings their often meager labor market skills could command. The early years of welfare reform would almost certainly have been far worse for women and children in the absence of the EITC. Its policy ascendance relative to the minimum wage is now well-established: whatever the minimum wage can do, the EITC can do more efficiently, with fewer negative consequences, and with better target efficiency.

The EITC is now a program that we clearly need and that we could ill do without. It has become a vital part, if not the central feature, of the safety net as it is now understood in the 2000s.

As we have documented amply in this book, we now know a great deal about the EITC and about the direct and indirect economic impacts it has on workers and families. There are many accomplishments and some issues that could be addressed. Every income-transfer program, including the EITC, alters individual incomes and wages and thus creates incentives and disincentives for work, marriage, fertility, and other behaviors. A decade's worth of high-quality research has consistently shown that the EITC has some positive effects on the labor force participation of the worst-off EITC workers—a first for any U.S. transfer program—and some negative effects on the labor force participation of the best-off EITC workers. There are some concerns about efficiency cost. Marriage penalties do exist on balance. Compared to AFDC, however, these negative impacts are orders of magnitude smaller. The EITC is truly an example of a well-designed, highly flexible government transfer program, one that has accomplished what used to be considered impossible—transfer income with relatively few economic distortions.

As we look forward to the next decade of the EITC, what do we see? We certainly expect the basic structure of the EITC with its characteristic phase-in, stationary, and phase-out regions to remain intact. Substantial future expansion of the program is unlikely in our view. Phase-in rates of 34 and 40 percent, the rates prevailing in 2001, are probably as high as they can be feasibly set without either imposing higher phase-out rates—which we would strongly oppose—or extending the recipient population much higher into the family income distribution with the higher costs that entails. Even our own proposal, offered in Chapter 8, makes only a modest increase in the phase-in rate to 42 percent for families with three or more children.

We do think it is well-worth making marginal adjustments to the program along the lines we proposed in Chapter 8—reducing the phase-out rate and establishing separate, slightly more generous benefit schedules for married couples and for families with three or more children. Of these changes, lowering the phase-out rate for families with two or more children, would accomplish the most, because it simultaneously mitigates negative labor supply incentives and reduces the marriage penalty. The EITC marriage relief in the tax act of 2001 is much less effective than what we propose. It is also worth addressing EITC tax simplification, especially the definition of a "qualifying child." Support for the EITC would be broader if compliance problems could be reduced.

Nothing we can foresee suggests that transfer policy or labor markets will change in ways that will make the EITC less important. The old world of AFDC, with unlimited lifetime receipt, is gone forever; TANF, with its lifetime receipt limits and work requirements, is here to stay. In the 2000s, many women with few labor market skills will undoubtedly be entering the labor market, probably in an economy less booming than the 1990s. Also here to stay, it appears, is the poorer labor market position of less-skilled, less-educated workers. Most economists believe that these labor market changes reflect underlying changes in labor demand driven by changes in technology, especially computerization. That trend is very unlikely to change in ways that would benefit less-skilled workers. Globalization of the economy is another contributing factor, and that, too, is unlikely to be reversed. Policies to promote human capital investment will be important, but there certainly will remain workers whose skills leave them without the ability to earn middle-class incomes.

In our view, continued, generous assistance to these workers is fully appropriate. It is very much in the American tradition of helping the "deserving poor," here expanded to include families above the poverty line but well below middle class. And, in that effort, the EITC will remain the policy instrument of choice for the foreseeable future.

Appendix A

The Algebra of the Earned Income Tax Credit

The EITC phases in according to labor earnings E but phases out according to income Y (from both labor and capital). If investment income exceeds a threshold, then the household is ineligible for the EITC. The EITC schedule is described by the following parameters:

E_m = earnings at which the phase-in range ends and the credit reaches its maximum,
C_m = the maximum credit,
Y_b = income at which the phase out begins,
Y_e = income at which the phase out ends as the credit reaches zero (*the EITC phase-out income*),
p_i = the phase-in rate,
p_o = the phase-out rate,
I = investment income,
I^* = investment income threshold.

Provided $I \leq I^*$, the credit C for a household with labor earnings E and total income Y is given by:

$C = p_i E$ if $E \leq E_m$,
$C = C_m$ if $E_m \leq E$ and $Y \leq Y_b$,
$C = C_m - p_o (Y - Y_b)$ if $E_m \leq E$ and $Y_o \leq Y \leq Y_e$,
$C = 0$ if $Y \geq Y_e$.
To obtain Y_e set $C = C_m - p_o (Y - Y_b) = 0$ and solve for Y to obtain:
$Y_e = (C_m/p_o) + Y_b = (p_i E_m/p_o) + Y_b$.

But if $I > I^*$, then $C = 0$.

Appendix B

The Effect of the EITC on Labor Supply: An Indifference Curve and Budget Constraint Approach

In this appendix, we present the effect of the EITC on labor supply using the standard indifference curve/budget constraint apparatus. We assume familiarity with standard labor supply analysis, emphasizing the way the EITC alters the budget constraint and how it affects labor supply choices. There are three cases to consider for hours of work, one for each range of the EITC, and four more for labor force participation.

We begin with the analysis of hours of work. It is best to regard these analyses as a model of the labor supply decision of a primary worker, that is, one who faces the entire EITC schedule. When we consider labor force participation issues, we focus primarily on the decision of a secondary worker.

Figure B.1 shows the case of a worker in a household with earned income sufficiently low in the absence of the EITC that it is operating on the phase-in range of the EITC. The budget line without the EITC is the lower line with a constant slope. With the EITC, the budget line is the upper kinked one, with slopes $w \times (1 + c)$ in the phase-in range, w in the stationary range, and $w \times (1 - p)$ in the phase-out range; w is the wage rate, c is the phase-in rate, and p is the phase-out rate. The vertical distance between the two budget lines shows the amount of the EITC cash grant. The two horizontal dotted lines identify the two income levels that define the three EITC ranges. The indifference curves have their conventional shape; they identify combinations of income and leisure that provide equal utility.

Equilibrium in the absence of the EITC is at A, with hours of work H_A. The EITC budget line generates a substitution effect because the net wage is now higher and an income effect because total income at the current labor supply is increased by the amount of the credit. The substitution effect is shown by the movement along the original indifference curve from A to A'; the dotted budget line, which is used to identify A', is the income-compensated budget line, containing just enough income to reach the original indifference curve at the new wage. The substitution effect increases hours of work. There is also an income effect, equal to the vertical distance between the income-compensated budget line and the new budget line. The income effect causes desired hours of work to fall, shown here as the movement from A' to B.

The net effect on desired hours of work is uncertain because the income and substitution effects conflict. As shown in the figure, the income effect is

Figure B.1 The Effect of the EITC on Hours of Work—A Household on the Phase-in Range

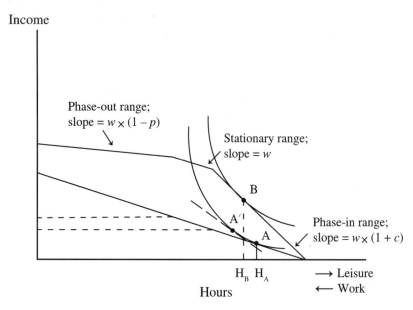

smaller than the substitution effect, so hours of work increase from H_A to H_B, but the opposite result is also possible. It is likely that the substitution effect will outweigh the income effect when A is located far down the budget line (i.e., representing very low earnings). In that case, the credit at A is smaller and thus the negative income effect is also smaller.

Figure B.2 shows the case for a primary worker whose current hours of work places him/her on the stationary range of the EITC. The original equilibrium point is A with hours of work H_A. Since the credit is constant along this range, the EITC operates as a pure income effect with no change in the net wage. Desired hours of work fall to point B with hours H_B.

Finally, Figure B.3 shows the situation for a worker whose current hours of work places him or her on the phase-out range of the EITC. Along the phase-out range, the EITC has the standard negative effects of a means-tested transfer program. The original equilibrium point is point A with hours of work H_A. The credit both lowers the individual's net wage to $w \times (1 - p)$ and raises the household's income by the amount of the credit. There is both a substitution effect and an income effect, and both operate to reduce desired hours of work. The substitution effect is shown as the movement from point A (on the no-EITC budget line) to point A' on the dotted, income-compensated

Figure B.2 The Effect of the EITC on Hours of Work—A Household on the Stationary Range of the EITC

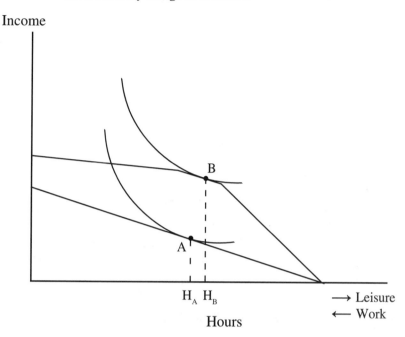

budget line. The income effect is the movement across indifference curves from A' to B on the new budget line. Desired hours of work fall to point B with hours H_B.

The effects of the EITC on labor force participation are shown in Figures B.4 to B.7. Figure B.4 is probably the most common and important case. It shows the case of a nonworking person in a household with no earned income. A typical case might be a household receiving AFDC or TANF. The original budget line includes nonlabor income shown by the upward shift of the budget line, so that income at zero hours of work is equal to some positive amount. The original equilibrium is the corner solution at A, with zero hours of work. In the situation shown here, the nonlabor income is lost and replaced by the familiar EITC budget line. There is no income effect in this case, because the household is made no richer by the EITC at its original equilibrium point. The substitution effect here is strong enough to induce participation in the labor market, and hours of work increase to point B with work hours H_B.

In Figure B.5, we show the situation for a nonworker in a household with earnings from another individual that leaves the household on the phase-in

Figure B.3 The Effect of the EITC on Hours of Work—A Household on the Phase-out Range of the EITC

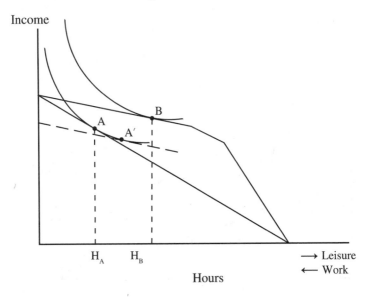

Figure B.4 The Effect of the EITC on Labor Force Participation—A Household with No Earners

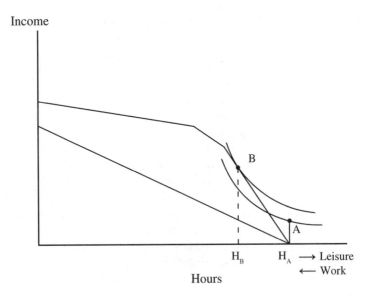

**Figure B.5 The Effect of the EITC on Labor Force Participation—A
Household on the Phase-in Range of the EITC**

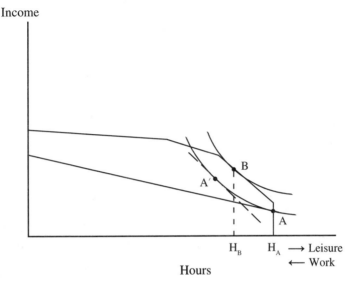

range. Here, and in Figures B.6 and B.7, we model the case as one of sequential labor supply decision making. This type of model simplifies the analysis
considerably and allows us to treat the earned income and EITC of the working family member as exogenous to the labor supply decision of the current
nonworker. The initial budget line without the EITC has a small vertical
portion reflecting the earnings of the other family member, and it is relatively
flat, reflecting a low wage rate. The initial equilibrium is at A with zero hours
of work. With the EITC the budget line is shifted up, reflecting the credit
based on the earnings of the other worker, and it is steeper, because the household is still operating along the phase-in range of the EITC.

There are conflicting effects in this case. There is a small income effect,
stemming from the credit already received, that acts to reduce participation.
Against this, however, is a positive substitution effect, stemming from the
higher net wage resulting from the phase-in rate. We have shown this to be
sufficient to induce participation but, in general, this outcome is not certain.

Figure B.6 shows the case of a worker in a household with other earnings
that place it on the EITC stationary range. In this case, the EITC may reduce
participation. There is no substitution effect because the credit is constant, at
least over the initial portion of the EITC budget constraint. There is an income effect stemming from the credit, however, and it could be substantial

Figure B.6 The Effect of the EITC on Labor Force Participation—A Household on the Stationary Range of the EITC

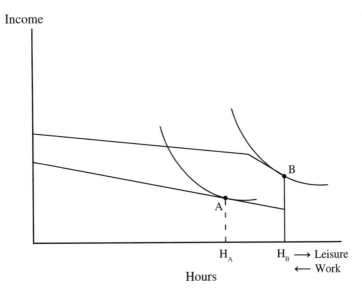

because the credit is at its maximum. The original equilibrium is at A with positive hours of work, H_A. The EITC alters the budget constraint first by shifting it vertically upward by the maximum amount of the credit and second by flattening it as the phase-out range kicks in. There is at least an income effect, and possibly also a substitution effect, depending where on the original budget constraint the second earner is located. In Figure B.6, the EITC is sufficient to cause withdrawal from the labor market (point B, where $H_B = 0$); it could, however, simply reduce hours of work while leaving them still positive.

Finally, Figure B.7 shows the case of a secondary worker in an EITC household on the phase-out range. Again, the original equilibrium is at A with work hours H_A. The EITC shifts the budget constraint up by the amount of the credit, but it now also flattens the buget constraint via the phase-out rate, which reduces the net wage. Here, there is both an income effect and a substitution effect, both reducing labor supply. The substitution effect is the movement from A to A'; the income effect is the movement from A' to B. Again, the figure shows a complete reduction in labor supply at point B, but a smaller decrease that leaves hours of work positive is also possible.

**Figure B.7 The Effect of the EITC on Labor Force Participation—A
Household on the Phase-out Range of the EITC**

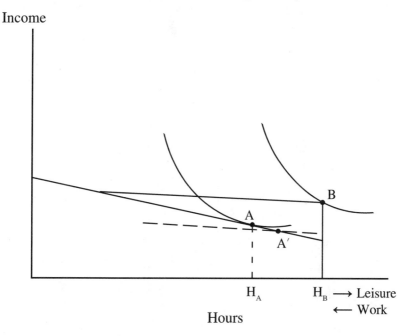

Appendix Table B.1 Effect of EITC on Labor Force Participation

Study	Data/Sample	Method	Findings	Comments
Dickert, Houser, and Scholz (1995)	Survey of Income and Program Participation, 1990 Families with children and low assets, not self-employed.	Structural labor force participation model that includes broad tax and transfer policy changes, including EITC and AFDC.	1993 EITC expansion increased LFPR of single parents 3.3 percentage points and of primary earners 0.7 percentage points; reduced LFPR of secondary earners by unspecified amount.	Careful modeling of taxes and transfers. Bivariate probit model estimated.
Eissa and Liebman (1996)	CPS, 1985–91. Single women, age 16–44. Examine impact of 1986 EITC expansion.	Natural experiment: Single mothers compared to single women without children. Similar comparisons for women without high school degree and women with high school degree. Reduced form analysis with controls for individual and policy variables.	2.4–4.1-percentage-point increase in LFPR for all single mothers, depending on sample and control group. Stronger results for less educated women, who are more likely to be affected by EITC. 1.9-percentage-point increase in LFPR for all single mothers (RF).	Reasonably strong effects for relatively small change in EITC. LFPR of single women without children is very high at baseline (>95%) so any increase may be infeasible.

Eissa and Hoynes (1998)	CPS, 1985–97. Married couples, both husband and wife are ages 25–54, wife has less than 12 years of education. Before and after 1993 EITC expansion.	Natural experiment: Married men and women with children compared to married men and women without children. Reduced form labor supply model with wage and nonlabor income effects.	Married women: 1.8–4.3-percentage-point decrease in LFPR, with larger effect for women with 2 + children (NE). 1.2-percentage-point decrease (RF). LFPR increases 9% on phase-in range, decreases 5–6% on flat and phase-out (RF). Married men: 0.7–1.6-percentage-point increase, larger effect for men with 2 + children (NE). 0.2-percentage-point increase (RF).	Careful and attentive to data and methods. Labor force participation effects for married men unlikely given their very high baseline rate.

(continued)

Appendix Table B.1 (continued)

Study	Data/Sample	Method	Findings	Comments
Meyer and Rosenbaum (1999, 2000)	CPS, 1985–97. Single mothers, age 19–44.	Natural experiment: LFPR of mothers compared with LFPR of single women without children. Structural labor force participation model that includes broad tax and transfer policy changes, including EITC and AFDC.	7–10-percentage-point increase in LFPR of single mothers between 1990 and 1996 (NE). Change in income taxes (largely EITC) increased LFPR of all single mothers 1.5 to 2.0 percentage points between 1992 and 1996, accounting for 35% of total change in LFPR for all single mothers (SM).	Very careful and exhaustive study with multiple outcome measures and attention to wide range of policy measures. Very difficult to fully characterize changes in AFDC regulations at state level in structural model.
Ellwood (2000)	CPS, 1980–98. Single and married mothers, age 18–44, 1986 and 1998.	Natural experiment: Low wage single mothers compared to higher wage single mothers and to low wage single women without children. Low wage married mothers compared to higher wage married mothers	Single mothers: 13–18-percentage-point increase in LFPR for low wage single mothers compared to higher wage single mothers; 23-percentage-point increase in LFPR for low wage single	Natural experiment results include impact of welfare reform and other policy changes that may also have increased LFPR.

and to low wage married women without children. Also examines behavior of low wage married women by whether husband's income created positive, negative, or no EITC work incentives. All wages are predicted; low and higher wage refer to quartile positions. Reduced form model to identify trend in labor force participation not due to changes in unemployment rate and welfare reform.

mothers compared to single women without children (NE). Approximately 30% of growth in Labor Forced Participation attributed to EITC (RF). Married mothers 3–7-percentage-point decrease in Labor Forced Participation of low wage married mothers (NE). 13-percentage-point increase in Labor Forced Participation for low wage women with positive EITC work incentives (NE). No impact on low wage married mothers compared to low wage married women without children (NE).

NOTES: NE = natural experiment; RF = reduced form; SM = structural model. LFPR = number of persons who are either employed or looking for work.

Appendix Table B.2 Estimated Effect on EITC on Hours of Work

Study	Data/Sample	Method	Findings	Comments
Hoffman and Seidman (1990)	PSID, 1988. All recipient households.	Simulation using structural labor supply estimates from Seattle and Denver Income Maintenance Experiments (SIME/DIME)	−2.1%, all recipients; +2.2% on phase-in; −2.3% on flat range; −2.8% on phase-out.	Assumes behavioral response to EITC is identical to income and substitution effects from SIME/DIME.
Dickert, Houser, and Scholz (1995)	Survey of Income and Program Participation, 1990. Families with children and low assets, not self-employed. Examine impact of 1993 EITC expansion.	Simulations using range of estimates from kinked budget set labor supply studies and from negative income tax experiments.	For all recipients, most estimates fall between −0.5% and −1.5%. Hours of work increase along phase-in range (2–6%) and decrease along flat (−1%) and phase-out (−1.5%) ranges. Largest negative effects for wives.	Very detailed attention to tax and transfer programs. Assumes behavioral response to EITC is identical to income and substitution effects from literature.

Eissa and Liebman (1996)	CPS, 1985–91. Single women, age 16–44. Examine impact of 1996 EITC expansion	Natural experiment comparison of single women with and without children.	Either small positive effect or no impact.	Short time period and relatively modest change in EITC.
Eissa and Hoynes (2000).	CPS, 1985–97. Married couples, both husband and wife are ages 25–54, wife has less than 12 years of education.	Reduced form labor supply model with varying sets of instrumental variables.	Married women: 1993 EITC expansion decreased average hours of work 1% to 6%. Large positive effect (8% to 50%) for workers on phase-in, small positive effect for workers on flat range, and negative (2% to 20%) for workers on phase-out. Married men: 1993 EITC expansion decreased average hours of work about 2%. 4% increase for workers on phase-in, no effect for workers on flat-range, and −3% to −4% for workers on phase-out.	Estimated effects for women are not very robust. No correction for selection bias in wage estimates. Describe estimates as "preliminary." Some implausible estimates.

Appendix C

The Efficiency Cost of the EITC

In this appendix, we examine the efficiency cost (or deadweight loss) of the EITC using the standard indifference curve/budget constraint apparatus. We assume familiarity with standard labor supply analysis; see Appendix B for a full discussion.

Figure C.1 shows a standard labor supply diagram with leisure and hours worked on the horizontal axis and income on the vertical axis. The EITC program is shown by the kinked budget line. The linear budget line is the budget line without the EITC. We focus here on an EITC recipient on the phase-out range.

In response to the EITC, the individual has moved from point A on indifference curve U_0 to point B on indifference curve U_1. The EITC induces the person to choose more hours of leisure (less hours of work), Z_1 instead of Z_0.

Figure C.1 The Efficiency Cost of the EITC for a Recipient on the Phase-Out Range

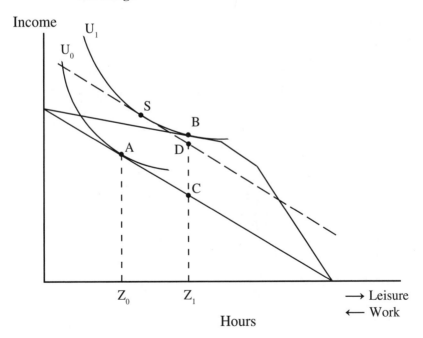

The amount of the EITC is *CB* (the difference between the person's income including the EITC, Z_1B, and the person's wage income, Z_1C). If instead of the EITC, the person were given a lump-sum income supplement of only *CD* (which is less than *CB*), the person would also have reached indifference curve U_1 (at point *S*). *CD* is defined as the equivalent variation; it measures how much better off (in monetary terms) the EITC has made this individual. Thus, the person's welfare gain from the EITC is *CD*, which is less than the EITC received of *CB*. The difference, *BD*, is the efficiency cost of the EITC, the difference between the cost of the program and the welfare gain to the recipient. To summarize: credit = *CB*, welfare gain (equivalent variation) = *CD*, and efficiency cost = *BD*.

Figure C.2 shows an EITC-ineligible taxpayer financing the EITC through a wage tax. In response to wage tax, the person has moved from point *A* on indifference curve U_0 to point *B* on indifference curve U_1. The wage tax in this example induces the person to choose more hours of leisure (less hours of work), Z_1 instead of Z_0. The amount of the tax is *CB*, which is the difference between the person's before-tax wage income (Z_1C) and the person's after-tax wage income (Z_1B). If instead of the wage tax, the person were given

Figure C.2 The Efficiency Cost of the EITC for a Taxpayer

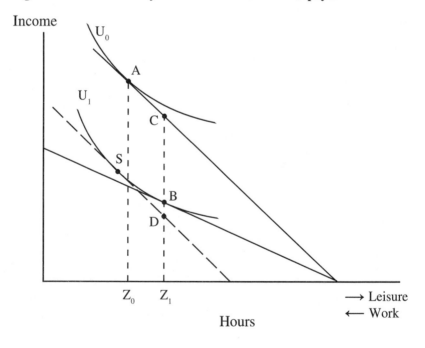

a lump-sum tax *CD* (which is greater than *CB*), the person would also have reached U_1, so, exactly as in Figure C.1, *CD* is the equivalent variation. Thus, the person's welfare loss from the wage tax is *CD*, which is greater than the tax of *CB*. The difference, *BD*, is the efficiency cost of the EITC to the taxpayer. To summarize: tax = *CB*, welfare loss (equivalent variation) = *CD*, and efficiency cost = *BD*.

The credit received by the recipient equals the tax paid by the taxpayer. Hence, the welfare loss to the taxpayer exceeds the welfare gain to the recipient.

Appendix D

Variations on Proposed EITC Reform

Table 1D. Alternative EITC Reform Plans

Family and Marital Status	Phase-in rate (%)	Income at which phase-in ends ($)	Maximum credit ($)	Income at which phase-out begins ($)	Phase-out rate (%)	Income at which phase-out ends ($)
Without reduction in phase-out rate						
Two children						
Single	40.0	10,020	4,008	13,090	**21.06**	**32,121**
Married	40.0	12,020	4,808	13,090	**21.06**	**35,891**
Three or more children						
Single	42.0	10,980	4,612	13,090	**21.06**	**34,989**
Married	42.0	12,980	5,452	13,090	**21.06**	**38,978**
Without separate married-couple schedule						
Married						
No children	7.65	**4,760**	**364**	5,950	7.65	**10,710**
One child	34.0	**7,140**	**2,428**	13,090	15.98	**28,283**
Two children	40.0	**10,020**	**4,008**	13,090	15.98	**38,171**
>Two children	42.0	**10,980**	**4,612**	13,090	15.98	**41,949**
Without third child benefit						
>Two children						
Single	**40.0**	10,020	**4,008**	13,090	15.98	**38,171**
Married	**40.0**	12,020	**4,808**	13,090	15.98	**43,178**

NOTE: Only family/marital status groups with changes are shown; bolded entries are changes from full reform plan.

References

Alm, James, Stacey Dickert-Conlin, and Leslie A. Whittington. 1999. "Policy Watch: The Marriage Penalty." *Journal of Economic Perspectives* 13 (3): 193–204.

Alston, Richard M., J. R. Kearl, and Michael B. Vaughan. 1992. "Is There a Consensus Among Economists in the 1990s?" *American Economic Review* 82(2): 203–209.

Angrist, Joshua D., and Alan B. Krueger. 1999. "Empirical Strategies in Labor Economics." In *Handbook of Labor Economics*, Vol. 3A, Orley C. Ashenfelter and David Card, eds. Amsterdam: Elsevier. pp. 1277–1366.

Barrow, Lisa, and Leslie McGranahan. 2000. "The Effects of the Earned Income Credit on the Seasonality of Household Expenditures." *National Tax Journal* LIII (4, part 2): 1211–1244. Also in Bruce D. Meyer and Douglas Holtz-Eakin (eds.) 2001. *Making Work Pay: The Earned Income Tax Credit and Its Impact on American Families.* Russell Sage Foundation: New York, pp. 329–365.

Blundell, Richard, and Thomas MaCurdy. 1999. "Labor Supply: A Review of Alternative Approaches." In *Handbook of Labor Economics*, Vol. 3A, Orley C. Ashenfelter and David Card, eds. Amsterdam: Elsevier. pp. 1559–1696.

Brown, Charles. 1988. "Minimum Wage Laws: Are they Overrated?" *Journal of Economic Perspectives* 2 (3):133–145.

Browning, Edgar K. 1987. "On the Marginal Welfare Cost of Taxation." *American Economic Review* 77:11–23.

———. 1995. "Effects of the Earned Income Tax Credit on Income and Welfare." *National Tax Journal* XLVIII (1): 23–43.

Browning, Edgar K., and William R. Johnson. 1984. "The Trade-off Between Equality and Efficiency." *Journal of Political Economy* 92: 175–203.

Burkhauser, Richard V., Kenneth A. Couch, and Andrew J. Glenn. 1996. "Public Policies for the Working Poor: The EITC Versus Minimum Wage Legislation." In *Research in Labor Economics*, Vol. 15, Solomon W. Polacheck, ed. JAI Press: Greenwich, CT. pp. 65–111.

Burtless, Gary. 1987. "The Work Response to a Guaranteed Income: A Survey of Experimental Evidence." In *Lessons from the Income Maintenance Experiments*, Alicia H. Munnell, ed. Federal Reserve Bank of Boston: Boston. pp. 22–52.

Card, David. 1992a. "Using Regional Variation in Wages to Measure the Effects of the Federal Minimum Wage." *Industrial and Labor Relations Review* 46(1): 22–37.

————. 1992b. "Do Minimum Wages Reduce Employment? A Case Study of California, 1987–1989." *Industrial and Labor Relations Review* 46(1): 38–54.

Card, David, and Alan B. Krueger. 1994. "Minimum Wages and Employment: A Case Study of the Fast-Food Industry in New Jersey and Pennsylvania." *American Economic Review* 84(4): 772–793.

————. 2000. "Minimum Wages and Employment: A Case Study of the Fast-Food Industry in New Jersey and Pennsylvania: Reply." *American Economic Review* 90 (5): 1397–1420.

Cherry, Robert and Max B. Sawicky. 2000. "Giving Tax Credit Where Credit Is Due." Economic Policy Institute Briefing Paper, Washington, DC.

————. 2001. "Progressive Tax Cuts That Republicans Can Support." *Challenge* 44(3): 43–60.

Congressional Budget Office. 1997. "For Better or For Worse: Marriage and the Federal Income Tax." Photocopy. Congressional Budget Office, Washington, DC.

Deere, Donald, Kevin Murphy, and Finis Welch. 1995. "Employment and the 1990–91 Minimum Wage Hike." *American Economic Review* 84(2): 232–237.

Dickert, Stacy, Scott Houser, and John Karl Scholz. 1995. "The Earned Income Tax Credit and Transfer Programs: A Study of Labor Market and Program Participation." In *Tax Policy and the Economy, Vol. 9*, James Poterba, ed. Cambridge, MA: MIT Press.

Dickert-Conlin, Stacy, and Scott Houser. 2000. "EITC and the Female Headship Decision." Photocopy, August, 2000, Syracuse University, Syracuse, New York.

Duncan, Greg J., and Saul D. Hoffman. 1990. "Welfare Benefits, Economic Opportunities, and Out-of-Wedlock Births Among Black Teenage Girls." *Demography* 27(4):519–535.

Eissa, Nada, and Hilary W. Hoynes. 1998. "The Earned Income Tax Credit and the Labor Supply of Married Couples." NBER Working Paper 6856, Cambridge, Massachusetts.

————. 1999. "Good News for Low-Income Families? Tax-Transfer Schemes and Marriage." Photocopy, University of California, Berkeley, California.

————. 2000. "Explaining the Fall and Rise in the Tax Cost of Marriage." Photocopy, University of California, Berkeley, California.

Eissa, Nada, and Jeffrey Liebman. 1996. "Labor Supply Response to the Earned Income Tax Credit." *Quarterly Journal of Economics* 111 (2): 605–637.

Ellwood, David T. 2000. "The Impact of the Earned Income Tax Credit and Social Policy Reforms on Work, Marriage, and Living Arrangements." *Na-*

tional Tax Journal LIII (4, part 2): 1063–1106. Also in Bruce D. Meyer and Douglas Holtz-Eakin (eds.) 2001. *Making Work Pay: The Earned Income Tax Credit and Its Impact on American Families.* Russell Sage Foundation: New York, pp. 166–195.

Ellwood, David T., and Jeffrey B. Liebman. 2001. "The Middle Class Parent Penalty: Child Benefits in the U.S. Tax Code." In *Tax Policy and the Economy,* Cambridge, MA: MIT Press, pp. 1–40.

Fitzgerald, John, Peter Gottschalk, and Robert A. Moffitt. 1998. "An Analysis of Sample Attrition in Panel Data: The Michigan Panel Study of Income Dynamics." *Journal of Human Resources* 33(2):251–299.

Gore/Lieberman. 2000. "Blueprint for America."

Greenstein, Robert, and Isaac Shapiro. 1998. "New Research Findings on the Effects of the Earned Income Tax Credit." Photocopy, Center on Budget and Policy Priorities, Washington, DC.

Hausman, Jerry. 1981. "Labor Supply." In *How Taxes Affect Economic Behavior*, Henry Aaron and Joseph Pechman, eds. Brookings Institution: Washington, DC, pp. 27–72.

———. 1985. "Taxes and Labor Supply." In *Handbook of Public Economics* Vol. I, Alan Auerbach and Martin Feldstein, eds. Amsterdam: North-Holland, 213–263.

Heckman, James. 1983. "Comment on the Hausman Essay." In *Behavioral Methods in Tax Policy Research*, Martin Feldstein, ed. Chicago: University of Chicago Press, pp. 70–82.

———. 1993. "What Have We Learned about Labor Supply in the Past Twenty Years?" *American Economic Review* 83 (2):116–122.

Hill, Martha S. 1992. *The Panel Study of Income Dynamics: A User's Guide.* Newbury Park: Sage Publications.

Hoffman, Saul D., and Greg J. Duncan. 1988. "A Comparison of Choice-Based Multinomial and Nested Logit Models: The Family Structure and Welfare Use Decisions of Divorced or Separated Women." *The Journal of Human Resources* 23 (4): 550–562.

Hoffman, Saul D., and Laurence S. Seidman. 1990. *The Earned Income Tax Credit: Anti-Poverty Effectiveness and Labor Market Effects.* W. E. Upjohn Institute for Employment Research: Kalamazoo, MI.

Holtzblatt, Janet, and Robert Rebelein. 1999. "Measuring the Effect of the EITC on Marriage Penalties and Bonuses," mimeo.

———. 2000. "Measuring the Effect of the EITC on Marriage Penalties and Bonuses." *National Tax Journal* LIII (4, part 2): 1107–1134. Also in Bruce D. Meyer and Douglas Holtz-Eakin (eds.) 2001. *Making Work Pay: The Earned Income Tax Credit and Its Impact on American Families.* Russell Sage Foundation: New York: pp. 166–195.

Hotz, V. J., and John Karl Scholz. 2000. "The Earned Income Tax Credit." NBER Conference Paper, July 15, 2000. Also in Robert A. Moffitt (ed.) In press. *Means-Tested Transfer Programs in the U.S.* Chicago: University of Chicago Press.

Howard, Christopher. 1997. *The Hidden Welfare State: Tax Expenditures and Social Policy in the United States.* Princeton University Press: Princeton, NJ.

Internal Revenue Service. 1997. *Study of EITC Filers for Tax Year 1994.* Washington DC: Internal Revenue Service.

———. 1999. "Audits to Assess Tax Administration at the Internal Revenue Service, Annual Plan Fiscal Year 1999." Available at <http://www.irs.gov/foia/display/0,,1%3d49%26genericID%3D16991,00.html>.

———. 2000. 1040 Instruction Booklet.

———. 2001. 1040 Instruction Booklet.

Johnson, Nicholas. 2001. "A Hand Up: How State Earned Income Tax Credits Help Working Families Escape Poverty in 2001." Photocopy, December Center on Budget and Policy Priorities, Washington, DC.

Joint Committee on Taxation. 2001. Report, Vol 2. Doc 2001–12006 (603 original pages), 2001 TNT 91–14.

Joint Committee on Taxation. 2001. *Summary of Provisions Contained in the Conference Agreement for H.R. 1836, the Economic Growth and Tax Relief Reconciliation.* May 16 CX-50-01. U.S. Congress: Washington, DC.

Katz, Lawrence F., and Alan B. Krueger. 1992. "The Effects of the Minimum Wage on the Fast-Food Industry." *Industrial and Labor Relations Review* 46(1): 6–21.

Killingsworth, Mark R., and James J. Heckman. 1986. "Female Labor Supply: A Survey." In *Handbook of Labor Economics* Vol 1, Orley Ashenfelter and Richard Layard, eds. Amsterdam: Elsevier Science Publishers B.V., pp. 103–204.

Kosters, Marvin. 1967. "Effects of an Income Tax on Labor Supply." In *The Taxation of Income from Capital*, Arnold Harberger and Martin Baily, eds. Washington, DC: Brookings Institution, pp. 301–321.

Liebman, Jeffrey B. 1998. "The Impact of the Earned Income Tax Credit on Incentives and Income Distribution." In *Tax Policy and the Economy*, James M. Poterba, ed., MIT Press: Cambridge, MA, pp. 83–119.

———. 2000. "Who Are the Ineligible EITC Recipients?" *National Tax Journal* LIII (4, part 2): 1165–1186. Also in Bruce D. Meyer and Douglas Holtz-Eakin (eds.) 2001. *Making Work Pay: The Earned Income Tax Credit and Its Impact on American Families.* Russell Sage Foundation: New York, pp. 274–298.

———. 2001. "The Optimal Design of the Earned Income Credit." In Bruce D. Meyer and Douglas Holtz-Eakin (eds.) 2001. *Making Work Pay: The*

Earned Income Tax Credit and Its Impact on American Families. Russell Sage Foundation: New York, pp. 196–233.

MaCurdy, Thomas, David Green, and Harry Paarsch. 1990. "Assessing Empirical Approaches for Analyzing Taxes and Labor Supply." *Journal of Human Resources* 25(3): 415–490.

McCubbin, Janet. 2000. "EITC Noncompliance: The Determinants of the Misreporting of Children." *National Tax Journal.* LIII (4, part 2): 1135–1164. Also in Bruce D. Meyer and Douglas Holtz-Eakin (eds.) 2001. *Making Work Pay: The Earned Income Tax Credit and Its Impact on American Families.* Russell Sage Foundation: New York, pp. 237–273.

Meyer, Bruce D., and Douglas Holtz-Eakin (eds). 2001. *Making Work Pay: The Earned Income Tax Credit and Its Impact on American Families.* Russell Sage Foundation: New York.

Meyer, Bruce D., and Dan T. Rosenbaum. 1999. "Welfare, The Earned Income Tax Credit, and the Labor Supply of Single Mothers." NBER Working Paper No. 736. Cambridge, Massachusetts.

———. 2000. "Making Single Mothers Work: Recent Changes in Policy for Single Mothers and their Effects." *National Tax Journal.* LIII (4, part 2) 1027–1062. Also in Bruce D. Meyer and Douglas Holtz-Eakin (eds.) 2001. *Making Work Pay: The Earned Income Tax Credit and Its Impact on American Families.* Russell Sage Foundation: New York, pp. 69–115.

Moffitt, Robert A. 1992. "Incentive Effects of the U.S. Welfare System." *Journal of Economic Literature* 30(1): 1–61.

———. (ed.) In press. *Means-Tested Transfer Programs in the U.S.* Chicago: University of Chicago Press.

Moffitt, Robert A., and Mark Wilhelm. 2000. "Taxation and the Labor Supply Decisions of the Affluent." In *Does Atlas Shrug?: The Economic Consequences of Taxing the Rich*, Joel Slemrod, ed. Cambridge, MA: Harvard University Press, pp. 193–234.

Mroz, Thomas. 1987. "The Sensitivity of an Empirical Model of Married Women's Hours of Work to Economic and Statistical Assumptions." *Econometrica* 55: 765–800.

National Center for Children in Poverty. 2001. "Untapped Potential: State Earned Income Credits and Child Poverty Reduction." Photocopy, Columbia University, New York.

Neumark, David, and William Wascher. 1999. "Using the EITC to Increase Family Earnings: New Evidence and a Comparison with the Minimum Wage." Photocopy, Michigan State University, East Lansing, Michigan.

———. 2000. "Minimum Wages and Employment: A Case Study of the Fast-Food Industry in New Jersey and Pennsylvania: Comment." *American Economic Review* 90 (5): 1362–1396.

Pencavel, John. 1986. "Labor Supply of Men: A Survey." In *Handbook of Labor Economics* Vol. 1, Orley Ashenfelter and Richard Layard, eds. Amsterdam: Elsevier Science Publishers B.V., pp. 3–102.

Poterba, James. 1998. *Tax Policy and the Economy.* MIT Press: Cambridge, MA.

Romich, Jennifer L., and Thomas Weisner. 2000. "How Families View and Use the EITC: Advance Payment versus Lump Sump Delivery." *National Tax Journal* LIII (4, part 2): 1245–1265. Also in Bruce D. Meyer and Douglas Holtz-Eakin (eds.) 2001. *Making Work Pay: The Earned Income Tax Credit and Its Impact on American Families.* Russell Sage Foundation: New York, pp. 366–391.

Rosenzweig, Mark R., and Kenneth I. Wolpin. 2000. "Natural 'Natural Experiments' in Economics." *Journal of Economic Literature* XXXVIII (5): 827–874.

Sawhill, Isabel, and Adam Thomas. 2001. "A Tax Proposal for Working Families with Children." The Brookings Institution, Policy Brief No.3, January, 2001.

Scholz, John Karl. 1994. "The Earned Income Tax Credit: Participation, Compliance, and Anti-Poverty Effectiveness." *National Tax Journal* 47 (March 1994): 63–87.

Seidman, Laurence S., and Saul D. Hoffman. 2001. "The Earned Income Tax Credit and the Child Tax Credit Under the Tax Act of 2001." *Tax Notes* 93(4):549–554.

Slemrod, Joel B. 2000. *Does Atlas Shrug? The Economic Consequences of Taxing the Rich.* Russell Sage Foundation: New York.

Smeeding, Timothy M., Katherine Ross Phillips, and Michael O'Connor. 2000. "The EITC: Expectation, Knowledge, Use, and Economic and Social Mobility." *National Tax Journal* LIII (4, part 2): 1187–1209. Also in Bruce D. Meyer and Douglas Holtz-Eakin (eds.) 2001. *Making Work Pay: The Earned Income Credit and Its Impact on American Families.* Russell Sage Foundation: New York, pp. 301–328.

Triest, Robert. 1990. "The Effect of Income Taxation on Labor Supply in the United States." *Journal of Human Resources* 25(3): 491–516.

———. 1994. "The Efficiency Cost of Increased Progressivity." In *Tax Progressivity and Income Inequality*, Joel Slemrod, ed. Cambridge University Press: Cambridge, pp. 137–169.

U.S. Committee on Ways and Means. 2000. *Green Book.* Washington, DC: U.S. Government Printing Office.

U.S. Treasury, Internal Revenue Service. 2000a. "Compliance Estimates for Earned Income Tax Credit Claimed on 1997 Returns." September, photocopy, U.S. Treasury, Washington, DC.

————. 2000b. "Treasury and IRS Announce New Initiatives to Improve EITC Compliance," September 22, photocopy, U.S. Treasury, Washington, DC.

————. 2000c. "General Explanation of the Administration's Fiscal Year 2001 Revenue Proposals." Photocopy, U.S. Treasury, Washington, DC.

Ventry, Dennis J. 2000. "The Collision of Tax and Welfare Politics: The Political History of the Earned Income Tax Credit, 1969–99." *National Tax Journal* LIII (4, part 2): 983–1026. Also in Bruce D. Meyer and Douglas Holtz-Eakin (eds.) 2001. *Making Work Pay: The Earned Income Tax Credit and Its Impact on American Families.* Russell Sage Foundation: New York, pp. 15–66.

Weber, Michael E. 1998. "Combining Parents and Dependents into Family Units." *SOI Bulletin* Fall 231–244.

Yellen, Janet. 1984. "Efficiency Wage Models of Unemployment." *American Economic Review* 74(2): 200–205.

The Authors

Saul D. Hoffman is a Professor of Economics and the Department Chair at the University of Delaware, where he has taught since 1977. He is also a Core Faculty Associate for the Program in Women's Studies, University of Delaware, and a Research Associate at the Population Studies Center, University of Pennsylvania. In addition to his work on the Earned Income Tax Credit, he has published extensively on the relationship between economic forces and demographic behavior, including research on the economic consequences of divorce and of teen and non-marital childbearing, and also on the impact of the welfare system on family structure. He is the author of "Welfare: A Special Report" in the 1995 *World Book Year Book*, and of a forthcoming textbook (with Susan Averett) for courses on Women and the Economy, entitled *Family, Work, and Pay: The Economic Analysis of Women's Issues*. Hoffman also serves on the Research and Effective Programs Task Force of the National Campaign to Prevent Teen Pregnancy.

Laurence S. Seidman is the Chaplin Tyler Professor of Economics at the University of Delaware, where he has taught since 1982. He received his Ph.D. in economics from the University of California, Berkeley. He is the author of *Automatic Fiscal Policies to Combat Recessions* (M.E. Sharpe, forthcoming 2003), *Funding Social Security: A Strategic Alternative* (Cambridge University Press, 1999), *Economic Parables and Policies* (M.E. Sharpe, 1998), *The USA Tax: A Progressive Consumption Tax* (MIT Press, 1997), and co-author (with Saul D. Hoffman) of *The Earned Income Tax Credit* (Upjohn Institute, 1990). He has published articles in economics journals including the *American Economic Review*, the *Journal of Political Economy*, the *Review of Economics and Statistics*, and the *National Tax Journal*. Seidman is also a member of the National Academy of Social Insurance.

Index

The italic letters *f*, *n*, and *t* following a page number indicate that the subject information is within a figure, note, or table, respectively, on that page.

About the Institute

The W. E. Upjohn Institute for Employment Research is a nonprofit research organization devoted to finding and promoting solutions to employment-related problems at the national, state, and local levels. It is an activity of the W. E. Upjohn Unemployment Trustee Corporation, which was established in 1932 to administer a fund set aside by the late Dr. W. E. Upjohn, founder of The Upjohn Company, to seek ways to counteract the loss of employment income during economic downturns.

The Institute is funded largely by income from the W. E. Upjohn Unemployment Trust, supplemented by outside grants, contracts, and sales of publications. Activities of the Institute comprise the following elements: 1) a research program conducted by a resident staff of professional social scientists; 2) a competitive grant program, which expands and complements the internal research program by providing financial support to researchers outside the Institute; 3) a publications program, which provides the major vehicle for disseminating the research of staff and grantees, as well as other selected works in the field; and 4) an Employment Management Services division, which manages most of the publicly funded employment and training programs in the local area.

The broad objectives of the Institute's research, grant, and publication programs are to 1) promote scholarship and experimentation on issues of public and private employment and unemployment policy, and 2) make knowledge and scholarship relevant and useful to policymakers in their pursuit of solutions to employment and unemployment problems.

Current areas of concentration for these programs include causes, consequences, and measures to alleviate unemployment; social insurance and income maintenance programs; compensation; workforce quality; work arrangements; family labor issues; labor-management relations; and regional economic development and local labor markets.